D0834327

Miss Charming's
Guide
for
Hip Bartenders
and
Wayout
Wannabes

Your Ultimate One-Stop Bar and Cocktail Resource

Cheryl Charming

SOURCEBOOKS, INC.®
NAPERVILLE, ILLINOIS

Published by Sourcebooks, Inc.
P.O. Box 4410, Naperville, Illinois 60567-4410
(630) 961-3900
Fax: (630) 961-2168
www.sourcebooks.com
Library of Congress Cataloging-in-Publication Data

Charming, Cheryl.
  Miss Charming's guide for hip bartenders and wayout wannabes : your ultimate one-stop bar and cocktail resource / Cheryl Charming.
   p. cm.
  Includes index.
  ISBN-13: 978-1-4022-0804-1
  ISBN-10: 1-4022-0804-9
  1. Bartending. 2. Cocktails. I. Title. II. Title: Guide for hip bartenders and way-out wannabes.

TX951.C474 2006
641.8'74--dc22
        2006024101

Printed and bound in the United States of America
CH 10 9 8 7 6 5 4 3 2 1

This book is dedicated to every style of bartender and wannabe bartender on earth.

Acknowledgments

*F*irst and foremost I'd like to raise a glass and toast my agent, June Clark. She never gave up in finding a publisher for this book, and I appreciate her efforts more than she knows.

Next, a Champagne pyramid of toasts to Sourcebooks, Inc., for having the guts to publish a book that is, quite frankly, the first of its kind. You've helped the F&B industry in more ways than you'll ever know. Special individual toasts go out to editor, Bethany Brown; project editor, Erin Nevius; publicist, Tony Viardo; copy editor, Rachel Jay; and awesome book designer, Dawn Pope. Cheers to all of you!

A special top-shelf toast goes to all of my cocktail culture friends and acquaintances that have supported and believed in me for many years. You know who you are. An ultra-premium straight up cheers to you!

And of course, a loving toast to my family and friends, who always wonder when I'm going to get a real job, but support and love me anyway.

Contents

Introduction

Once upon a time in a land far, far away, while taking a shortcut through the meadow, a raven-haired girl accidentally dropped a bunch of ripe grapes and a carving knife into a patch of wild mushrooms. The yeast from the mushrooms began to ferment the sweetness of the grapes with much help from the yellow ball of fire in the sky. The next day the girl retraced her steps to locate her lost carving knife and, once found, realized she dropped her grapes as well. She decided to rest for a spell, partake of some grapes, and watch white puffs dance in the sky. She felt warm and loved. Later, the clan medicine woman noticed a change in the girl's manner and sought answers. The secret of alcohol is born, then used in ceremonies, celebrations, worship, and medicine for many years to come. All live happily ever after.

Of course no one knows when, how, or who first discovered alcohol, but scientists and archeologists tell us that it dates back to 7000 B.C. And of course, if you're a believer of the *Lost Continent* then it goes back even further.

What we do know is that humans are social beings and social gathering structures have been part of daily life for a long time. The Greeks had symposiums for the intellectual upper class; frescos show men reclining being served food and wine, while playing games as flute girls and various entertaining acts roamed the room. The Romans were less formal due to so much traveling and actually preferred setting up portable tavernae (taverns). Soon permanent tavernae were built on all roads that Roman troops traveled. All roads lead to Rome! Barmaids served soldiers wine, food, music and danced, and if so desired, then led them to rooms with harlots. Roman troops also carried grapevines with them on every journey to make wine on the road. England began creating their own taverns, and since grapes didn't grow well in their area, they made ale. Soon taverns were found in every town with women given the responsibility of making the beer and wine because it was considered an extension of bread making. Even then, women were the servers at the banquet of life.

Taverns, inns, and public drinking houses (pubs), alehouses, and taprooms pretty much stayed the same from the 1000s to the 1700s. All had fireplaces for warmth, lanterns for light, furniture for sitting, and lots of drink while discussing current events, complaining about the weather, telling stories, and making wagers.

It's mind boggling to think about the many hats a tavern keeper and his ale-wife had to wear. They had to own land in which to grow carbs to make beer, wine, mead, and cider, as well as food for guests. This meant they owned farm animals and tended a garden. They had to provide rooms to house people and stables with hay and water for horses. And they also had to be literate enough to keep books and bills and collect payments due as well as manage the hired help. To multitask, a kitchen dog was placed in a wheel called a *turnspit dog,* and the dog would walk inside the wheel turning the meat as it roasted over the fire. Tavern floors were often made of sand, and it was common to have a portcullis grate around the bar area. For wagering, there was the tavern puzzle jug, which was a drinking jug with several holes with only one working hole to drink from. So the tavern keeper was the barkeeper as well as many other keepers. Maybe that's where the term, *He's a Keeper* comes from?

We know what taverns, pubs, and drinking houses looked like in the 1600s because Dutch artist Jan Steen painted many daily life scenes on the subject. After viewing his paintings you begin to realize that drinking houses basically had the same things we have today: alcohol, drinking vessels, tables, chairs, music, flirting, fire, food, laughter, games, gambling, and even a tavern keeper flairing a long pour from a wine jug into a Martini shaped glass. However, there were a few differences: lots of children, messes, dogs, cats, chicks, and pigs. On second thought, maybe not.

The 1800s were magical years for barkeeps, barmaids, and bartenders in bars, pubs, taverns, saloons, and inns across America. The times brought on civilized behavior with new technological advances. One could order a *Sling, Grog, Flip, Sazerac, Manhattan, Rob Roy, Toddy, Tom Collins, Cobbler, Crusta, Smash, Sour,* and more. Popular spirits and mixers were beer, wine, cider, whiskey, apple brandy, apple-jack, gin, rum, bitters, egg whites, Port, absinthe, amaretto, rye, scotch, Bacardi, mint, vermouth, soda water, brandy, anisette, Sherry, syrups, juices, Southern Comfort (known then as Cuff & Buttons), Jack Daniel's, and Coca-Cola. The position of a bartender, even though blue-collar, was seen as aristocracy of the working class. In those days you had to be a bartender apprentice for several years before you could be a bartender. The first known celebrity bartender was Jerry Thomas. Jerry learned the craft in New Haven, Connecticut, then traveled west to San Francisco. He then traveled back east to New York and opened four saloons. The first one can still be seen at Broadway and Ann Street below the Barnum's Museum. After that he traveled and worked as a head bartender in St. Louis, San Francisco, Chicago, Charleston, South Carolina, and New Orleans. With a set of solid silver bar tools he set sail for England and France. Thomas published *How to Mix Drinks, or the Bon-Vivant's Companion* in 1862 and then the first bartender guide, *The Bartender's Guide or How to Mix All Kinds of Plain and Fancy Drinks in 1887.* He was considered the world's first flair mixologist because he created a cocktail called the *Blue Blazer* in which he poured a flaming drink back and forth from cup to cup.

By the early 1900s most saloons were owned by the breweries. Barkeeps made $10–$15 dollars a week with Sunday being the busiest. Drink making was appreciated, and bartending was turned into an art form. The Waldorf–Astoria in NYC set the standard for quality classic cocktails. Even though some states had already made the sale of alcohol illegal, the booze biz was going strong. No one had any idea of the enormous changes that were just around the corner. Then on January 16, 1920, at one minute past midnight, prohibition started. By nationwide law, it was prohibited to manufacture, import, export, or sell alcoholic beverages (exceptions being medical and religious). This created a booming business for bootleggers and their moonshine, but also created a dark underworld of organized crime (Mafia), homemade hooch (bathtub gin), and secret bars called speakeasies. There were over 100,000 speakeasies in Manhattan alone during prohibition (1920–1933). Bartenders who weren't afraid to risk a temporary job due to raids were forced to create new cocktails to mask the nasty burn of the bootlegged moonshine, so honey, sugar, juices, egg whites, vermouth, and bitters were commonly found behind bars. Canada, Cuba, and Mexico's alcohol business benefited from prohibition through whiskey, rum, Tequila, and tourists. NASCAR was conceived from bootleggers building powerful automobile engines to outrun the law through the Appalachian Mountains to run their moonshine. After prohibition, American bartenders were able to use quality spirits again, but the good bartenders that knew how to make drinks before prohibition were few and far between. Some had died or were too old and couldn't remember. On December 5th, 1933, at 3:32 p.m. (the day of the repeal), it's been said that only one out of ten bartenders knew how to bartend. Bartenders were searched for everywhere, even imported. It was then that people realized that much training and practice was in order to develop the skill of drink making again in America. Thank goodness England's and France's bartenders could lend a helping hand.

Within a year, Hollywood shined the glamorized cocktail torch towards the silver screen. Cocktails became sophisticated and elegant in the movies. And due to all the tropical locations where affluent Americans had spent time during prohibition, they fell in love with the tropics. Donn the Beachcomber left his life of bootlegging in New Orleans and opened the first tiki bar in Hollywood. Donn created the pupu platter, and his drink, *Zombie*, was served at the 1939 New York World's Fair. Pat O'Brien stayed in New Orleans, moved his speakeasy, renamed it *Pat O'Brien's*, and invented the *Hurricane*. And the one-legged Trader Vic opened up his restaurant in San Francisco and invented the *Mai Tai*. In the 1940s–1950s tiki bars burst with popularity. Men returning home from World War II (1939–1945) flocked to them because it reminded them of the Polynesian Islands. Smirnoff's *Moscow Mule* swept the nation and *Rum & Coca-Cola* became popular when the Andrew Sisters released a song of the same name in 1941. This was also the time that many gangsters from prohibition laid the foundation for the mega-drinking city we know today as Las Vegas. With the combination of war-free times, new home appliance technology, supermarket style liquor stores, the swinging, boozing Rat Pack, and James Bond ordering a *Smirnoff Vodka Martini* shaken not stirred, cocktails flourished through the mid-1960s.

In 1965 Alan Stillman opened the first American casual dining bar and grill called TGI Friday's in New York City. It focused on American cuisine, bar food, and alcoholic beverages. It became *the* meeting place for professional singles and was an enormous success. *Lifetime* magazine credited Friday's with ushering in the *Singles' Era*. The New York City gay community followed suit creating their own singles' bars/discos the very same year. Of course, since these were not gay-friendly times, their bars were underground. The deejays in the discos played music by unknown black artists and record companies soon saw that they could promote soon-to-be-hits through the deejays. Disco was born; however, the Vietnam War (1965–1973) created sad, political, drug-induced times slowing down all the fun. But in 1973, after the war ended, TGI Friday's opened a store in Dallas, Texas, and took the city by storm. Within a week, police had to come and ring the bar-and-grill with barricades to handle the nightly hordes of singles. Hundreds of imitative bar-and-grills opened, but only four have survived the test of time: Ruby Tuesday's, 1973; Chili's, 1975; Bennigan's, 1976; and Applebee's, 1980. TGI Friday's created an industry and was the first to create an extensive range of alcoholic beverages. Kahlua, Bailey's, pop-a-top beer, the first light beer from Miller, and the Long Island Iced Tea are all big hits. At the same time, discos were now able to sweep the nation while developing strong record company relations. Bartenders were making spin-offs from the froufrou drinks TGI Friday's had on their menus, and the other copycat bar-and-grills followed suit. Margaritas and Tequila Sunrises were hugely popular too because of the Eagles and Jimmy Buffet singing about them in their songs. And in 1979, bartenders everywhere wanted to ring the neck of a guy named Rupert Holmes who released "The Piña Colada Song."

In the 1980s, discos faded away, and the happy hour became a common ritual in America. Bars set up buffets of free nibbles to attract more business and to appease the new enforcement of anti–drunk driving laws. Wine of the time—Burgundy, Chablis, and Rosé—was served in six-ounce glasses so that they could be filled to the top and was often served in half and full carafes. People adjusted their refrigerator shelves to fit in the convenient wine-in-a-box and their four-packs of Bartles and Jaymes wine coolers. The introduction of Peachtree Schnapps, Midori, and Captain Morgan Spiced Rum exploded possibilities. The popular drinks of the time were Fuzzy Navel, Long Island Iced Tea, Sex on the Beach, Strawberry Daiquiri, Melon Colada, Midori Sour, Sloe Comfortable Screw, Jelly Bean, White Russian, Russian Quaalude, Flaming Dr. Pepper, B-52, Alabama Slammer, Melon Ball, Golden Cadillac, Freddy Fudpucker, and any tropical drink. Blush replaced Rosé, and White Zinfandel replaced Blush. The industry began launching many new liqueurs to keep up with America's sweet tooth—which resulted in the decline of the craft of bartending. The classic cocktail was sometimes ordered by patrons over the age of forty but still thrived only in obscure hotel bars in Europe and Singapore because, quite frankly, their countries didn't have a demand for prepackaged, sweetened mixers and candy-flavored liqueurs.

In 1986 TGI Friday's hosted the very first flair bartender contest, *Bar Olympics* in Woodland Hills, California. This led to Hollywood making the 1988 film *Cocktail* that starred Tom Cruise igniting flair bartending worldwide.

In the late 1980s and into the 1990s the microbrew kick started a whole new appreciation of what we drink. It was all about savoring and not guzzling. Next it was the wine boom. All of a sudden common wine choices were Shiraz, Pinot Noir, Pinot Grigio, Merlot, Cabernet, Chardonnay, and Syrah. Spirit sales declined, and I'm sure many company roundtable meetings were held all over the globe to figure out what to do. The result was to follow the current trend and bump up the quality of spirits. Just when bartender's heads had stopped spinning from all the new beers and wines they had to learn, the new elite Single Malt Scotch showed its peaty head. One by one, each category of spirit reinvented itself. Bourbon was refined to Single Batch and Single Barrel, vodkas turned boutique, fine Tequilas and rums emerged, gins were improved, and flavored infusions never lost steam.

With the new superior line of spirits, some bartenders naturally progressed into modern mixologists, handmaking the classics of yesteryear as well as new modern classics.

Dale DeGroff made it his mission to resurrect the craft of bartending in America. His pioneering efforts have led him to be founding member and president of the The Museum of the American Cocktail.

In 1998, HBO aired a show called *Sex in the City* and exploded the flavored Martini craze to a new dimension by making the Cosmopolitan its mascot cocktail. All of a sudden the shooters of yesterday were being sipped in Martini glasses of today: savored not guzzled.

With hip-hop and *Girls Gone Wild* videos igniting a raunchy sexploitation of women in the 1990s, it was a natural progression for Hollywood to put out a bartender film at the turn of the century called *Coyote Ugly* where half-dressed cowgirls work as NYC take-no-crap bartenders, slinging whiskey and dancing on the bar top. Rappers singing about Courvoisier, Bacardi, Gin & Juice, and Coke & Rum skyrocketed liquor sales to whole new levels. Cognac was once considered a drink for old men sitting in overstuffed leather chairs smoking cigars, but rap songs completely changed this category for a whole new generation. Its category switch can be compared to gin being the crack cocaine of London in the 1700s and then considered elegant and sophisticated as movie stars drank it in Martini glasses on the silver screen in the mid 1990s. In 2002—after forty years—James Bond explodes another cocktail by resurrecting the classic *Mojito*. And in 2004, the hit independent film *Sideways* had bartenders' tongues turning sideways saying Pinot Noir one hundred times a night.

Modern mixologists, flair bartenders, bar-top booty-shaking cowgirls, and just plain ol' bartenders working local gin joints are part of the new millennium. Over 316,000 establishments are licensed for on-premise alcohol sales in America, and that means about 1.5 million bartenders nationwide. What will happen next in the world of bartending? Only time will tell.

1

The History of Booze

Whole books have been written on each of the following subjects, so my goal is to share the most important facts about each in the simplest way possible.

In our modern world, we casually meet for drinks all the time and never consider the liquid history that passes through our lips. Kings, queens, pirates, explorers, and people from all walks of life throughout history drank pretty much the same things we drink today. Alcohol has been around for a long time, and the process to produce it has basically remained the same. How many things can you say that about?

Fermentation

The chosen sugars/carbohydrates are grown, harvested, cleaned, and ground up, then cooked until broken down into a mash. The mash is sprinkled with yeast, which absorbs all the sugar and leaves the alcohol. The creation process stops here for wine and beer.

Distillation

Liquor goes through another process after fermentation: *distillation*. A *still* is a copper contraption (or a bathtub, in the days of prohibition and in some parts of Kentucky today) that boils the alcohol you get from the fermentation process. The steam rises and is directed through a coiled copper tube. The condensation of the steam drips down and is collected—this is the liquor. Of course these processes involve temperatures, harvesting at certain seasons, and time-tested techniques, so don't go trying this at home.

Alcohol
In chemistry, the most common alcohol comes in either ethanol or methanol form. The main thing to know is that ethanol is potable (drinkable) and methanol is not.

Other Uses
The fermentation process is used to produce many different things, such as cheeses, penicillin and other medications, B-complex vitamins, and citric acid. Alcohol itself has different forms and can be used as a cleaner, antiseptic, or sedative.

It's believed that distillation was used to make perfumes and elixirs before being used to make alcohol.

Vodka = Wheat, rye, corn, potatoes, beets, sugar, or any vegetation. Vodka can be made practically anywhere in the world.

Gin = Grains such as wheat or rye, but is then redistilled with herbs and botanicals.

Rum = Sugarcane or molasses.

In 1516, *The Reinheitsgebot Law* was enacted in Bavaria, Germany, requiring that beer be made from malt, hops, yeast, and water only.

There are over 20,000 brands of beer brewed in 180 styles worldwide:

Ale: Stout, porter, wheat, bitter, lambic, brown, cream, and pale.

Popular ale brands: Guinness, Sierra Nevada, Full Sail, Hefeweizen, Bass, Sam Adams Boston Ale, Sam Adams Cherry Wheat, Sam Adams Cream Stout, Killians, Rolling Rock, Pete's Wicked Ale, Pyramid, Red Hook, and Yuengling Porter.

Lager: Bock, dry, light, pilsner, ice, malt, amber, and export.

Beer

Beer is the first alcohol known to man. Ancient civilizations drank, worshiped with, and paid workers with beer. It was considered food. Of course, you can't compare it to the beer of today, because their beer was consumed warm and usually had grain floating in it. Today beer is either one of two types: ale or lager. *Ale* is top-fermenting, and *lager* is bottom-fermenting.

How It's Made

1. A malt has to be made by soaking barley with water; this allows it to germinate (grow).
2. The malt is cleaned, ground, mixed with corn grits, then cooked. The sugary liquid it produces is called wort (wert).
3. The wort is put into kettles and boiled with hops. Hops comes from an herbal vine and is where beer gets its flavor. It also serves as a preservative.
4. The wort is moved to a cooler, where either ale yeast or lager yeast is added to begin fermentation. The wort is chilled even more to stop fermentation, and the yeast is removed.
5. Flavors can be added now; then it's filtered, pasteurized, and stored in bottles, cans, casks, or kegs.

Beer Facts

- The first beer brewery in the U.S. opened in Manhattan in 1623.
- The first Oktoberfest was held in 1810 in Munich, Germany.
- Beer is usually stored in dark glass bottles because they found that ultraviolet rays convert the hop oils into a bad-smelling chemical.
- Home brewers experiment with beer aged in used Jack Daniel's white oak barrels, chocolate, peanut butter, espresso beans, candied ginger, oysters, seaweed, and wild bacteria.
- In an effort to serve cold beer in the 1100s, Germany brewed cold lagers and stored them in caves, and England brewed warm ales and stored them in cellars.

Wine

History and art show us that many civilizations have had love affairs with wine. It's been used in ceremonies, religion, parties, as medicine, at events, in the home, basically everywhere. With a population of one million, the Romans really expanded the wine culture. Many things happened over the hundreds of years of history with wine, but just know that the Church and French monks are responsible for reviving it after its last fall.

Today there is such reverence of wine that many people seem intimidated by it. There's so much one can learn that it can boggle the mind.

Fake It Like a Wine Pro

- Wine is mostly made with grapes, but other fruits can also be used. The fruit is grown, harvested, cleaned, crushed, pressed, fermented (with yeast), and then aged. Wine is just fruit juice whose sugar has been naturally converted to alcohol.
- Wines made from grapes are pretty much named for the kind of grape that is used, like Chardonnay, Cabernet, and Merlot. Some other wines are named by the region in which they are grown, like Burgundy and Bordeaux.
- When you hear people say "Ah, that was a very good year," it means that the quality of wine was enhanced by environmental conditions such as the climate, soil, weather conditions, and rain, or lack thereof. It will also determine the price of the wine.
- A wine's vintage is the year the grapes were harvested.
- Rosé, white zinfandel, and blush wines get their pink color from the skins being left on the grapes during the beginning of the fermentation process. The longer the skins are left on, the darker the wine. All wine juice begins as clear.
- In most cases, white wine is served chilled, and red wine is not.

Popular lager brands: Budweiser, Michelob, Miller, Sam Adams Boston Lager, Fosters, Stella Artois, Carlsberg, Labatt, Molson, Moosehead, Beck's, Red Stripe, Corona, Heineken, Zima, Icehouse, Smirnoff Ice, Red Dog, Colt 45, Mickey's, Lone Star, Falstaff, Pabst, Schlitz, and Yuengling Lager.

The exception: The Anchor Steam Brewery in San Francisco uses a brewing process that produces a beer that's half-lager/half-ale (half top-fermenting and half bottom-fermenting yeast).

Beer is the only alcohol that is packaged in many forms—kegs/barrels, bottles, and cans—and served in many types of glasses—steins, yards, half-yards, mugs, pints, tankards, goblets, thistles, pitchers, and more.

The Most Popular Red Wine Grapes
Cabernet Sauvignon (cab-er-NAY soh-vihn-YAWN)
Grenache (gra-NAHSH)
Merlot (mer-LOW)
Pinot Noir (PEE-no NWAR)
Sangiovese (sanj-eo-VAY-zay)
Syrah (see-RAW), also called Shiraz in Australia (sha-RAWZ, but in Australia they say sha-RAZZ)
Zinfandel
Gamay (gah-MAY).

Chardonnay (shar-doh-NAY)
Chenin Blanc
(SHEN-ihn BLAHN)
Gewürztraminer
(ga-virtz-tra-meener)
Pinot Gris/Pinot Grigio
(PEE-noh gree/gree-gee-o)
Pinot Blanc
(PEE-noh BLAHN)
Riesling (REEZ-ling)
Sauvignon Blanc (soh-vihn-YAWN BLAHN)
Viognier (vee-on-YAY)

Wine Facts

• There are 20 million known acres of grapes worldwide.

• There are over 10,000 types of grapes existing in the world.

• There are an average of 600 grapes in a bottle of wine.

• California exports wine to 164 countries.

• American wine drinkers consume more wine on Thanksgiving Day than any other day of the year.

• Only three grapes are used to make Champagne: pinot noir, pinot meunier (mehr-n-YAY), and chardonnay.

• Red wine glasses have a bigger bowl than white wine glasses.
• Basic pairings of wine and food are whites with light food like fish and reds with hearty food like steak.
• Even though wine is made all over the world, France and California are the top producers.
• Grapes are also used to make Champagne, Sherry, Port, Madeira, vermouth, brandy, Cognac, and grappa.
• A sommelier (sum-ul-YAY) is a trained and knowledgeable wine professional usually working at a fine restaurant. A Master Sommelier is certified, which is quite an honor.

Wine is bottled many different ways. Cheap corks are made from bits and pieces of cork glued together. Expensive corks are solid pieces of cork that tend to be longer than the cheap variety. Twin-top corks sandwich cheap cork in between expensive cork, so the wine touches only the expensive stuff. Synthetic/man-made corks are great for young wines. Screw caps have a reputation of being used on cheap wines, but this has changed lately. A substitute for the screw cap is the crown cap (like a beer bottle).

Other Wine-Based Alcohols

Champagne

A blind Benedictine monk named Dom Pérignon (dom-pay-ree-NYON) is credited with inventing Champagne. The quote that's always attributed to him at the moment of discovery is "Come quickly, I'm tasting the stars!" Bubbly wines were already around at the time, but his was called Champagne because the grapes were grown in the Champagne region of France. In 1804, Madame Clicquot invented pink Champagne, the mushroom-shaped cork, and a way of removing sediment from bottles called *riddling*.

- Champagne takes about one and half years to go through processing and aging.
- The most popular Champagne brands are Dom Pérignon, Mumms (mooms), Moët & Chandon (mow-ET-a Shan-DAWN), Cristal (kris-TALL), Perrier-Jouët (PAIR-ee-a JOO-ette, the pretty flowered bottle with real gold etching), and don't forget the Champagne that James Bond drank, Bollinger (bowl-ahn-JAY).
- The most popular sparkling wines are Prosecco (praw-SAY-co, used in a Bellini), Asti Spumante (AH-stee spoo-MAHN-teh) from Italy, and Korbel (core-BELL) from America.
- The two most popular Champagne glasses are the saucer and the flute. The tall flute came out in the 1970s to help keep the bubbles longer. Two variations on the flute are the tulip and the trumpet.
- Popular Champagne drinks are Mimosas, Champagne cocktails, Kir (rhymes with ear), and Kir Royale.

Also, Champagnes come in levels from sweet to dry: doux, demi-sec, sec, extra dry, brut, brut zero, ultra brut, and extra brut.

Brandy and Cognac

Basically, brandy and Cognac (CONE-yak) are wines that have been distilled. The most important thing to know about them is that all Cognac is brandy, but not all brandy is Cognac. Cognac is made from grapes in the Cognac region of France, while brandy can be made from any grapes or fruit anywhere.

- The most popular grape brandies are Armagnac (ar-mahn-YAK) and Cognac (KON-yak) from France and Pisco (PEE-skoh) from South America.
- The most popular fruit brandies are applejack from America, Calvados (KAL-vah-dohs) apple brandy from France, Framboise (frahm-BWAHZ) raspberry brandy from France, Kirsch (KEERSH) cherry brandy from Germany, Poire (PWAHR), a Swiss pear brandy, and Slivovitz (SLIHV-uh-vihts), a German plum brandy.

Champagne Facts

- Unlike most wines, Champagnes are named after the houses that produce them.

- If it's not made from grapes grown in the Champagne region of France, by law the bottle must say sparkling wine.

- A good temperature to serve Champagne at is 44° F.

- Champagne corks can pop out at 100 mph.

- A 750 ml bottle of Champagne has an average of 50 million bubbles.

- Champagne bottle sizes range from 6 ounces to 508 ounces.

- If a raisin is dropped into a glass of Champagne it will bounce up and down between the top and the bottom of the glass.

- It has been reported that Marilyn Monroe once filled her tub with 350 bottles of Champagne and took a bath.

- Pomace brandy is made from the residue of wine, stems, and seeds. The most popular are grappa (GRAHP-pah) from Italy and marc from France.
- The most popular drinks made with brandy are *Stingers, Brandy Alexanders, Apricot Sours, Between the Sheets,* and *Sidecars.*

Cognac

Cognacs are distilled twice and then poured into oak casks made from Limousin or Troncais oak. (Limousin and Troncais are forests in the Cognac region of France.) The aging process is very expensive because almost 60 percent of the Cognac evaporates. A term called *the angels portion* or the *angel's share* is associated with the evaporation. They say that when you visit Cognac, you can actually smell the evaporating Cognac in the air from the casks below.

Popular Cognac brands are Courvoisier (core-VAS-see-A), Hennessy (HEN-na-see), Martell (mar-TELL), and Remy Martin. Some bars serve one and a half ounces, others two ounces, while still others turn a brandy snifter on its side and pour until the spirit reaches the rim.

The King of Cognacs

King Louis the XIII, produced by Remy Martin, is considered the king of Cognacs. Only grapes from the Grande Champagne region are used, and it's aged in barrels that are several hundred years old. It can range in age from forty to one hundred years, and it's packaged in a Baccarat crystal bottle. It sells for $1,500 or more, and in bars across the globe it can sell for $120 to $300 a serving.

Fortified Wines

Port

Port is made in the Douro Valley, which is in North Portugal (however, other countries make versions of it). It was invented out of the need to have wine that could survive long sea voyages without spoiling. Brandy is added to wine, and then it's aged. A proper serving is two and a half to three ounces.

There are two basic groups of Port: wood-aged and bottle-aged. The wood-aged ports found in most bars are tawny and ruby. Ruby is sweeter then tawny. Popular Port brands are Sandeman, Lindemans, and Noval.

Sherry

Most Sherry comes from Jerez, in southwest Spain. It also has brandy added to fortify and preserve it. There are two types of Sherry: fino (fee-NO), which is light and dry, and oloroso (O-lo-ROW-so), dark and full-bodied. A proper serving is two and a half to three ounces.

Sherry is made using the *solera* system. Basically, wine is taken from the young Sherry casks and blended with the wine in the older Sherry casks, and vice versa. They say that the young wine refreshes the old wine, and old wine educates young ones. Popular Sherry brands are Dry Sack and Harvey's Bristol Cream.

Madeira

Madeira (ma-DEER-uh) fortified wine is produced from grapes grown on the southern coast of Madeira Island, which is about 360 miles west of Morocco in Northern Africa and 540 miles southwest from Portugal. Portugal has owned the island since 1974.

Madeira was used to toast the signing of the Declaration of Independence—it was looked upon as something very magical and special. To reach the New World, ships carrying Madeira had to pass through the tropics and the heat literally baked the wine, giving it a soft, deep, pleasant burnt taste. Soon, pipes filled with Madeira were installed with ship ballasts and sent on tropical voyages. The heat mixed with the constant rocking made this wine last for years without spoiling.

Brandy and Cognac are spirits but were discussed with the wines because of their relationship with it.

Russia and Poland fight, to this day, about who invented it first.

Vermouth

Vermouth is a fortified white wine that has a spirit added (usually brandy) and is aromatized with herbs and botanicals such as seeds, plants, flowers, and the like. It comes in two types: dry (white) and sweet (red). Sweet vermouth has caramelized sugar added to make it sweet and give it its color. The most popular drinks made with vermouth are the classic *Martinis* and *Manhattans*. Popular brands are; Martini & Rossi (Italy), Cinzano (Italy), and Noilly Prat (Noy-ee praht, France).

Dubonnet (America) and Kina Lillet (lee-LAY, France) are aperitif wines, but are often used in the place of vermouth in Martinis. The most popular Martini that uses Kina Lillet is from Ian Fleming's first book, *Casino Royale,* where James Bond asks for a dry Martini in a deep Champagne goblet. He says, "Three measures of Gordon's, one of vodka, half a measure of Kina Lillet. Shake it very well until it's ice cold, and then add a large thin slice of lemon-peel. Got it?"

Spirits

Spirits have had many names throughout time; some of the first were *ardent waters* ("ardent" means "to burn") and *the water of life*. The water of life was translated into many languages, the most popular being *eau-de-vie* (oh-duh-VEE) and *aquavit* (AH-kwah-veet). Other slang names are hooch, booze, firewater, moonshine, and potion.

Vodka

Vodka has been around since the 1300s, but it didn't taste like the vodka we know of today because it was flavored with herbs. Vodka can be made from potatoes, beets, grains, sugar, or any vegetation anywhere in the world. It's filtered through charcoal and un-aged, creating a colorless and almost tasteless and odorless spirit. The *Moscow Mule* is credited to introducing vodka (Smirnoff) to America in the 1940s. Screwdrivers were popular in the 1950s, and when James Bond ordered a Vodka Martini in the 1962 film, *Dr. No,* it skyrocketed vodka to the top. It's still the number-one spirit sold in America. The basic steps in making vodka are fermentation, distillation, filtration, dilution, and bottling.

The most popular vodka brands are Absolut (Sweden), Stolichnaya (STOW-lee-sha-NI-ya, Stoli for short), Smirnoff (SMEAR-nahf), Finlandia (Finland), Skyy (California), and the new, turn-of-the-century upscale vodkas: Belvedere, Chopin, Van Gogh, Grey Goose, etc. The most popular drinks made with vodka are *Screwdrivers, Cape Codders, Bloody Marys, Seabreezes, Baybreezes, Sex on the Beach, Lemondrops, Kamikazes, Cosmopolitans, Black and White Russians,* and *Madras.*

Fun Uses for Vodka

1. To remove a bandage painlessly, saturate the bandage with vodka—the alcohol dissolves the adhesive. **2.** To clean the caulking around bathtubs and showers, fill a trigger-spray bottle with vodka, spray the caulking, let it sit five minutes, and wash clean. The alcohol in the vodka kills mold and mildew. **3.** To clean your eyeglasses, simply wipe the lenses with a soft, clean cloth dampened with vodka. The alcohol in the vodka cleans the glass and kills germs. **4.** Prolong the life of your razors by filling a cup with vodka and letting your the blades soak in the alcohol after shaving. The vodka disinfects the blades and prevents rusting. **5.** Spray vodka on vomit stains, scrub with a brush, then blot dry—gone. **6.** Using a cotton ball, apply vodka to your face as an astringent to cleanse the skin and tighten pores. **7.** Add a jigger of vodka to a twelve-ounce bottle of shampoo. The alcohol cleanses the scalp, removes toxins from hair, and stimulates the growth of healthy hair. **8.** Fill a sixteen-ounce spray bottle with vodka and use it to kill bees or wasps. **9.** Pour one-half cup vodka and one-half cup water in a plastic baggie and freeze it for a slushy, refreshable ice pack for aches, pain, or black eyes. **10.** Fill a clean mayonnaise jar with freshly picked lavender flowers, fill the jar with vodka, seal the lid tightly, and set it in the sun for three days. Strain the liquid through a coffee filter, then apply the tincture to aches and pains. **11.** Make your own mouthwash by mixing nine tablespoons of powered cinnamon with one cup vodka. Seal in an airtight container for two weeks. Strain through a coffee filter then mix with warm water and rinse your mouth. Don't swallow. **12.** Using a Q-tip, apply vodka to a cold sore to help it dry out. **13.** If a blister opens, pour vodka over the raw skin as a local anesthetic that also disinfects the exposed dermis. **14.** To treat dandruff, mix one cup vodka with two teaspoons crushed rosemary, let sit for two days, strain through a coffee filter, and massage into your scalp and let dry. **15.** To treat an earache, put a few drops of vodka in your ear. Let it sit for a few minutes, then drain. The vodka will kill the bacteria that's causing the pain. **16.** To relieve a fever, use a washcloth to rub vodka on your chest and back as a liniment. **17.** To cure foot odor, wash your feet with vodka. **18.** Vodka will disinfect and alleviate a jellyfish sting. **19.** Pour vodka over an area affected by poison ivy to remove the poison oil from your skin. **20.** Swish a shot of vodka over an aching tooth. Allow your gums to absorb some of the alcohol to numb the pain. **21.** If all else fails, just turn the bottle up and drink it—nothing will matter anymore!

Gin

It's said that a Dutch professor and physician named Dr. Sylvius invented gin in the 1650s; however, many alcohol historians aren't quite sure. Some think that Italian monks had something to do with it because the juniper berry grows bountifully in Italy. Later in England, many things happened involving gin: The Gin Act, Gin Lane, and Gin Madness. Laws were passed, taxes were imposed, and gin became the liquid crack of London in the 1700s and 1800s. It turned London into a slum full of misery and despair. In the 1900s, Hollywood portrayed gin as a glamorous and sophisticated spirit served in a Martini glass. In its basic form, gin is really just vodka, but it's redistilled with herbs and botanicals, the juniper berry being the most detectable.

The most popular brands of gin are Bombay, Beefeater, Gordon's, Boodles, Tanqueray, and Plymouth. The most popular drinks made with gin are classic *Martinis, Tom Collinses, Pink Ladys, Gibsons*, and *Gin and Tonics*.

Rum

No other spirit conjures up tropical, sea-swept images like rum does. It's made from sugarcane or molasses and comes in varying shades from light/silver to medium/gold to heavy/dark, as well as flavored varieties. The first time the term *rum* was ever used was in 1672. And in 1862, Don Facundo Bacardi made the first light rum in Cuba. Popular rum brands are: Bacardi, Myers's, Appleton, Captain Morgan, and Mount Gay.

Popular rum drinks are *Daiquiris, Mai Tais, Hurricanes, Piña Coladas, Rum Punches, Zombies, Blue Hawaiians, Planters' Punches, Bahama Mamas*, and *Mojitos*.

Gin Facts
- Bombay Sapphire's bottle is a translucent light blue with the herbs and botanicals listed down the sides.

- The dark green Tanqueray bottle is said to be modeled after a British fire hydrant or a cocktail shaker. Most believe it's the latter, because the Tanqueray 10 bottle looks like a cocktail shaker as well.

- The first Seagram's gin bottle was textured with starfish and seashells.

- Sloe gin is not gin.

Of all the gin joints in all the towns in all the world, she walks into mine.
—Casablanca

Rum Facts
- Rum was issued daily to every sailor in the British Navy from 1651 until 1970.

- In medieval England, rum was often served with breakfast.

- In the 1800s, rum was considered excellent for cleaning hair.

- Bacardi is the most popular rum worldwide.

Tequila

Tequila is made from cacti…nope! This is a myth. Tequila is made from the agave (ah-GAHV-ee) plant.

You should know that mescal can be made from any agave plant or many types combined; however, Mexican law states that Tequila must be made from at least 51 percent the *blue* agave plant. Premium Tequilas are made from 100 percent blue agave and will say so on their labels.

The Four Types of Tequila

Blanco (BLAWN-ko): white Tequila aged less than two months. It's usually cheap and has a burning taste.

Reposado (ree-poh-SAH-doh): In Spanish, it means *rested*. It's aged in charred oak casks for two to twelve months, which gives it a golden color and makes it taste mellower than straight-out-of-the-still white Tequila. This is excellent Tequila for Margaritas because it gives the drink a bite to balance the tartness and sweetness of the lime juice and orange liqueur.

Joven (HO-ven): white Tequila blended with gold Tequila (usually reposado). This is a good Tequila for Margaritas too, but it's best to use the ones that say 100 percent agave on the bottle, because the cheap ones will add coloring to their white Tequila to make it look gold.

Añejo (on-YAY-ho): This is the smoothest Tequila available; it's the Cognac of Tequilas. It's aged for more than a year in barrels of 350 liters or smaller and is meant for sipping.

The most popular Tequila brands are Jose Cuervo, Sauza, Patron, Tres Generaciones, and Herradura. The most popular drinks made with Tequila are *Margaritas, Tequila Sunrises,* and *Bloody Marias.*

- So what's up with the worm? The worm is only found in mescal. Well, it's really not even a worm—it's a butterfly/caterpillar larva that's found naturally hanging out on agave plants. It's also supposed to be an aphrodisiac, but most think it's just a big marketing ploy.
- The traditional method of drinking Tequila is salt-Tequila-lime/lick-sip-bite. You can see now how the words *lick-sip-bite* easily gave conception to the Tequila body shot: lick a choice body part of your partner, sprinkle salt on the wet spot, and put the lime in their mouth, meat side out. Lick the salt, shoot the Tequila, then bite into the lime.
- Agave plants take up to ten years to grow.
- Bing Crosby imported the first 100 percent blue agave Tequila, Herradura, to America in 1950.
- Sauza's Hornitos derives its name from the horno, the traditional stone or brick oven used to soften piñas.
- *One Tequila, two Tequila, three Tequila, floor!* —Unknown

In the 1500s, the Spanish conquered the Aztecs and founded a town named Tequila. At the time there was only a honey wine alcohol being drunk, but the Spanish broke out their copper stills and Tequila was born. In the 1700s, the king of Spain granted land to Jose Antonio de Cuervo to cultivate the agave plant. Then for a short while liquor was outlawed in Mexico, but a new Spanish king lifted the prohibition and granted the second generation of the Cuervo family the first license to produce Tequila for a commercial market. Tequila became an icon of Mexican nationality, pride, and culture and has been recognized worldwide ever since.

Whiskey

Scotland and Ireland fight to this day about who first made whiskey. Whiskey, simply put, is aged grain alcohol fermented from malt or grain, distilled, then aged in wooden barrels whose color and flavor it absorbs. Whiskies and whiskeys include Bourbon, rye, Scotch whisky, Irish whiskey, single malt whisky, Canadian whisky, corn whiskey, Tennessee whiskey, and so on.

The four main countries that produce whiskey/whisky are Ireland, Scotland, America, and Canada. America and Ireland spell the drink whiskey, while Scotland and Canada spell it whisky. No one has a good answer why. (A few other countries produce whiskey, like Japan, Wales, and Spain but not nearly at the volume as these four countries.)

American Whiskey Facts

Single barrel Bourbon is the bottling of *one single barrel* of Bourbon.

Single batch Bourbons are bottlings from a *batch of barrels* that have been mixed prior to the bottling. Sour mash just means that some of the yeast mixture from one batch is used for another batch. It's the same when you make sour dough bread.

Jack Daniel's whiskey is filtered through 10 feet of sugar maple charcoal prior to aging. That's where it gets its flavor.

Southern Comfort is classified as a liqueur. No, it does not have a whiskey base to it. It's made with peaches and apricots.

The *Mint Julep* is the most popular drink made with Bourbon. It's the drink mascot of the Kentucky Derby.

Ireland

- Ireland produces Irish whiskey. Popular ones are Jameson and Bushmills.
- There are only three distilleries in all of Ireland. Bushmills has been there since 1608, making it the oldest distillery in the world. They dry their grain with kilns.
- Bailey's Irish Cream is a cream liqueur made with Irish whiskey. Irish cream is used in recipes like B-52, Mudslide, Nutty Irishman, Orgasm, and an Irish Car Bomb.
- Most times it is served neat, on the rocks, or with water or soda. Lemon twists are a common garnish.

Scotland

- Scotland produces blended Scotch whisky and single malt whisky. Some popular blended Scotch whiskies are Chivas Regal, J&B, Cutty Sark, Johnnie Walker, Dewar's, and Pinch. Popular single malt Scotch whisky brands are: Glenlivet, Glenmorangie, Laphroaig, and Glenfiddich. Scotch whisky is known for its smoky flavor, which comes from drying the malted barley over peat fires. Scotland is divided into four geographical flavors: Lowlands, Highlands, Speyside, and The Islands.
- Scotch is served neat, on the rocks, or with water or soda water. Sometimes guests request a lemon or lemon twist. Every once in a while you'll get an order for a Scotch sour.
- Scotland has a liqueur made with Scotch whisky, heather honey, and herbs called Drambuie.
- When a European orders whiskey, they usually mean Scotch whisky. Double check with them.

Canada

- Canada produces Canadian whisky and rye such as Crown Royal, Canadian Club, Seagram's VO, Black Velvet, Canadian Mist, and Highwood.
- Canada blends many whiskies together for their blended whisky. By law, whisky in Canada must be aged for at least

three years. Most people think of rye whisky when they think of Canada. Often, a guest from Canada will ask an American bartender for a rye and coke or a rye and ginger.

• Popular recipes include whisky sours and whisky highballs.

America

America produces Bourbon, corn whiskey, rye, and Tennessee whiskey.

• Popular whiskey brands from America are Jack Daniel's, Wild Turkey, Jim Beam, Evan Williams, Maker's Mark, Booker's, Woodford Reserve, Knob Creek, Seagram's 7, Old Overholt, Van Winkle, Basil Hayden's, Old Crow, Ezra Brooks, George Dickel, and Early Times.

• The U.S. government specifically defines and recognizes twenty-nine different types of whiskeys. Most people are familiar with only six. There are strict laws governing just what a whiskey must be to be labeled as such. For example, at least 51 percent of the grain used in making the whiskey must be corn. Also, Bourbon must be aged for a minimum of two years in new, white-oak barrels that have been charred. Nothing can be added at bottling to enhance flavor, add sweetness, or alter color.

The Deal with Bourbon

Bourbon can be made anywhere in the United States, but Kentucky is the only state that can put the words "Kentucky Bourbon" on the bottle. Way back when, whiskey made in Bourbon County, Kentucky, was sent down the river to New Orleans with the barrels stamped with the word "Bourbon." Thus, whiskey and Bourbon became synonymous.

Popular Liqueurs and Their Flavors

Absinthe (AB-sinth): Anise/licorice
Advocaat (ad-vo-KAHT): Eggnog
Amaretto: Almond
Annisette (ANN-eh-set): Anise/licorice
Blue Curacao (CURE-uh-sow, sow rhymes with cow): Orange
Chambord (Sham-BOARD): Black raspberry
Coffee liqueur: Chocolate coffee
Cointreau (KWAHN-troh): Orange
Crème de banana: Banana
Crème de cocoa (ca-KAY-o, ca KAH-o): Chocolate; Comes in dark/brown and white/clear
Crème de cassis (ca-CEASE): Black currant
Crème de menthe: Mint; Comes in green and white/clear
Crème de noyaux (noy-YOH): Almond
Drambuie (dram-BOO-ee): Honey, Scotch whisky, and herbs
Frangelico: Hazelnut
Galliano (gall-LEEYAH-no): Anise, herbs, and spices
Goldschlager: Cinnamon
Grand Marnier (marn-YAY): Orange Cognac
Irish cream: Irish whiskey, chocolate, coffee, vanilla, and cream
Licor 43: Citrus vanilla
Limoncello: Sweet lemon
Malibu: coconut rum
Midori (mi-DOOR-ee): Honeydew melon

Pernod (purr-NO):
    Licorice/anise
Parfait Amour (par-fay uh-
    MORE): Roses, violets,
    vanilla, and spices
Passoã (pass-SO-a):
    Passion fruit
Rumple Minze (ROOM-pull
    MINTS): Peppermint
Sambuca: Licorice/anise
Sloe gin: Sloe berries
Southern Comfort: Peach,
    apricot, and honey
Tequila Rose: Strawberry
    Tequila cream
Triple sec: Orange
Tuaca (tuh-WAH-kuh):
    Vanilla orange caramel
    brandy

Liqueurs and Cordials

Liqueurs (lih-KYOOR), cordials (CORE-jull), crèmes, and schnapps are very sweet, flavorful, and usually low-proof spirits. Liqueurs come in every flavor imaginable. Always keep in mind that for every brand-name liqueur there is also another less expensive copycat version of it on the market.

Mixers and Garnishes

2

The first known mention of the word "cocktail" was found in *The Farmer's Cabinet* on April 28, 1803. It said, "Drank a glass of cocktail—excellent for the head...Call'd at the Doct's. found Burnham—he looked very wise—drank another glass of cocktail."

The first known definition of the word cocktail can be found in the *The Balance and Columbian Repository*, a Hudson, New York, newspaper on May 6, 1806: "Cocktail is stimulating liquor composed of spirits of any kind, sugar, water, and bitters."

Mixers

Orange juice, cranberry juice, pineapple juice, grapefruit juice, lemon-lime juice (sweet-n-sour mix), Bloody Mary mix, strawberry mix, olive juice, V8 juice, and tomato juice.

Some common mixed drinks that call for juice are: *Screwdriver, Bloody Mary, Cape Codder, Greyhound, Seabreeze, Baybreeze, and Madras.*

Sweet Mixers

Simple syrup, grenadine, maraschino syrup, coconut cream, flavored syrups, liqueurs and cordials, honey, gomme (GAWM, a French simple syrup), orgeat (OAR-zhat), and lime cordial (which is a syrup made from lime juice and sugar).

Some common drinks that call for sweet mixers are: *Tequila Sunrise, Piña Colada, Mai Tai, Gimlet, Kamikaze, and Daiquiri.*

Savory Mixers

Hot sauces, Worcestershire sauce (WOOS-tuhr-sheer), beef bouillon, steak sauce, Clamato juice, and clam juice.

Bitters

Mention the word "bitters" to a cocktail connoisseur, modern mixologist, or bar chef, and their eyes light up. Almost every bar has a bottle of the most popular bitters, Angostura (ang-uh-STORE-ah), from Trinidad. It has a funky paper label that doesn't form fit to the top part of the bottle, and though almost all bartenders would recognize it, I'd guess that a full 80 percent know nothing about this mysterious potion. They've probably coated a lemon wedge with it and given it to a guest to suck for hiccups, jerked several dashes in a short glass of soda water to cure a stomachache, and they've probably even tried to read the writing on the label on a slow afternoon only to discover that this stuff is, wow, 90 proof!

Bitters is made from the distillation of aromatic herbs, spices, bark, roots, and seeds. Common ingredients include dried orange peels, myrrh, saffron, caraway seeds, cardamom seeds, coriander seeds, chamomile, rhubarb, and bark.

Some common savory mix drinks are: *Bloody Mary, Bloody Bull, Bloody Caesar, Bloody Maria, Red Eye,* and *Prairie Fire.*

Dairy Mixers

Milk, cream, half-and-half, whipped cream, ice cream, hot chocolate, yogurt, unsalted butter, eggnog, eggs, and egg white (however, a lot of bars don't allow the use of raw eggs due to the chance of salmonella).

Some common dairy mix drinks are: *Grasshopper, Brandy Alexander, White Russian, Hot Buttered Rum,* and *Pisco Sour.*

Carbonated Mixers

Cola, diet cola, soda water (also called seltzer and club soda), tonic water, ginger ale, ginger beer, Perrier, Pellegrino, Champagne, sparkling wine, beer, and lemon-lime soda such as Sprite or 7-Up.

Some common carbonated mix drinks are: *Bourbon & Coke, Rum & Coke, 7&7, Presbyterian, Vodka Tonic, Gin & Tonic, Moscow Mule,* and *Shandy.*

Dry Mixers

Sugar, brown sugar, raw sugar, powdered sugar, sugar cube, salt, celery salt, chili pepper, cayenne pepper, white pepper, cocoa powder, cloves, cinnamon, spicy seasonings, powdered hot chocolate, and powdered apple cider.

Novelty Mixers

Red Bull, Jell-O, Mountain Dew, Kool-Aid, Gatorade, flavored colas, Yoo-Hoo, Fresca, and food coloring.

Sundry Mixers

This is my miscellaneous category for all the mixes that just didn't quite fit into one of the others.

Bitters, vanilla extract, flower waters, horseradish, and wasabi. Common drinks using sundry mixes are: *Ramos Fizz, Old Fashioned, Manhattan, Bloody Mary,* and *Piña Colada.*

Garnishes

Most girls can relate to garnishes: they are the accessories of the cocktail world, like jewelry and handbags are to our outfits.

Lime

The lime wedge is by far the preferred and most professional way to cut a lime. Cut the lime lengthwise. You don't have to cut the ends off first. When you don't cut the ends, it allows the wedge to be held and squeezed without getting the meat all over you or your guest's fingers, plus it just looks prettier because you kept the natural curve of the lime intact. Hold one of the halves meat-side towards you and cut a slit across the inside of the lime. This will create slits in your wedges so that you can slip one on the rim of a glass. Repeat with the other half. Make three cuts to get four wedges.

All bars have their own policies about lime wedges. Some will want you to place the lime on the rim of the glass for sanitary reasons. After all, when you think about it, a bartender's hands are pretty nasty. You are touching so many gross things: money, dirty glasses, dirty bar towels, ashtrays. If you set the fruit on the rim, allowing the guest to decide if they want the lime squeezed, simply lay an extra cocktail napkin down for them to wipe their hands with. If you're allowed to squeeze the fruit, cup your other hand around the drink when you do it so no one gets squirted.

Handmade Simple Syrup
Makes 3 cups

2 cups sugar
2 cups water

Heat the sugar and the water in a pan on the stove while stirring. When it starts to a boil, reduce the heat and continue to stir for another 5 minutes. Remove from the heat and let it cool. The result is simple syrup. It can be stored in the fridge for a long time.

You can also make a no-cook simple syrup by filling a bottle half with sugar and half with lukewarm water. Shake, then after the cloudiness clears, shake again. For sugar-free simple syrup, replace sugar with Splenda.

Insider tip: Keep the orange juice and sweet-n-sour mix closest to you—they are the most used of the mixers.

Margaritas should have lime juice, and a whiskey sour should have lemon juice.

There are many different types of bars, but I'm willing to bet that if you chose one bar and laid all their garnishes and decorations side-by-side, you could tell what type of bar it was even if you had never been there. High-end bars will always have the freshest and largest selection of garnishes, and low-end bars will always have only the basic four. All other bars fall in-between.

Lemons

Lemons win for the most uses. It's automatically used for a *Long Island Iced Tea, Long Beach Tea, Texas Tea, Chocolate Cake Shot, Lynchburg Lemonade,* and tomato juice. It can also be requested for a Tequila shot, iced water, vodka soda, scotch & water, scotch & soda, and really anything else that the guests wants.

Lemon Twists
Peel-Off Twists
There are a few ways to cut lemon twists. The most common is to make peel-off twists. Simply take a lemon (try to pick a long one) and make incisions through the skin, stopping at the meat all the way around the lemon. Now, some bartenders cut off both ends and then cut the incisions, but this just makes a juicy mess all over their hands. The size of the twists is up to you, but don't make them too thin. After you've made the incisions, cut off one end. At this point the twist can be pulled off when needed. Some bartenders cut both ends off, but that just makes a shorter twist, and it's not necessary because the twist will rip right off.

Curly Twists
Another way to make lemon twists is to remove the meat of the lemon from the skin, then roll up the skin and cut it into pieces (like cinnamon rolls). It makes long, curly twists. There are a few ways to get the whole skin off the lemon. One is to cut the ends off, then make an lengthwise incision half way through the lemon. Use your fingers to separate the rind from the meat. Another way is to omit the halfway incision and use a spoon—just stick it between the skin and the meat and run it around the lemon until it separates. Also, you could always soak a couple lemons in hot water while cutting your other fruit. The heat loosens the skin from the meat, so when you remove the skin it slips off easily.

Maraschino Cherries

Yes, maraschino cherries come from real cherries. They are named after the marasca cherry, which is used to make cherry liqueurs. There are three basic steps taken to turn a fresh-harvested batch of cherries into maraschino cherries. First, they soak in a solution of brine, sodium metabisulfite, calcium chloride, and citric acid. The sodium metabisulfite transforms into sodium dioxide, the calcium keeps the cherry firm, and the citric acid balances the pH of the solution. It's similar to the process of turning cucumbers into pickles. During this process, the cherries lose their color. Next, the cherries are sorted by size and pitted with a star-shaped needle. They are then rinsed and packed into jars with corn syrup, water, flavored syrup (usually almond), preservatives, and red food color #40. You'll also see some upscale bars with green maraschino cherries that are peppermint flavored.

Olives

The olive tree is the oldest tree in continuous cultivation. Olives are used in the classic *Martini* and sometimes *Bloody Marys*. Some high-end bars remove the pimento (which is a pickled pepper) and stuff them with blue cheese, anchovies, or almonds. For a classic *Martini*, one unspeared olive or two olives speared through the side with a cocktail pick is proper.

Cocktail Onions

Cocktail onions are pickled pearl onions, which are small, white, and mild-flavored. They are generally only used to make a Gibson (a classic *Martini* with onions instead of olives).

Sweet-n-Sour Mix
Makes 6 cups

Sour mix is probably the most confusing mixer for most novice bartenders because we're so accustomed to buying it in pre-mixed bottles. If you've looked at drink recipe books, you'll see some recipes that call for fresh squeezed lemon or lime juice and a spoonful of sugar. Basically, this is sweet-n-sour mix made to order.

Sweet-n-Sour Mix
Juice from 6 lemons
Juice from 6 limes
4 cups of sugar
6 cups water

When you mix the juice and simple syrup together you're striving to reach a perfect balance of sweet with sour. Keep taste-testing until you find your preference because not all lemons and limes yield the same amount of juice.

29

Oranges

Oranges can be found in most medium- to high-end bars. The most popular use for them as a garnish is to make flags: a cherry speared on an orange slice with a cocktail pick.

You'll find flags garnishing a *Tom Collins, Whiskey Sour, Amaretto Sour,* and some tropical drinks. You'll also find an orange slice muddled with sugar and bitters to make an *Old Fashioned.*

There are a couple of ways to cut oranges. To me, the typical half-wheel orange is too much of a garnish. I like to cut them one more time to have a quarter orange. After all, we're just enhancing the drink, not feeding the guest.

Pineapple

You really only find pineapple garnishes in bars located in sunny places. It's considered very exotic and is somewhat expensive. The most famous cocktail it garnishes is the *Piña Colada.*

Like the orange you don't really need a huge slice, so I like to cut them in quartered sizes. Make a pineapple flag by spearing a cherry on it.

Celery

Celery is used in a *Bloody Mary.* Take the bunch and cut off the bottom ends, then rinse all the stalks. I like to cut them off at an angle (like how you cut flowers) so they have interesting pointed ends. Some people hack off the tops, but I think it looks nice to keep the leaves. One whole stalk is really too much for a drink, so slice the stalk lengthwise to make two pieces from one. You can skewer many items to the celery stalk, like scallions, olives, cherry tomatos, peppers, peel-n-eat-shrimp, etc.

Strawberries

Strawberries are a high-ticket item—especially when they aren't in season—but high-end bars or tourist bars in warm climates will stock them. They can be used to garnish a *Strawberry Daiquiri*, glass of *Champagne*, *Mimosa*, or muddled to make a *Strawberry Mojito*.

Bananas

You will mostly find bananas in tropical bars; they are used to make *Banana Daiquiris*. Lots of bartenders will cut off the top 1/4 of the banana (skin and meat), make a slit in the bottom of it, then set it on the rim of the glass. The rest of the banana is used to make the drink.

Mint

A sprig of mint consists of about three leaves. Mint leaves are used for *Mint Juleps* and *Mojitos*.

Other garnishes include:
   Kiwi, star fruit (I love this one!), sugar, pepper, kosher salt, coconut flakes, chocolate syrup, chocolate shavings, cocoa powder, chili powder, raw horseradish, scallions, cherry tomato, cocktail shrimp, pickled okra, pickled green beans, pickled asparagus, peppers, nutmeg, whipped cream, cookies, rock candy, swizzle sticks, and coffee beans.

Drinks that get an automatic cherry are *Manhattan, Amaretto Sour, Whiskey Sour, Tom Collins,* and *Shirley Temple.* Other drinks that might get a cherry are *Piña Colada, Sour Appletini,* tropical and exotic drinks, and whipped cream drinks.

Modern mixologists have created cocktails using such random foods as grapes, blueberries, raspberries, blackberries, rose petals, flowers, basil, sugared ginger, cucumber, cinnamon sticks, edible pearl dust, and oysters on the half shell. If you shake a clear drink made with the edible pearl dust, it will have a beautiful, shimmering luster. There's also a vodka from Canada called Pearl, so you could design a cocktail with a pearl theme and maybe add a rim of edible gold flake. Just look on the Internet for the edible pearl dust and gold flake.

Here are some nontoxic flowers that you can use as a garnish: Angelica, anise hyssop, apple blossoms, arugula blossoms, banana blossoms, basil blossoms, bee balm blossoms, borage, marigolds, carnations, chrysanthemum, chamomile, citrus blossoms, dandelion, elderberry, fuchsia, hibiscus, honeysuckle, hyacinth, jasmine, lavender, sage blossoms, roses, petunia, primrose, and sunflower petals.
Some toxic flowers to avoid include: Daffodil, lily, sunflower, azalea, mistletoe, morning glory, periwinkle, wisteria, wild cherry blossoms, narcissus, poinsettia, peony, rhododendron, African violet, and baby's breath.

Without a doubt, the lime wedge is at the top of the garnish heap. It's automatically used for a gin & tonic, vodka tonic, rum & tonic (Older people order rum & tonic. Limes are NOT automatically used for a rum & coke. They are used for a *Cuba Libre*, which is a rum & coke with a lime), *Cape Codder, Seabreeze, Margarita*, soda water, and Perrier. It can also be used for a *Bloody Mary*, shot of Tequila, and muddled for a *Mojito* or *Caipirinha*.

Garnishing Tips

Garnishes are put into a fruit tray. It's ideal for a bartender to set the fruit tray behind the bar so guests aren't constantly sticking their nasty fingers into it, thinking it's a free buffet (a bartender's pet peeve). Some bartenders put ice underneath the containers of the tray to keep the fruit cool. If the tray has to be on the bar top, try to keep the olives near you—they're the #1 thing most guests zoom in on.

Keep in mind:
- Cutting boards that are used to cut meat should never be used to cut garnishes.
- You will always need more limes than lemons in your fruit tray.
- Some bars may require you to wear a cut-resistant glove with a rubber glove. Just a rubber glove on one hand is nice too because it keeps your fingers from being stained from the cherries and keeps the burning citrus off.
- In most bars, you'll have to cut backup fruit in case you run out.
- Try to preassemble or prep any garnishes so that it does not slow you down throughout your shift.

Recipes to Remember

3

Of all the chapters in this book, this is the one I'm most excited about because it's not like most bar guides. The majority are filled with three hundred pages of crazy, random drink recipes that no real bartender will ever be asked to make. Guests under the age of twenty-five love to order the crazy club drinks with wild names, but past twenty-five, guests tend to order beer, wine, or standards because they've drank enough to know what they like. There are some exceptions however; establishments carry their own specialty menus that you'll have to learn (but they're just spin-offs from the drinks in this chapter), and there are different types of bars in many geographic locations. For example, you'll probably be making more tropical drinks in Florida, and more hot drinks in Wisconsin. And high-end bars will be making more classic cocktails than low-end bars.

> Memorize these recipes the same way you would memorize anything else: repetition. Try making and using flash cards.

The recipes are grouped into ten categories: Juicy, Creamy, Sour, Tropical, Hot, Stick, Shots, Classic, Highballs and Miscellaneous. This way you can see how the drinks relate to each other as families, which will make them easier to remember. You will also notice that some drinks are mentioned several times in different categories: another memory trick. Buying a pocket-sized address book with alphabetical tabs is highly recommended. Write these drinks in the address book, and as time goes by simply add more and more recipes to your collection. Having these essential recipes at your fingertips is very comforting.

Drink-Making Terms

Build: Fill a glass with ice and pour in the ingredients.

Stir: Fill a glass with ice, build, then stir with a straw. In the case of stirring a classic Martini or Manhattan, you are stirring the mixture in a shaker glass of ice with a bar spoon, then straining with a julep strainer.

Roll: Fill a glass with ice, build the drink, then pour it into a shaker tin or glass and quickly back into the original glass, without shaking. It's like a chemistry-set pour.

Shake: Fill a glass with ice, build the ingredients, then pour everything into a shaker tin and shake. Pour everything back into the original glass.

Well, call, premium, and **ultra premium:** Refer to the quality and/or price level of spirits you offer at your bar. Behind the bar, for example, the vodka that you keep in your speed rail/well is the *well* vodka. Smirnoff will probably be the *call* vodka, then Absolut is typical *premium* vodka. Ketel One is considered *ultra premium* vodka (sometimes called super premium or boutique). Just so you know, there wasn't an ultra premium category until the Grey Goose, single batch–type *boutique* spirits hit the market.

Back: An extra glass of something to accompany a drink. For example, you may get an order for a Bourbon on the rocks with a water back. What they want is Bourbon on ice with a short glass of water set about an inch behind the Bourbon.

Chaser: An extra glass of something to drink right after a shot of liquor. A common chaser is beer.

Shake and Strain: Pour ingredients into a shaker tin filled half with ice, shake, and strain into the glass. This method is typical for shooters and Martinis.

Shake and Strain over Ice: Pour ingredients into a shaker tin filled half with ice, shake, and strain into a glass of ice.

Float: Gently pour on top of a drink. You're floating it on top.

Layer: Spirits and/or ingredients poured on top of one another to create layers. An object, such as a bar spoon, is often used to break the fall so that the new ingredient layers gently on top of the spirit below. Before you begin to layer, gather all your bottles and line them up next to you.

Blend: To mix in an electric blender.

Rim: To add something to the rim of the glass, like salt to a Margarita glass.

Chill: To chill a glass, add ice and then water to the glass, and allow it to chill while you are making the drink. When ready, empty the glass and pour in the drink. Mostly, you are chilling Martini/cocktail glasses. A lot of bars these days keep Martini glasses in coolers, so you don't have to hand-chill them.

Muddle: To crush up ingredients such as fruit with a muddler to extract essential oils and flavors.

Flame: To set a drink on fire. The most common method is to float 151 rum on top of a drink, then light with a match (don't use a lighter—lighter fluid goes into the drink). Other popular spirits used for flaming are Grand Marnier and Sambuca, and cinnamon sprinkled on top of a flame creates a mini-firework show. Other spirits can be flamed if you heat them up slightly first and then put them into a heated glass as well. Whatever liquor you're setting on fire, be careful.

On the rocks: Over ice.

Straight Up: Chilled in a shaker tin and strained. The term *up* is the same as *straight up*.

Neat: Room-temperature; pour straight from the bottle. No ice.

Drink-Making Tips:

- Always serve a cocktail on a beverage napkin to absorb the condensation.
- Never fill a cocktail to the brim. Somewhere between 1/4" and 1/2" from the rim is proper.
- Anytime an ingredient is mentioned, try to use the highest possible quality of that ingredient. Of course, when you work for an establishment you have to use what they provide, but at home parties and handmade cocktail bars you can use the best.
- Some drinks have geographical or preferential differences in measures and ingredients. This is nothing to have a fight over: just make it the way your boss wants you to or agree with the other bartenders so that it's made consistently. Always make it the way a guest prefers.
- If possible, always make a guest's drink in front of them. This presentation makes a little a show for them and makes more sense than making the drink and then trying to carry it to them.
- If possible, preheat coffee glasses with hot water for a few seconds before making a coffee drink.

Free Pour: Making drinks by *freely pouring* out of the bottle without a measuring device.

Speed Rail: A long stainless-steel shelf about the height of your knees that holds the most commonly used well liquors. It's usually connected to the ice well.

Experienced and professional bartenders always grab and pour a bottle by the upper neck, and many times they wrap a finger around the pour spout in case it slips out.

- When you get several orders at once, the first thing you should do is grab your glassware, ice them (if needed), and set them in order on the bar mat in front of your well. This way, if you forget what you're making, all you have to do is glance at the glassware and nine times out of ten you'll remember.
- If a drink has one spirit on the rocks (or two spirits without a mixer, like a rusty nail) then it gets *one* straw or cocktail stir stick to stir the drink and help the ice melt. It's then sipped from the rim of the glass. Drinks with mixers served in short highballs or Old-Fashioned glasses get two cocktail straws for stirring and sipping.
- Other ways straws are used are to *mark* drinks. Let's say a server needs a coke and a diet coke. How will the server know which is which? Stick a small cocktail straw in one of them to differentiate. Once your system is established then you can keep marking drinks, and the server will know what they are. Another good system is lining up the drinks in the exact order they were given.
- Servers are generally responsible for garnishing their own drinks.
- Alcohol portions normally add up to two ounces or less. It's very rare for drinks to contain more than that.
- When guests ask for cream, they mean half-and-half.
- Never shake carbonated mixers unless you enjoy mini-explosions.
- If a draft beer has been sitting long enough for the head to go down, covertly stick in a straw and swirl it around to beat the head back up before serving.
- When a guest lays a napkin on top of their drink, it means that they will be returning.

When you look at recipe websites and books, sometimes they give instructions in *parts*. A part is an equally divided section of the whole. Let's say that your recipe says, mix together one part vodka, one part orange juice, and one part cranberry juice. That's three *parts,* right? You're just going to mix equal parts of all those ingredients together.

The Drink Families

Juicy Drinks

Screwdriver

It's said that the *Screwdriver* got its name from American oil-riggers who were working in the Middle East in the 1950s. They stirred this drink with a screwdriver.

Glass: Highball; however, some bars want it made in a tall Collins glass, and others may want it in a short Old-Fashioned glass.

    1 1/2 ounces of vodka

    Fill with orange juice

Mixing Method: Build.

Garnish: None. If you work in a bar with a decent budget then you'll use an orange slice or a flag.

Note: If you float half an ounce of Galliano on top of a *Screwdriver* it makes it a *Harvey Wallbanger*. It's said the drink got its name from a California surfer named Harvey who would request this drink and, after drinking a few, would walk into a wall.

Cape Codder (Cape Cod)

The *Cape Codder* gets its name from the cranberries grown near Cape Cod, Massachusetts. When harvest time rolls around in October, farmers flood the cranberry fields to make the cranberries float to the top.

Glass: Highball; however, some bars want it made in a tall Collins glass, and others may want it in a short Old-Fashioned glass.

    1 1/2 ounces of vodka

    Fill with cranberry juice

Mixing Method: Build.

Garnish: Lime wedge.

Note: When someone orders a *vodka and cranberry* it does

Screwdriver/Orange Juice Family:

Sloe Screw: vodka, sloe gin, and orange juice (some omit the vodka)

Sloe Comfortable Screw: vodka, sloe gin, Southern Comfort, and orange juice

Sloe Comfortable Screw Up Against the Wall: vodka, sloe gin, Southern Comfort, Galliano, and orange juice

Alabama Slammer: shooter or drink made with vodka, sloe gin, Southern Comfort, amaretto, and orange juice

Hairy Navel: vodka, peach schnapps, and orange juice

Melon Ball: vodka, melon liqueur, and orange juice

Bocce Ball (BOTCH-ee): amaretto and orange juice

Mimosa: Champagne and orange juice

Cape Cod/Cranberry Family:

Woo Woo: vodka, peach schnapps, and cranberry juice

Scarlett O'Hara: Southern Comfort and cranberry juice

37

Washington Apple: shooter or Martini made with equal parts of Crown Royal, Apple Pucker, and cranberry juice

Red Snapper: shooter made with equal parts of Crown Royal, amaretto, and cranberry juice

---

Greyhound Family:
Salty Dog: vodka, grapefruit juice, and a salted rim.

not automatically get a lime wedge, but lime wedges do automatically garnish a *Cape Cod.*

Madras (MAD-dress)

A *madras* is just the combination of a *Screwdriver* and a *Cape Codder* without the lime.

Glass: Highball; however, some bars want it made in a tall collins glass, and others may want it in a short Old-Fashioned glass.

1 1/2 ounces of vodka

Fill with equal parts of orange and cranberry juice.
Mixing Method: Build.
Garnish: None. If you are in an upscale bar then you might get an orange slice or flag.

Greyhound

Glass: Highball; however, some bars want it made in a tall Collins glass, and others may want it in a short Old-Fashioned glass.

1 1/2 ounces of vodka

Fill with grapefruit juice
Mixing Method: Build.
Garnish: None.
Note: Pink grapefruit juice can be used. Also, you'll find that some people will just order a *vodka grapefruit* instead of asking for a *greyhound.* If they order a *sweet vodka grapefruit* or *sweet greyhound* then they want a little grenadine or simple syrup added.

Seabreeze

A *Seabreeze* is the combination of a *Greyhound* and a *Cape Codder.*

Glass: Highball; however, some bars want it made in a tall collins glass and others may want it in a short Old-Fashioned glass.

    1 1/2 ounces of vodka

    Fill with equal parts grapefruit and cranberry juice.

Mixing Method: Build.

Garnish: Lime.

Note: This drink is supposed to get just a splash of cranberry juice, but most people want a little more than that. Guests that want just the splash will usually order it as a splash.

Baybreeze

The *Baybreeze* is also called the *Hawaiian Seabreeze.* When you substitute the grapefruit juice in a *Seabreeze* with pineapple juice, you've made a *Baybreeze.*

Glass: Highball; however, some bars want it made in a tall collins glass, and others may want it in a short Old-Fashioned glass.

    1 1/2 ounces of vodka

    Fill with equal parts of pineapple and cranberry juice

Mixing Method: Build.

Garnish: None, but if you are working in an upscale bar then you'll probably use a pineapple slice. If you are in a nightclub then it's common for a cherry to be dropped on top if the guest is female.

Baybreeze/Pineapple Juice Family:

Pearl Harbor: vodka, melon liqueur, and pineapple juice

Hollywood: vodka, Chambord, and pineapple juice

Surfer on Acid: shooter of equal parts of Jägermeister, coconut rum, and pineapple juice

Malibu & Pineapple: Malibu rum and pineapple juice

Fuzzy Navel Family:
Hairy Navel:
vodka, peach schnapps,
and orange juice

Sex on the Beach Family:
Redheaded Slut:
peach schnapps,
Jägermeister, and cranberry
juice

Fuzzy Navel

The *Fuzzy Navel* became extremely popular in 1984 when DeKuyper Peachtree Schnapps hit the market.

Glass: Highball; however, some bars want it made in a tall Collins glass, and others may want it in a short Old-Fashioned glass.

> 1 1/2 ounces of peach schnapps
> Fill with orange juice

Mixing Method: Build.

Garnish: None, but if you are working in an upscale bar then you'll probably use an orange slice or flag.

Sex on the Beach

There are about five different ways to make a *Sex on the Beach;* this is the original recipe. Also, some recipes call for more vodka than peach schnapps, but I've found that it tastes better with equal amounts.

Glass: Tall.

> 1 ounce of vodka
> 1 ounce of peach schnapps
> Fill with equal parts of cranberry and orange juice

Mixing Method: Build.

Garnish: None, but if you are working in an upscale bar then you'll probably use an orange slice or flag.

Note: By now, you can see how these juicy drinks are closely related. This drink is just a *Fuzzy Navel* and a *Cape Codder* combined without the lime. Other *Sex on the Beach* recipes add melon and/or raspberry liqueur and pineapple juice.

Cosmopolitan (Cosmo)

The *Cosmopolitan* was probably the most popular cocktail of the late twentieth century; just when it was starting to die off, the hit TV show *Sex in the City* skyrocketed its fame worldwide and carried it into the twenty-first century.

Glass: Martini.

    1 1/2 ounces of citrus vodka

    1/2 ounce of Cointreau

    1/4 ounce lime juice

    1/2 ounce cranberry juice

Mixing Method: Shake and strain, or stir.

Garnish: Lime wedge, lime wheel, lemon twist, or lemon wheel are the most common.

Note: The *Cosmo* is basically just a combination of a *Cape Codder* and a *Kamikaze*. Many bars across the nation have their own way of making this cocktail. Some swear that you should only use fresh-squeezed lime juice and splash the cranberry to just color it pink, while others will use a full ounce of cranberry juice. Again, it's what the guest wants.

Tequila Sunrise

They say that the *Tequila Sunrise* was created in Mexico in the 1950s for welcoming tourists to Acapulco and Cancun. They also say that a Mexican bartender who stayed up all night drinking with his friends was found in the bar when the boss walked in the next day. His explanation to the boss is that he wanted to concoct a drink that looked like the sun was rising. The drink gained popularity again in the 1970s, when the Eagles released a song of the same name.

Glass: Highball.

    1 1/2 ounces of Tequila

    Fill with orange juice

    Pour in 1/2 ounce of grenadine and it will sink to the bottom

Mixing Method: Build.

Garnish: None.

Tequila Sunrise Family:

Freddy Fudpucker: Tequila, orange juice, and grenadine

The Top Juicy Drinks You Must Know:

Alabama Slammer
Baybreeze
Bloody Mary
Cape Codder
Cosmopolitan
Fuzzy Navel
Greyhound
Madras
Malibu & Pineapple
Screwdriver
Seabreeze
Sex on the Beach
Sloe Screw Family
Tequila Sunrise

Top Juicy Drinks You Must Know in a Nightclub:

Redheaded Slut
Red Snapper
Surfer on Acid
Washington Apple
Woo Woo

Bloody Mary Family:

Red Snapper: gin and Bloody Mary mix (not to be confused with the hip-hop *red snapper,* made with cranberry juice)

Bloody Bull: vodka, Bloody Mary mix, and beef bouillon

Bloody Caesar: vodka and Clamato

Bloody Maria: Tequila and Bloody Mary mix

Red Beer: tomato juice and beer (Bloody Mary mix and beer is popular too)

Bloody Mary

The juice extractor hit the market in 1921, and tomato juice came out the very same year. It's said that Paris bartender Pete Petiot was the first to mix vodka and tomato juice. Supposedly he named it after a Chicago bar, Bucket of Blood, and a regular named Mary who would visit him there. He then took his *Bloody Mary* to the King Cole Bar in New York City and embellished it with pepper, Worcestershire sauce, Tabasco, lemon, lime, and raw horseradish and sold it as a hangover cure. The name changed to *Red Snapper,* then *Morning Glory,* and then back to *Bloody Mary.* This cocktail is also considered a classic.

Glass: Highball, but many glasses are used for this drink.
　1 1/2 ounces of vodka
　Fill with Bloody Mary mix
Mixing Method: Build then roll. Do not shake.
Garnish: *Bloody Marys* win hands down for the most garnishes that can be used. They can include celery, green olives, scallions, cherry tomatoes, jumbo cocktail shrimp, rimmed with salt, Cajun spice or celery salt, pickled okra, pickled green beans, pickled asparagus, lime, lemon, pepperoncini pepper, carrot, dill pickle, beef jerky, or oyster on the half shell. And hot sauce, Worcestershire, wasabi, raw horseradish, beef bouillon, chili powder, white pepper, bitters, and a splash of Guinness can all be added to the drink.
Note: You can use store-bought Bloody Mary mix then embellish it, or make it from scratch.

A Charming Secret

My secret ingredient is A-1 steak sauce. Every single person always makes a comment on the taste. I've even had guests from the restaurant side come hunt me down asking about the mix I used. When guests are at the bar, I have a small platter filled with goodies such as Worcestershire, hot sauce, bitters, salt and pepper, lemon, and lime wedges. The look on a guest's face when you set the small platter next to their drink is priceless. They feel so pampered.

Creamy Drinks

White Russian

The name of this drink comes from the war between the White Russians and the Red Army in the Russian Civil war of 1918 to 1921.

Glass: Highball.
    1 ounce of vodka
    1 ounce of coffee liqueur
    3 ounces of half-and-half
Mixing Method: Build then shake softly.
Garnish: None.
Note: Omit the cream and you've made a *Black Russian.* There are many variations concerning the measurement portions. There's supposed to be more vodka than coffee liqueur, but I've found over the years that people like a balance between the two. Kahlúa is the most popular coffee liqueur, but you're only supposed to use it if a guest calls for it; most bars will have a cheaper coffee liqueur that they want you to use. You can also replace the cream with milk, soy milk, or anything else creamy.

Mudslide

Glass: Can come in many glasses because it can be made many ways.
    1 ounce of vodka
    1/2 ounce of coffee liqueur
    1/2 ounce Irish cream
    Fill with half-and-half
Mixing Method: Various.
Garnish: Sometimes chocolate syrup and whipped cream for the frozen variety.
Note: As you can see, the *Mudslide* is just a *White Russian* with Irish cream added. The most popular Irish cream is

White Russian/Coffee Liqueur Family:
Black Russian: vodka and coffee liqueur

Kahlúa and Cream: Kahlúa and half-and-half

Sombrero: coffee liqueur and half-and-half

Angel Tip: Layered shot of coffee liqueur and cream

Smith & Kerns: coffee liqueur, half-and-half, and a splash of soda water on top

Smith & Wesson: vodka, coffee liqueur, half-and-half, and a splash of soda water on top

Colorado Bulldog: vodka, coffee liqueur, half-and-half, and a splash of cola on top in a tall glass

Mind Eraser: vodka, coffee liqueur in a rocks glass of ice with soda water on top; should be quickly sucked down

Dirty Mother: brandy and coffee liqueur

Dirty White Mother: brandy, coffee liqueur, and half-and-half shaken

Separator: brandy, coffee liqueur, and half-and-half built

Toasted Almond: amaretto, coffee liqueur, and half-and-half

Roasted Toasted Almond: vodka, amaretto, coffee liqueur, and half-and-half

Brave Bull: coffee liqueur and Tequila

Girl Scout Cookie: coffee liqueur, white crème de menthe, and half-and-half

---

Mudslide Family:
Orgasm: amaretto, coffee liqueur, and Irish cream (some places add a little cream)

Screaming Orgasm: vodka, amaretto, coffee liqueur, and Irish cream (some places add a little cream)

B-52 Bomber (also just called a *B-52*): shot layered with coffee liqueur, Irish cream, and Grand Marnier

Blow Job: shot layered with coffee liqueur, Irish cream, and whipped cream

Nutty Irishman: Irish cream, Frangelico, and half-and-half

Russian Quaalude: vodka, Irish cream, and Frangelico shaken and strained as a shot

Baileys Irish Cream. A *Mudslide* on the rocks can be made in a tall, Collins, or Old-Fashioned glass. When frozen, you can use cream, but some establishments use vanilla ice cream or a pourable ice cream mix. Almost every chain restaurant and bar has a spin-off *Mudslide*. Many twirl chocolate syrup inside the glass before pouring and add whip cream and a cherry. *Mudslide Martinis* can be made with two ounces of cream then shaken and strained.

Bushwacker

Glass: Whatever frozen glass you are using.
- 1 1/2 ounces dark rum
- 1 1/2 ounces coffee liqueur
- 1 ounce of coconut cream
- 2 ounces of half-and-half

Mixing Method: Blended.

Note: This is just the basic foundation recipe for a *Bushwacker*. The most important thing is the creamy coconut taste; the amount of each ingredient is flexible. Some bartenders add Irish cream and amaretto. The most popular coconut cream is Coco Lopez. Some guests like more of this ingredient and some less. Some bars do not have the budget for Coco Lopez and will substitute Piña Colada mix or add coconut rum to get the coconut taste into the drink. It can also be made with ice cream.

Chocolate Martini

Glass: Martini.
- 1 ounce vodka
- 1 ounce white or dark crème de cocoa
- 2 ounces of half-and-half

Mixing Method: Shake then strain.

Garnish: Can be rimmed with cocoa powder, sprinkled with chocolate shavings, insides swirled with chocolate syrup.

Note: This is a basic *Chocolate Martini* recipe; every establishment has their signature version. For instance, you can use different flavored vodkas such as vanilla and different chocolate liqueurs including white chocolate liqueur.

I like to rim the glass in hot chocolate powder (it's sweeter than cocoa powder), then squirt a little chocolate syrup in the bottom. Use a drinking straw to pull six to eight chocolate lines straight up the glass. You can do it really fast by twisting the stem around with the fingers on one hand and pulling up the chocolate lines with the other hand. A clear or milky Martini looks awesome with this presentation.

Creamsicle

Glass: Tall.

> 1 ounce vanilla vodka
> 1/2 ounce triple sec
> Fill with orange juice and half-and-half.

Mixing Method: Shake, or build and roll.

Garnish: None.

Note: You can vary this recipe by replacing the vanilla vodka with vanilla schnapps, Licor 43, or anything else with a vanilla taste. The main concern is to have a balance of vanilla, orange, and cream.

Nuts & Berries

Glass: Rocks.

> 1 ounce raspberry liqueur
> 1 ounce Frangelico
> 2 ounces of half-and-half.

Mixing Method: Shake or build and roll.

Garnish: None.

Chocolate Martini/Chocolate Liqueur Family:

Brandy Alexander: brandy, white crème de cocoa, and half-and-half if up or on the rocks; can also be blended with ice cream. Gets a sprinkle of nutmeg.

Grasshopper: green crème de menthe, white crème de cocoa, and half-and-half

Golden Cadillac: white crème de cocoa, Galliano, and half-and-half

Banshee: white crème de cocoa, banana liqueur, and half-and-half

Pink Squirrel: white crème de cocoa, crème de noyaux, and half-and-half

---

The Top Creamy Drinks You Must Know:
B-52
Brandy Alexander
Chocolate Martini
Grasshopper
Kahlúa & Cream
Mudslide
Orgasm
Sombrero
White Russian

The One-Liquor
Sour Family:

Amaretto Sour: amaretto and sour mix

Vodka Sour: vodka and sour mix

Scotch Sour: scotch and sour mix

Apricot Sour: apricot brandy and sour mix

Midori Sour: Midori and sour mix

Collins Family:
Vodka Collins: vodka, sour, soda water

John Collins: whiskey, sour, and soda water

Singapore Sling #1: gin, sour mix, soda water, bitters, and a cherry brandy floater

Singapore Sling #2: gin, Cherry Heering, Cointreau, Benedictine, pineapple juice, lime juice, grenadine, and bitters

Sloe Gin Fizz: sloe gin, sour mix, half soda, half Sprite/7-Up

Sour Drinks

Sweet-n-sour mix has many names in the mixer aisle of your local store—sour mix, margarita mix, whiskey sour mix—but they are basically all just sweetened lemon-lime water. Sour drinks should be shaken and have a frothy top. Also, a *Stone Sour* means that the mixer is half sour mix and half orange juice.

Whiskey Sour

Glass: Highball, Old-Fashioned, or whatever your establishment requires.

    1 1/2 ounces of whiskey

    4 ounces of sour mix

Mixing Method: Shake.

Garnish: Flag, with the minimum garnish being a cherry.

Tom Collins

Glass: Collins glass or tall thin glass.

    1 1/2 ounces of gin

    Fill with equal parts of sour mix and soda water.

Mixing Method: Shake the gin and sour, then top with the soda water.

Garnish: Flag, with the minimum garnish being a cherry.

Note: Most guests prefer the taste of half soda water and half Sprite/7-Up.

Long Island Iced Tea

The *Long Island Iced Tea* is a controversial drink. Bartenders hate to make it (we have to pick up five bottles of booze!) and guests think that they can catch a buzz from drinking only one. It became famous in the late 1970s disco era and is said to have been invented by a man named Robert Butt from Long Island, New York. The gimmick of the drink is that it looks and tastes like nonalcoholic iced tea.

> 1/2 ounce vodka
>
> 1/2 ounce gin
>
> 1/2 ounce rum
>
> 1/2 Tequila
>
> 1/2 ounce triple sec
>
> 2 ounces of sour mix
>
> 1/2 to 2 ounces of cola

Mixing Method: Shake or roll.

Garnish: Lemon wedge.

Note: The #1 mistake bartenders make when pouring this drink is adding too much sour. When guests taste a lot of sour, they think you cheated them by not putting in much alcohol.

For a low carb *LIIT,* you can use fresh squeezed lemon juice, Splenda or Equal, and diet cola.

Lynchburg Lemonade

Glass: Tall.

> 1 1/2 ounces of Jack Daniel's
>
> 1/2 ounce triple sec
>
> Fill with equal parts of sour and Sprite/7-Up

Mixing Method: Roll.

Garnish: Lemon wedge.

LIIT Family:

Long Beach Tea: (also called *California Tea*): vodka, gin, rum, Tequila, triple sex, sour, and cranberry juice

Miami Iced Tea: vodka, gin, rum, triple sec, peach schnapps, cranberry juice, and Sprite or 7-Up

Electric Iced Tea: vodka, gin, rum, Tequila, Blue Curacao, sour, and Sprite/7-Up

Daiquiri Family:

Bacardi Cocktail: Bacardi light rum, sour mix, and grenadine (by law it must be made with Bacardi)

Between the Sheets: rum, brandy, triple sec, and sour mix

Sidecar: brandy or Cognac, triple sec, and sour mix. Can be served with a sugared rim.

Margarita Family:

Top Shelf Margarita: use any premium Tequila and triple sec that the guests call or that your establishment says to use

Golden Margarita: use gold Tequila

Golden Grand Margarita: use gold Tequila and Grand Marnier

Blue Margarita: substitute Blue Curacao for the triple sec

Daiquiri

Okay. Here's the deal with the *Daiquiri*. The name comes from a beach in Cuba. A man named Jennings Cox was working in an iron mine as an engineer near Daiquiri Beach. One weekend, while entertaining some Americans, he ran out of gin and quickly mixed up some rum, fresh lime juice and sugar (sounds like a rum sour, huh?). The drink became a hit and was then served at the Army and Navy Club in Washington, D.C. The rest is history.

Glass: Cocktail.

> 1 1/2 ounces of rum
>
> 1 ounce simple syrup
>
> 1 ounce fresh lime juice

Mixing Method: Shake and strain.

Garnish: None, but some add a lime wedge.

Note: Most guests think that a *Daiquiri* is a term for a frozen drink, or most times, a *Strawberry Daiquiri*. Honestly, I didn't know what it was until I worked on a cruise ship, and I had to make trash cans full of Daiquiris for fifteen hundred passengers. Be prepared, because many guests will walk up to your bar and ask for a Daiquiri, and 99 percent of the time, they don't want this drink.

Margarita

This is by far the most popular drink worldwide, and many people claim to have invented it. If you're currently working as a bartender then you probably make around five thousand Margaritas a year—double if you work in a tropical location and triple if you work in a Mexican restaurant.

Glass: Many glasses can be used, but many establishments use real Margarita glasses with their unique sombrero-like shape.

> 1 1/2 ounces of Tequila
>
> 1/2 ounce of triple sec
>
> 1/8 ounce lime juice
>
> 4 ounces sour mix

Mixing Method: Can be served up, on the rocks, or blended.

**The Top Sour Drinks
You Must Know:**
Amaretto Sour
Lemondrop
Long Beach Tea
Long Island Iced Tea
Lynchburg Lemonade
Margarita
Midori Sour
Sour Appletini
Tom Collins
Whiskey Sour

Garnish: A salted rim and a lime wedge. For presentation's sake some establishments will use lime wheels.

Note: The lime juice called for in this recipe is not fresh squeezed, it's sweetened lime juice like Rose's Lime Cordial. This margarita recipe is the way most bars in America make it.

- A lot of bartenders are confused about flavored Margaritas. A Margarita is Tequila, orange liqueur, and lime juice. To make flavored Margaritas, simply replace the orange liqueur with another flavored liqueur or mixer. For example, if you use Chambord (sham-BOARD) instead of the triple sec, you'll make a *Raspberry Margarita;* if you use Midori, it's a *Melon Margarita;* and if you replace the orange liqueur with strawberry mix, you've got a *Strawberry Margarita.*
- To make unforgettable blended frozen Margaritas, blend the nonalcoholic portions and pour into the glass, leaving room for the alcohol on top. When you blend with the alcohol already added, the melted ice waters down the drink.
- Cointreau is the true upgrade of triple sec. A lot of bartenders think Grand Marnier is the upgrade. Grand Marnier is orange flavored, yes, but it's a Cognac-based orange liqueur: meaning you are putting Cognac in your Margarita, making it a cross between a *Margarita* and a *Sidecar.*
- Coarse salt called *kosher salt* is used for Margaritas, not table salt.

Lemondrop Martini

Glass: Martini.

    1 1/2 ounces citrus flavored vodka

    1/2 ounce triple sec

    2 ounces sour mix

Mixing Method: Shake and strain.

Garnish: Sugared rim with a sugarcoated lemon wedge.

Sour Apple Family:
Caramel Appletini: vodka, sour apple liqueur, butterscotch schnapps, and sour mix

Washington Appletini: Crown Royal, Apple Pucker, and cranberry juice (some bartenders use Southern Comfort instead of Crown Royal)

There's a basic bar *Punch Mix* that some bartenders will premix for maximum efficiency. It's a combination of orange juice, pineapple juice, sour mix, and grenadine. So if a guest asks for a Rum Punch, you would add rum to this mix. Many tropical drinks use this bar punch mix.

The Top Tropical Drinks You Must Know:
Bahama Mama
Blue Hawaiian
Hurricane
Mai Tai
Piña Colada
Planter's Punch
Rum Runner
Strawberry Daiquiri
Zombie

Sour Appletini

Glass: Martini.

    1 ounce citrus flavored vodka

    1 ounce sour apple liqueur

    2 ounces sour mix

Mixing Method: Shake and strain.

Garnish: Dropped cherry; however, handmade cocktail bars will actually use a slice of green apple.

Note: There are slight variations on this recipe. Some bartenders add triple sec, others add apple juice, and others leave out the sour mix and bump up the alcohol portions.

Tropical Drinks

Hurricane

The Hurricane is said to have been invented in the 1940s at Pat O'Brien's in New Orleans. At the time, you had to buy several cases of rum in order to get a case of whiskey, so the owner had to figure out a way to use up the extra rum. He poured the concoction in hurricane lamp-shaped glasses, and the rest is history. The recipe has changed a few times and occasionally contained Galliano, bitters, Cognac, and absinthe, but the basics—rum and fruit juices—are what have lasted.

Glass: Hurricane glass.

    1 ounce of light rum

    1 ounce dark rum

    1 ounce passion fruit juice

    Fill with bar punch

Mixing Method: Some shake then strain into a glass of ice, and some build then roll.

Garnish: Flag and a cherry at the minimum.

Note: Most bars don't carry passion fruit juice, so they just omit it. Also, some bars add a 151 rum floater. No original recipes have ever called for the floater, but it's believed to have started in the 1980s to distinguish it from a *Planter's Punch*.

The Pat O'Brien's powdered mix that you find in stores is not owned by Pat O'Brien's anymore. The company that bought it also purchased the rights to use the Pat O'Brien name. The official Pat O'Brien's mix is sold in bottles and can be found at their website.

Planter's Punch

Planter's Punch has always been associated with Myers's Jamaican Dark Rum. The bottle even had the recipe on the back label for many years.

Glass: Tropical glass.

    2 ounces dark rum

    Fill with bar punch mix.

Mixing Method: Some shake then strain into a glass of ice, and some build then roll.

Garnish: Flag and a cherry at the minimum.

Note: Some recipes don't call for pineapple juice.

Zombie

The *Zombie* was created by Donn Beach (born Ernest Raymond Beaumont Gantt), owner of the tiki-themed Don the Beachcomber Restaurant in Hollywood, California. The drink was first served at the 1939 World's Fair in New York and was also known as *Tahitian Rum Punch*.

Glass: Tropical glass.

    1 ounce light rum

    1 ounce dark rum

    1 ounce apricot brandy

    Fill with bar punch mix

    1/2 ounce 151 float

Mixing Method: Some shake and strain into a glass of ice, then float, and some build and roll, then float.

Garnish: Flag and a cherry at the minimum.

Note: There have been other ingredients in the recipe in the past, like papaya juice, Cherry Heering, Pernod, applejack, passion fruit juice, and orange Curacao, but most modern bars don't carry these items or even get asked for the drink. Generally, bartenders just make a *hurricane* with apricot brandy and a 151 rum floater.

Donn's original recipe had light rum, gold rum, 151 rum, lime juice, lemon juice, pineapple juice, passion fruit syrup, brown sugar, and bitters and was garnished with a mint sprig.

Now, I know most modern bars don't carry orgeat (OAR-zhat, nonalcoholic almond-flavored syrup) or Curacao syrup (CURE-uh-sow, nonalcoholic orange-flavored syrup)—what do you think happened to them? Amaretto replaced the orgeat, triple sec replaced the Curacao, and the fresh lime juice and rock candy syrup was replaced by sweet-n-sour mix. The gold rum was even replaced by dark rum. So a real Mai Tai should be goldish with a dark top (just like the Mai Tais Angela Lansbuy served at a party for Elvis Presley in the 1961 film *Blue Hawaii*).

Somehow pineapple juice crept into the recipe over the years, and grenadine followed soon after.

Mai Tai

Mai tai means *out of this world* in Tahitian. Vic Bergeron, also known as Trader Vic (and Donn Beach's rival), claims to have invented the *Mai Tai* in 1944. Donn Beach says the same thing, but evidence seems to lean towards Trader Vic. His original recipe uses Jamaican light and gold rum, fresh lime juice, a few dashes of orange Curacao syrup, French orgeat, and rock candy syrup. The gold rum floats on top of the drink.

Glass: Tropical glass.

#1:

    1 ounce light rum

    1 ounce dark rum float

    1/2 ounce triple sec

    1/2 ounce amaretto

    2 ounces sour mix

Mixing Method: Some shake and strain into a glass of ice, then float; some build and roll, then float.

#2:

    1 ounce light rum

    1 ounce dark rum

    1/2 ounce triple sec

    1/2 ounce amaretto

    2 ounces sour mix

    2 ounces pineapple juice

    1/2 ounce grenadine

Mixing Method: Some shake and strain into a glass of ice; some build and roll.

Garnish: Flag and a cherry at the minimum.

Rum Runner

Glass: Tropical glass.

    1 ounce dark rum

    1/2 ounce 151 rum

    1 ounce crème de banana

    1 ounce blackberry brandy

    1 ounce grenadine

    1 ounce Rose's Lime Cordial

Mixing Method: Blend.

Garnish: Anything tropical.

Note: Of course, there are slight variations for the *Rum Runner*, but the common ingredients are always banana liqueur, blackberry brandy, lime, cherry, and rum. This recipe happens to be the best recipe I've ever tasted. You'll notice in most bars that the banana liqueur and blackberry brandy always sit next to each other, and the reason is this drink. When making it on the rocks, most add pineapple juice to fill in the gaps.

Piña Colada

In Spanish, *Piña Colada* means strained pineapple. The Piña Colada is probably the most popular tropical drink of all time. It's said to have been invented on August 15, 1954, at the Caribe Hilton's Beachcomber Bar in San Juan, Puerto Rico. Allegedly, bartender Ramon Monchito Marrero Perez invented it and served it in coconuts and pineapples. At the time, the drink was not blended. That came a little bit later, when the coconut cream Coco Lopez made its way to the Beachcomber Bar. The Piña Colada is the official drink of Puerto Rico.

Glass: Tropical drink glass.

    1 1/2 ounces of rum

    4 ounces of Piña Colada mix

Mixing Method: Blend.

Garnish: Pineapple and cherry flag and just a cherry at the minimum. Please don't add an orange.

Note: The very best *Piña Colada* mix is mixture of Coco Lopez and pineapple juice. You'll need about 1 cup of Coco

In the 1500's, *Rum Runners* were pirates who shipped illegal rum to colonies that were heavily taxed. During prohibition in the 1920's, the most famous Rum Runner was Captain William McCoy because he didn't add water to his spirits like the others. This is one story of how we got the phrase *the real McCoy.*

Piña Colada Family:
Chi Chi: just a Piña Colada made with vodka instead of rum

A Charming Secret:
I like to add some half-and-half, a capful of vanilla extract, then float dark rum on top.

Lopez for every 3 cups of pineapple juice. You can make flavored coladas by adding strawberry mix for a *Strawberry Colada* or Midori for a *Melon Colada.*

Bahama Mama

There are many, many recipes for a *Bahama Mama,* but it's basically a cross between a *Piña Colada* and a *Rum Punch.*

Glass: Tropical drink glass.
   1 ounce of light rum
   1 ounce of dark rum
   2 ounces of Piña Colada mix
   2 ounces of bar punch mix
Mixing Method: Blend.
Garnish: Pineapple and cherry flag, anything tropical, or just a cherry.
Note: You'll see a lot of recipes that use coconut rum as a replacement for the coconut flavor of the Piña Colada mix, then add pineapple juice. Some other recipes will have banana liqueur and coffee liqueur.

Strawberry Daiquiri

Glass: Tropical drink glass.
   1 1/2 ounces of rum
   4 ounces of strawberry mix
Mixing Method: Blend.
Garnish: Strawberry, lime wedge, sugared rim, or whipped cream with a cherry on top. Depends where you work.
Note: Most bars have a standard Daiquiri mix they use, but it's usually just overly sweet, strawberry-flavored liquid like the stuff in the mixer section of your local store. Bars in tropical locations tend to bump it up a notch and stock better and meatier brands. However, the very best is using fresh-crushed ripe strawberries, fresh lime juice, and simple syrup blended together to make a pourable strawberry mix. Also, it's easy to make other flavors of Daiquiris without mixers. For example, you can make a peach Daiquiri by using peach schnapps, lime juice, orange juice, and a touch of grenadine. Just think about all the different flavored liqueurs available to you: the options are unlimited.

Blue Hawaiian

Bartender Harry Yee from Hawaii invented this drink in 1957. His original recipe has equal part pineapple juice and sour mix and is garnished with a pineapple and orchid.

Glass: Tropical drink glass.
    1 ounce of light rum
    1 ounce of Blue Curacao
    Fill with pineapple juice
Mixing Method: Shake.
Garnish: Pineapple slice, pineapple flag, or a cherry at the minimum.

Hot Drinks

Irish Coffee

An Irish bartender named Joe Sheridan invented the *Irish Coffee* at Shannon Airport in Dublin. In 1952, a San Francisco reporter named Stanton Delaplane took the recipe back to Jack Koeppler, who owned the Buena Vista Cafe. Today the bar claims to serve 2000 *Irish Coffees* a day.

Glass: Irish coffee mug.
    1 1/2 ounces of Irish whiskey
    3 packets of sugar
    4 ounces of hot black coffee
Mixing Method: Build.
Garnish: Whipped cream.
Note: If you have it, try to use brown sugar. The Buena Vista recipe is: preheat the glass, pour black coffee three-quarters full, drop in three sugar cubes, stir to dissolve, add a jigger of Irish Whiskey, and add real whipping cream to the rim using a spoon.

The Top Hot Drinks You Must Know:
Irish Coffee
Italian Coffee
Keoke Coffee
Mexican Coffee

Irish Coffee Family:
Italian Coffee: amaretto and coffee

Mexican Coffee: Kahlúa and coffee

Keoke Coffee (key-O-Key): brandy, coffee liqueur, and coffee (also called a *Coffee Nudge* in Northwest America)

Bailey's and Coffee: Bailey's Irish Cream and coffee

Hot Nutty Irishman: Irish cream, Frangelico, and coffee

Hot Girl Scout Cookie: coffee liqueur, white créme de menthe, and coffee

Many guests want to try some different hot drinks, so here are a couple that I've found guests love.

Tuaca, hot apple cider topped with whipped cream.

Coffee liqueur, raspberry liqueur, hot chocolate, topped with whipped cream.

Others you probably won't make but should know, are:

Hot Toddy: whiskey, hot water, lemon, and honey.

Hot Buttered Rum: dark or spiced rum, hot water or hot apple cider, spoon of unsalted butter, honey, cinnamon, and cloves.

Stick Drinks

Stick drinks are the drinks that require a muddler. Muddling releases the oils in what you are crushing and releases its flavor.

The Top Stick Drinks You Must Know:
Mint Julep
Mojito
Old Fashioned

Mojito

The *Mojito* (mo-HEE-toe) is said to come from Havana, Cuba, specifically the La Bodeguita del Medio restaurant that opened in 1942.

Glass: Highball.

1 1/2 ounces of light rum

4 lime wedges

3 packets of sugar

4 mint sprigs (one saved for a garnish)

Soda water

Mixing Method #1: Muddle the limes, sugar, and mint in a shaker glass, then add ice and rum. Shake and strain into a highball or tall glass filled with crushed or cracked ice. Top with soda water.

Build Mixing Method #2: Muddle the limes, sugar, and mint in a highball or tall glass, add the rum then crushed or cracked ice and top with soda water.

Garnish: Mint sprig.

Note: Sadly, a lot of bars replace the time-consuming muddling method with mint syrup. It will not be as refreshing a drink if you use syrup. And the most important thing about *Mojitos* is they are not served in a short, stubby glass.

Mint Julep

The Mint Julep is the official drink of the Kentucky Derby.

Glass: Highball.

    2 ounces of Bourbon

    3 packets of sugar

    4 mint sprigs (one saved for a garnish)

Mixing Method: Muddle the sugar and mint in a shaker glass, then fill with ice and add the Bourbon. Then shake and strain over a highball glass of crushed or cracked ice.

Garnish: Mint sprig.

Note: It's said that spearmint leaves are better than peppermint when making this drink. Also, some say that you should infuse a handful of mint leaves in the bottle of Bourbon for a couple of days in place of muddling the mint.

Old Fashioned

This is a controversial drink, but don't worry about it too much because you won't get many orders for it. This recipe is pretty standard in most bars. There are even bars that will tell you that they don't make it, but that's mainly because they don't know how.

Glass: Rocks.

    2 ounces of Bourbon, whiskey, or rye

    2 packets of sugar

    Orange slice and one cherry

    2 dashes of Angostura bitters

Mixing Method: Muddle the sugar, orange, and cherry in the rocks glass then fill with ice. Add the whiskey.

Garnish: None.

Note: No matter what you've been told, do not put a splash of water or soda water on top. Also, the cherry really serves no purpose other than decorative. The original *Old Fashioned* is built with a spoon of sugar, two dashes of bitters, spoonful of water, ice, rye whiskey, and garnished with a lemon peel.

Caipirinha Family:
Caipirissima: a caipirinha made with rum

Caipiroska: a caipirinha made with vodka

Buttery Nipple Family:
Slippery Nipple: sambuca and Irish cream

Slippery Dick: banana liqueur and Irish cream

Caipirinha

The Caipirinha (ki-pee-REEN-ya) comes from Brazil. It's made from a popular Brazilian liqueur called cachaça (ka-SHA-suh). There are about four thousand different brands of cachaça in Brazil, but probably only 5 percent of American bars stock it.

Glass: Rocks.
> 2 ounces of cachaça
> 4 lime wedges
> 3 packets of sugar

Mixing Method: Muddle the limes and sugar in a shaker glass, then add ice and the cachaça and shake. Pour everything into a rocks glass.
Garnish: None.

Shots & Shooters

Technically, shots and shooters are slightly different from each other. Shooters have a mix to them, like a *Woo Woo* or a *Lemondrop*. Since they have a mix, they require a larger glass than just a shot glass; rocks glasses work well. Shots fit into a shot glass and are usually 100 percent alcohol, like a *B-52* or a shot of Tequila. However, what they have in common is that you drink both in one gulp.

B-52

This layered shot gets its name from B-52 Stratofortress bomber planes built for the American Air Force in 1954. The planes lasted until 1991 when President Bush took them off alert duty.
Glass: Shot.
> 1/2 ounce coffee liqueur
> 1/2 ounce Irish cream
> 1/2 ounce Grand Marnier

Mixing Method: Layer in the order given.
Garnish: None.
Note: If you replace the Grand Marnier with Crown Royal, it's called a *Duck Fart*.

58

Blow Job

This shot started in the late 1980s. Its novelty has lasted for twenty years.

Glass: Shot.

> 1/2 ounce coffee liqueur
> 1/2 ounce Irish cream

Mixing Method: Layer in the order given.

Garnish: Whipped cream. If it's your first *Blow Job,* a stemless cherry on top of the whipped cream.

Note: The novelty of this shot is that a guest places both hands behind his or her back then leans over the shot and sucks out the whipped cream. Then they wrap their mouth around the glass and drink the shot using only their mouth. Hands stay behind the back the whole time. Recipes for this shot vary. Some bartenders don't bother with the layering and just pour a shot of coffee liqueur, others use different liquors, but really, it's all about *how* you do the shot.

Buttery Nipple

Glass: Shot.

> 1/2 ounce butterscotch schnapps
> 1/2 ounce Irish cream

Mixing Method: Layer in the order given.

Garnish: None.

Shot of Tequila

Glass: Shot.

> 1 1/2 ounces of Tequila

Mixing Method: Neat; however, current trends lean towards chilled.

Garnish: Can be salt and lime wedge.

Note: There are many ways that you can present the salt and lime wedge (some guests will ask for lemon). The easiest all-in-one method is to salt 1/4 of the shot glass rim and put the wedge on the other side.

Body shots are very popular with Tequila, so you may have guests ask for a saltshaker. What they do is lick a part of their partner's body, sprinkle the salt on the wet spot, and place the lime meat side out in teeth of their partner's mouth. Then the guest will lick the salt, drink the Tequila, and take a bite of the lime.

The original *Boilermaker* is a shot of Bourbon or whiskey dropped in a beer. Make sure to ask the drinker how they would like it.

Boilermaker Family:
Flaming Dr. Pepper: 1/8 ounce grenadine, 1 ounce amaretto, 1/4 ounce of 151 rum in the shot glass, and a half glass of beer. Light the shot, drop it in, and chug. It's supposed to taste like Dr. Pepper.

Irish Car Bomb: Irish cream and Irish whiskey in the shot glass, dropped into half a glass of Guinness

Jäger Bomb: shot of Jägermeister dropped into Red Bull

Slammer

Glass: Rocks.

   1 1/2 ounces Tequila

   3 ounces of Sprite/7-Up

Garnish: None.

Mixing Method: Pour the Tequila and the soda in a rocks glass, then lay a cocktail napkin on top and slam it on the bar top—it will fizz up. Then chug.

Garnish: None.

Liquid Cocaine

Glass: Shot glass.

   1/3 ounces of Jägermeister

   1/3 ounces of Goldschlager

   1/3 ounces of Rumple Minze

Mixing Method: Pour all 3 in a shot glass.

Garnish: None.

Note: These three items are normally kept cold behind the bar.

Chocolate Cake

Glass: Shot glass.

   3/4 ounce of citrus vodka

   3/4 ounce of Frangelico

Mixing Method: Shake and strain.

Garnish: Lemon wedge.

Note: You drink the shot then bite into the lemon, and for some weird reason it tastes like chocolate cake. Well, there is a very small amount of cocoa in the Frangelico, but with all the lemon it seems like it would be impossible to taste.

Boilermaker

Glass: Shot glass and a beer glass.

   1 1/2 ounces Bourbon or whiskey

   1/2 glass of beer

Mixing Method: Pour a shot of Bourbon in the shot glass and fill half of a glass with beer. Drop the shot in the beer and chug.

Garnish: None.

Kamikaze (ka-mee-KA-zee)

Glass: Rocks. Can be served on the rocks for sipping or chilled straight up as a shooter. You should ask before making the drink unless the guest specifies.

1 1/2 ounces of vodka

1/2 ounce of triple sec

1/4 ounce of lime juice

Garnish: Lime wedge.

Note: A *Kamikaze* is just a *Vodka Gimlet* with triple sec added.

Lemondrop

Glass: Rocks.

1 1/2 ounces citrus flavored vodka

1/2 ounce triple sec

2 ounces sour mix

Mixing Method: Shake and strain.

Garnish: Sugared rim with a sugarcoated lemon wedge.

Note: There's another kind of *Lemondrop* that is a shot made with a sugar-rimmed shot glass and chilled citrus vodka only.

A Charming Secret:

I have a favorite decadent Lemondrop I make for special guests. You need a saucer, sugar, book of matches, sliced lemon, citrus vodka, and Grand Marnier. Lay the lemon slice on the saucer and cover with sugar. Pour some Grand Marnier on top of the sugar to make it flammable, then light it. As the sugar is being crystallized into the lemon, chill a shot of citrus vodka. By the time you're done the flame will have died down. Drink the chilled shot then bite into the warm sugary lemon. Pick up the saucer and pour the leftover Grand Marnier into the shot glass and drink.

Purple Hooter

Glass: Rocks.

1 ounce vodka

1 ounce raspberry liqueur

2 ounces sour mix

Mixing Method: Shake and strain.

Garnish: None.

Note: Some bartenders put equal amounts of pineapple juice and sour mix to distinguish it from a *Grape Crush/Grape Nehi*.

Purple Hooter Family:

Grape Crush (also called *Grape Nehi*): vodka, raspberry liqueur, sour, and Sprite/7-Up; can be a shooter or tall drink.

Older Shots and Shooters:

Russian Quaalude: vodka, Irish cream, and Frangelico shaken and strained

Cement Mixer: Irish cream and Rose's lime juice. It feels gross in your mouth and is often used as a gag shot.

Prairie Fire: shot of Tequila with 5 dashes of Tabasco

Jelly Bean: equal amounts of blackberry brandy and anisette or sambuca

Snake Bite: Yukon Jack and Rose's Lime Cordial shaken and strained

Watermelon: Southern Comfort, crème de noyaux, and orange juice shaken and strained

Snowshoe: shot of chilled Wild Turkey and peppermint schnapps

Woo Woo

Glass: Rocks.
   1 ounce vodka
   1 ounce peach schnapps
   2 ounces cranberry juice
Mixing Method: Shake and strain.
Garnish: None.

Washington Apple

Glass: Rocks.
   1 ounce Crown Royal
   1 ounce sour apple liqueur
   2 ounces cranberry juice
Mixing Method: Shake and strain.
Garnish: None.

Red Snapper

Glass: Rocks.
   1 ounce Crown Royal
   1 ounce amaretto
   2 ounces cranberry juice
Mixing Method: Shake and strain.
Garnish: None.

Redheaded Slut

Glass: Rocks.
   1 ounce Jägermeister
   1 ounce peach schnapps
   2 ounces cranberry juice
Mixing Method: Shake and strain.
Garnish: None.

Surfer on Acid

Glass: Rocks.
   1 ounce Jägermeister
   1 ounce coconut rum
   2 ounces pineapple juice
Mixing Method: Shake and strain.
Garnish: None.

Mind Eraser

Glass: Rocks.
    1 ounce vodka
    1 ounce coffee liqueur
    Fill with soda water
Mixing Method: Build over ice.
Garnish: Large straw.
Note: Stick the straw in and quickly suck it down.

SoCo & Lime

Glass: Rocks.
    2 ounces of Southern Comfort
    1/2 ounce Rose's Lime Cordial
Mixing Method: Shake and strain.
Garnish: None.

Jell-O Shots

To make Jell-O shots, simply replace the cold water portion of the Jell-O box directions with alcohol. You want to pour the mixture into small portion cups (1 to 2 ounce cups can be bought in bulk at restaurant supply stores). Paper portion cups are better than plastic because you can squeeze them into your mouth.

Here are the Jell-O flavors as of 2006:
Apricot, Berry Blue, Black Cherry, Cherry, Cranberry, Cranberry-Raspberry, Grape, Pineapple, Lemon, Lime, Mixed Fruit, Orange, Peach, Raspberry, Strawberry, Strawberry-Banana, Strawberry-Kiwi, Wild Strawberry, Green Apple, Watermelon, Wild Berry, and Magical Twist.

And sugar-free flavors include:
Black Cherry, Cherry, Cranberry, Lemon, Lime, Mixed Fruit, Orange, Peach, Raspberry-Strawberry, Strawberry-Banana, Strawberry-Kiwi, and Wild Berry. Imagine the possibilities!

Classic Drinks

Martini

By far, the Martini is king of the cocktails. No one knows when, who, or where the first *Martini* was created. What we do know is that Jerry Thomas published a cocktail recipe called a *Martinez* in *The Bartender's Guide* in 1887. It consisted of gin, sweet vermouth, maraschino liqueur, bitters, and a lemon twist. In 1907, William Boothby published a *Dry Martini Cocktail* in his book, *The World's Drinks and How to Mix Them.* That recipe consisted of gin, French dry vermouth, orange bitters, a lemon peel, and an olive. During prohibition Martinis flourished because gin doesn't require aging like whiskey does, so it was available in speakeasies as soon as it was made. At the time, Martinis were being made with equal amounts of gin and dry vermouth. Through the years the amount of dry vermouth decreased, and by the 1950s Hollywood movie stars were swirling a couple of drops of dry vermouth in the glass on the silver screen. Then all hell broke loose when Ian Fleming wrote about a fictional British spy named James Bond in the novel *Casino Royale.* Bond orders a cocktail called a *Vesper* (the name of his love interest) made of gin, vodka, and Kina Lillet aperitif: shaken, not stirred, with a lemon twist. By the second Bond novel the handsome and debonair spy was drinking *Vodka Martinis* with a coined catch phrase: *shaken, not stirred.*

Glass: Martini or rocks.

   2 ounces of gin

   1/4 ounce dry vermouth

Mixing Method: Shake and strain, or stir and strain, depending on what the guest wants.

Garnish: Lemon peel or green olive.

Note: If you'd like to try the original *Martini,* add a dash of orange bitters. When a guest orders a *Dry Martini* it means that you only use a couple of drops of dry vermouth. When they order it *very dry* or *extra dry* it means that you don't use any vermouth at all. An *in & out* or *upside down Martini* is when you swirl a few drops of vermouth around the inside of the glass to coat it, then pour it out. A *Perfect Martini* (or perfect anything for that matter) means to use half dry vermouth and half sweet vermouth. A *Dirty Martini* means that you add olive juice. And a *Martini* garnished with cocktail onions is called a *Gibson. Martinis* can also be requested on the rocks.

Shaken or Stirred?

When you shake a Martini, the melting ice adds water to the cocktail, which is essential. Shaken Martinis are light and airy on the tongue because you've added air to the mix while shaking. Martini connoisseurs call this *bruising the gin.* The initial look will be a little hazy.

When you stir a Martini for half a minute, it creates a heavy, silky feel on the tongue. The look is very translucent. This is the way Martinis were made before James Bond was created.

Manhattan

There are many stories of people claiming to have invented the *Manhattan,* but all agree on where it was invented: Manhattan. What we do know is that it was first made with rye whiskey since it was plentiful at the time (late 1800s). Today it can be made with a favorite Bourbon or whiskey, and in Minnesota and Wisconsin it's made with brandy.

Glass: Martini or rocks.

    2 ounces of rye, Bourbon, or whiskey

    1 ounce of sweet vermouth

    2 dashes of bitters

Mixing Method: Stir and strain. Never shake a Manhattan. You want it clear and cold.

Garnish: Cherry.

Note: A *Perfect Manhattan* calls for half sweet vermouth and half dry vermouth with a lemon twist. A Manhattan can be requested on the rocks, and if you replace the whiskey with Scotch whisky you've made a *Rob Roy.*

Rusty Nail

Glass: Rocks.

    1 1/2 ounces of Scotch whisky

    3/4 ounce of Drambuie

Mixing Method: Build.

Garnish: None.

More Martini Facts

- Martini connoisseurs recommend starting with room-temperature liquor to get the best dilution of water from the ice. Honestly, it's all just dependent on how you like it. Lots of people like a small amount of water added to their Martini.

- A *Martini Mister* is a small stainless steel refillable spray canister that you fill with dry vermouth to mist the top of your Martini.

- There is much debate over how many olives a Martini should get. Most of the experts agree with one dropped to the bottom or two speared on a cocktail pick. Three or more olives are unacceptable unless requested by the guest.

- Olive stuffers can be found in upscale bars. The most popular ingredient to stuff in olives is blue cheese.

- The reason gin and dry vermouth go so well together is that gin is infused with herbs and botanicals and dry vermouth is a fortified wine, meaning that herbs have been added.

- The flavored Martinis of today make Martini connoisseurs' toes curl. It's said that Absolut Citron started it all with the *Cosmopolitan* because up until that time no other cocktail was strained into a Martini glass. Within just a couple of years Martini bars and Martini menus popped up everywhere, but the flavored Martinis of today are really just the shooters of yesterday. Instead of being chugged, they're being sipped from elegant glasses.

- You'll find that *Dirty Martini* lovers like different strengths of dirtiness (more or less olive juice), so I've learned to ask if they would like it R, X, or XXX rated? They always understand (and smile).

Note: You will find that *Rusty Nail* drinkers have a preference when it comes to the ratio of scotch to Drambuie; always ask what they prefer.

Just so you know, Drambuie is a Scotch-based honey and herb liqueur. Its proof is very high (80 proof) for a liqueur so it makes this cocktail very potent.

Stinger
Glass: Rocks.
   2 ounces of brandy or Cognac
   1 ounce of white crème de menthe
Mixing Method: Shake and strain into a rocks glass of ice.
Garnish: None.
Note: Some older guests may request for the *Stinger* to be made with crushed ice. If you replace the brandy with vodka it is called a *White Spider*.

Godfather
Glass: Rocks.
   1 ounce of blended Scotch whisky
   1 ounce of amaretto
Mixing Method: Build.
Garnish: None.
Note: Replace the scotch with vodka, and you've made a *Godmother*.

Vodka Gimlet
(The G sounds like the G in gum)

Glass: Rocks.
   1 1/2 to 2 ounces of vodka
   1/2 ounce lime juice
Garnish: Lime wedge.

Note: Most bars use sweetened lime juice like Rose's Lime Cordial, but a little simple syrup and fresh-squeezed lime juice also works well. Gimlet purists will just use fresh-squeezed lime juice. This cocktail was originally made with gin, so you might get some requests for a *Gin Gimlet*.

Champagne Cocktail

Glass: Champagne.
    1 sugar cube soaked with bitters (about 6 dashes)
    Fill with Champagne
Mixing Method: Build.
Garnish: Lemon twist.

Mimosa

Glass: Champagne.
    2 ounces of orange juice
    Fill with Champagne
Mixing Method: Build.
Garnish: Strawberry.
Note: The *Mimosa* is a traditional brunch cocktail and is often included in a buffet brunch's price.

Bellini

Glass: Champagne.
    1 ounce of white peach purée
    5 ounces of Prosecco (sparkling wine from Italy)
Mixing Method: Pour the peach puree into a mixing glass with ice cubes, then slowly add the Champagne. Gently stir with a bar spoon by dragging the puree up from the bottom, much like folding egg whites. Strain into a Champagne fluted glass.
Garnish: None.
Note: This cocktail is usually only found in high end bars that make their own white peach puree and stock Prosecco. Some cheat and use peach nectar and sparkling wine and pass it off as a *Bellini*.

As far as we know, Jerry Thomas first listed a *Champagne Cocktail* in his 1862 book, *How to Mix Drinks*. However, the recipe has evolved over the years.

It's said that the *Mimosa* was invented in Paris at the Ritz Hotel in 1925. They would also sometimes add a tablespoon of Grand Marnier and call it a *Grand Mimosa* or a *Buck's Fizz*. If you replace the orange juice with cranberry juice, it's called a *Hibiscus*.

The *Bellini* is said to have been invented in Harry's Bar in Venice, Italy, in 1945 and named in 1949 by Giuseppe Cipriani.

Kir (rhymes with ear)

The *Kir* is named after a French mayor of Dijon named Felix Kir, who lived from 1876 to 1968.

Glass: Champagne.
    1/4 ounce crème de cassis
    Fill with white wine
Mixing Method: Build.
Garnish: Lemon twist.
Note: Crème de cassis is a black currant liqueur. When you replace the white wine with Champagne, you've made a *Kir Royale*. When using white wine, Chablis or Chardonnay is preferred. Substitute the crème de cassis in a *Kir Royale* with Chambord, and you've made a *Kir Imperial*.

Cuba Libre

During the Spanish-American war, Teddy Roosevelt was commander of the 1st U.S. Volunteer Cavalry Regiment called the Rough Riders. While the Rough Riders were in Cuba fighting the Spanish in 1898, this drink was invented and named after the battle cry, "Free Cuba."

Glass: Highball.
    1 1/2 ounces of light rum
    Juice from a lime wedge
    Fill glass with Coca-Cola
Mixing Method: Squeeze the juice from a lime wedge over the ice, rim the glass with the same lime and throw it away, then build the rest of the ingredients.
Garnish: Lime wedge.
Note: Notice that a *Cuba Libre* (KOO-buh-LEE-bray) is just *Rum & Coke* with lime.

Highballs

Originally, when a guest walked up to the bar and asked for a highball, the bartender grabbed a bottle of rye whiskey and mixed it with ginger ale. Today, highball is just a name for a spirit mixed with a carbonated mixer.

Miscellaneous Drinks

Shandy: pilsner beer and Sprite/7-Up
Black & Tan: half pint of Bass beer with Guinness slowly layered on top.

Handmade Recipes

Fake Absinthe

Makes 1 pint

2 1/2 teaspoons dried wormwood
1 pint vodka
2 teaspoons chopped angelica root
3 teaspoons crushed anise seed
3 crushed cardamom pods
1/2 teaspoon ground coriander
1/2 teaspoon crushed fennel seed
1/2 teaspoon marjoram

Place the wormwood in the vodka for two days, filter, add the remaining herbs, and let sit for one week. Filter, then bottle. Serve over a sugar cube in the bottom of a cordial glass. Wormwood can be found on the Internet. Real absinthe has been illegal in America since 1912. It has hallucinogenic properties.

The Most Popular Highballs:
Vodka Soda, Vodka Tonic, Gin & Tonic, Rum & Coke, Bourbon & Coke, Whiskey & 7, Bourbon & Water, Scotch & Water, and *Scotch & Soda.* Other mixers include Sprite or 7-Up, ginger ale, and Diet Coke.

Garnishes for Highballs:
Tonics always get a lime wedge, and the most common requests from guests are lemon wedges and lemon twists for scotch.

A *Presbyterian* (*press*) means that the mixer is half ginger ale and half soda water. For example, if a guest orders a *Bourbon Press,* they want Bourbon with half ginger ale and half soda water.

Spirits You Can Serve in a Brandy Snifter Besides Cognac and Brandy:
Sambuca with three coffee beans dropped in, Grand Marnier, Drambuie, amaretto, single malt scotch, a premium rum or Tequila, Brandy Alexander; really any quality liqueur.

Sangria

Serves 8

    2 bottles of red wine

    2 ounces blackberry brandy

    1 cup orange juice

    1 cup pineapple juice

    1/2 cup cherry juice

    3 cups maraschino cherries.

    2 cups seasonal fruit cut into wheels.

Combine all the ingredients and refrigerate, then add the fruit when you're ready to serve.

White Sangria

Serves 4

    1 cup water

    3/4 cup sugar

    6 cinnamon sticks

    2 bottles non-dry white wine

    1 cup sparkling water

    1 cup apple juice

    1 cup white cranberry juice

    3 oranges cut

    2 cups cherries

    3 apples cut

Heat the water, sugar, and cinnamon sticks to a simmer for five minutes, then remove from heat. Mix in all remaining liquid ingredients and refrigerate. Add the fruit when ready to serve.

Coffee Liqueur

Makes 2 bottles

    5 cups sugar

    8 cups water

    1 1/4 cups instant coffee

    6 tablespoons vanilla extract

    1/2 bottle (750 ml) vodka

Heat the sugar and the water to boiling, then remove it from the heat and allow to cool. Mix it with all the other ingredients and bottle it. Let it sit undisturbed in a cool, dark place for one month.

Irish Cream

Makes 1 bottle

>   1 cup Irish whiskey
>   1 (14 ounce) can Eagle Brand condensed milk
>   1 cup whipping cream (the real stuff)
>   4 eggs
>   2 tablespoons chocolate flavored syrup (like Monin)
>   2 teaspoon instant coffee granules
>   2 teaspoons vanilla extract

Combine all ingredients and blend until smooth. Store in a tightly covered container in refrigerator. You can serve it in twenty-four hours, and it'll last a month; just stir before serving.

Infused Gin, Rum, and Vodka

Makes 1 bottle

>   1 bottle of gin, rum, or vodka
>   Spice, fruit, or herb of your choice

Get a large-mouthed glass container to make an infusion. Place your chosen spice, fruit, or herb in the container, then add the alcohol. Close the lid and place it somewhere away from direct sunlight, the let it sit from four days to two weeks, depending on what you're infusing it with. Strain, then bottle.

>   2 weeks: whole chili peppers, pineapple, fresh ginger, and lemongrass
>   1 week: cantaloupes, strawberries, peaches, mangoes, pitted cherries, raspberries, blueberries, and blackberries
>   4 days: vanilla beans, lemons, oranges, grapefruit, limes, mint, garlic, tarragon, basil, oregano, dill, and thyme

4 Getting the Job

Are you ready to take a big bite? This chapter—right here in the middle—is most certainly the *meat* of this book. If you want to work as a bartender, this chapter gives you straight up information, tips, hints, and facts. Open wide.

When bartenders ask me what to write for their *objective* on their resumes, I always tell them to say, *to provide an excellent experience for guests at your establishment.*

Entry-Level Bars

When I guest speak at bar schools, it always amazes me that most students have no idea that there are so many different types of bars. In their minds, they thought that there were only chain restaurants and dance clubs. Every profession has an entry level—here are some great places for you to start your bartending career.

Service Bartender

A service bartender can be found in restaurants that don't have an exposed bar but offer alcohol on their menu. Servers come to your small space to get drinks. The only tips you receive are from the servers. Comedy clubs, busy Asian restaurants, restaurants that have two or more floors, and places that provide entertainment normally have service bars.

Banquet and Caterer Bartender

Banquet and caterer bartending jobs are perfect for a beginner. The company organizes the events and you tend bar. (The bars are generally portable, so there's a little muscle involved in

Keep This in Mind
Most professions are either mental or physical. Bartending is both. Here's the deal: There are many bars where a guest can order a Rum & Coke in your town, right? So why would someone want to keep ordering a Rum & Coke from *you?*

Restaurants and bars are built every single day for one purpose and one purpose only: to make money. And American bartenders work for tips, generally $1 a drink or 15 percent of the bill. Your bottom line is to sell as much as you can because the more you sell, the more you make.

People like bartenders. They like to be your friend; they like to say they know you; they tell you lots of secrets, ask your advice, hook you up with all kinds of big ticket goodies…no doubt, it's a cool job. In their towns, bartenders are mini-celebrities, which is fitting. In order to make money, you have to provide an excellent guest experience so people tip you. There's a lot of acting in this line of work. Why do you think so many actors wait tables and getting all of your supplies and stock together.) Every event is different, but most times it's just a basic bar setup, which means you won't be making any frozen or blended drinks (just high-balls, juice drinks, bottled beer, and wine), and you don't have to deal with collecting cash, running tabs, or making change. Sometimes it's a cash bar, but you usually only operate out of a simple cash drawer. Payment is different all over, but it's usually a percentage of the sales of the event or a flat fee.

Daytime Bartender

Many restaurants that have bars are constantly looking for daytime bartenders because most of the money is made at night. Daytime bartenders can get a small lunch rush but spend most of their day stocking the bar for the nighttime bartender. Sometimes they overlap into the happy hour to help during that rush. This is a great way to get your foot in the door, pay your dues, prove yourself, build a clientele, and get paid to learn. Plus, there will be many times when a nighttime bartender will want a shift off here and there, and you'll be the first one asked. Try Mexican restaurants; they seem to always need a daytime bartender for some reason.

Pub or Tavern Beertender

At pubs and taverns you generally just serve beer. Use these jobs to polish your people skills, memory, and many of the things on the bartender quality list. Tips can be good, but these places are generally populated by regulars, so get used to seeing the same ol' faces.

Hotel Bars

Most hotel bars are pretty boring. You are totally dependent on the occupancy of the hotel. When it's dead, it's really dead. Even when the hotel is full the bar might be dead unless it's full of people that like to drink. Most times, locals don't visit hotel bars unless they are really nice bars. But for a beginner bartender, this is a great stepping-stone to greater opportunities.

tend bar before they become famous? One very important concept to grasp is that it really helps to look at your customers as if they are *guests* in your home. When this sinks in, then everything else falls into place.

The Top Ten Bartender Qualities
1. Personality.

2. Good grooming.

3. Great memory.

4. Knowledge of liquor, beer, wines, cocktails, and your local area.

5. Good money-handling skills with average math skills.

6. Responsible and dependable team player.

7. Fast and efficient.

8. Something unique.

9. Physical strength.

10. A people person with good eye contact and a firm handshake.

Private Party Bartender

Tending bar at private parties is great because you're working for yourself. Prices are settled on beforehand, you use what the host provides, and guests are always in a happy mood. The down side is that you almost have to be working at a bar already to be able to advertise yourself. As a beginner bartender, I would ask for $100 for every three hours they need you.

Movin' On Up

These bars are places you'll move to once you have some experience under your belt. And trust me, you want these jobs—the money is much better!

Chain Restaurants

Most of these positions are hired from within—people are waiting in line to move up. Chain restaurants want you to learn their menu and pay your dues before you get behind the wood. But here's a secret: if you can find a place that's just opening, your chances are 99 percent better. You can make great money and also get the opportunity to travel and transfer to other stores. The downside is that chains have so many corporate rules. But every job has its good and bad.

High-Volume Bartender

These are the busy nightclub bartenders that move to a nonstop heavy beat—most of the time they're reading lips. Money can be huge, even after tipping out the bar backs and splitting tips. The downside is that you almost always have to work holidays and weekends, you come home smelling like an ashtray, and your hearing begins to be affected. You generally have to be hired from within or know somebody to get these jobs.

Tourist Bartender

Working at a tourist bar spot is the greatest: tourists are generally happy, they have lots of money to spend, and the clientele is constantly changing. By far my favorite!

Pool and Beach Bars

Unless you live in a super warm climate, this is only seasonal employment. Every pool and beach bartender is addicted to the weather channel. Job retention is great because the money can be huge, so it can be hard to make your way into the good ones. I love these bars because of the constant connection with nature.

Airport Bars

I've never worked an airport bar, but I've talked with some airport bartenders, and they seem to do pretty well moneywise. Of course, not every airport bar is the same. The biggest complaint seems to be the time it takes to get to the bar because they have to park so far out in the parking lot.

Cruise Ships

If you're an American, forget about it. I know, I know. You see the ads in the paper all the time. Trust me, they're all a scam. I worked on a cruise ship for six years in the Caribbean, but I was part of an experiment. Cruise ships have people of many nationalities working for them because of the currency exchange. For example, when I worked on the ship the daily pay for a cocktail server was $10. The cocktail servers were all from Thailand—one American dollar was equivalent to $25, so they sent 95 percent of their money home. You're not going to get an American to work for $10 a day; it's cheaper to hire people from other countries. I knew people that would work the cruise ships for fifteen to twenty years and retire very rich in their country.

Now, there are places you can try. The Delta Queen Steamboat Company, which goes up and down the Mississippi, is American-owned.

Other bars include piano lounges, country bars, brew pubs, country clubs, jazz bars, wine bars, strip clubs, karaoke bars, VIP bars, flair bars, sports bars, French bistros, tapas bars, gay bars, neighborhood bars, biker bars, poetry reading bars, pool halls, street bars, Irish pubs, British pubs, outdoor bars, cantinas, salsa bars, ski resort bars, Amtrak bar cars, excursion bars, dive bars, tiki bars, and more.

1. Be in the industry. This means that you're already working as a host/hostess, server, busser, cook, cocktail server, or bar back. Managers prefer to hire within because they know your work habits, your dependability, and how you work with others. Make friends with the bartenders: run errands for them, pick up their food, tip them well, and have them quiz you on drinks. Trust me, it'll pay off.

2. Work for a bartender. High-volume nightclubs are so busy that they need bar backs. A bar back is a busy bartender's backbone. They keep the ice bin filled, fill the juices, wash glasses, empty the trash, change the kegs, run for backups, and do anything else the bartender needs. Oh, and they are masters of staying out of the bartender's way. Bartenders will tip you out very well, if you're good. The next best foot-in-the-door position is to be a cocktail server. Take these positions, sponge everything, and get paid to learn.

Bartending School

Some bartending schools can be helpful, but they're not the only way to learn about bartending, and they cannot guarantee you a job. As a matter of fact, you won't even be able to put it on your resume or application because managers and real bartenders will roll their eyes. It's sad for the good bartender schools, because the bad ones have given their business a bad name.

Also, you don't have to learn the hundreds of drinks they make you memorize, which is my biggest complaint about bar schools. I've been making the same thirty drinks for almost three decades! My second complaint is that most don't even employ people that actually work as a bartender. The truth is that you don't need to know the history of spirits to be a bartender. You can learn and absorb all of that later. A skeleton bartender needs to know about standard drinks, glassware, bar tools, mixers, garnishes, and the POS system. That's it. You build from there.

Let's say that you do shell out $600 for bartender school, and some bar somewhere gives you a chance. Most times what will happen is that the people already working there that have been waiting in line to move up will be pissed because you haven't paid your dues. On top of that, the bartenders that you work with will make your life a living hell because they will be pissed that they have to train a new bartender, and they have to split their money with you.

Bar School Boot Camp

I propose that you create your own *Bar School Boot Camp.* Here are some things to consider.

1. Before you can get your foot through the door, ya gotta knock. Take this book and go to a bar that has a nice bartender working the day shift. Be there between 2 p.m. and 4 p.m. (between lunch and dinner is a bar's slowest time). Great places to try first are chain restaurants or

any restaurant with a bar. You're searching for a *BarMentor* (half bartender and half mentor). You might have to check out a few of places until you feel a connection with someone, but it'll happen. Order something to eat, and have this book just lying there. While you're waiting for your food, start thumbing through the book. (Here's a secret: most bartenders like people with books. So often guests look to bartenders to entertain them, but when you bring your own source of entertainment the bartender will immediately like you.) Here's what I predict, the bartender will ask, "Whatcha reading?" And the door opens.

This is your opportunity to make a real connection with a real bartender. Tell them that you want to be a bartender one day, and you're trying to learn everything there is about bartending. Then ask them how they learned. Let them say as much as they want because bartenders don't get to talk about themselves too often; this will be a refreshing change for them. Making a good connection like this is one of the best things you can do. You'll be able to return and ask questions and get real information and instruction from someone who is actually doing what you want to do.

The best bar managers, owners, and bartenders I've ever seen have worked their way up from being dishwashers, bussers, cooks, and servers.

---

2. Somehow, someway, get several empty liquor bottles. Frat house trashcans are excellent for this. Clean them inside and out, fill them with water, and put pourers on them. You can even get creative and add food coloring. (A few drops of tea work well for the whiskeys.) Next, go to your local thrift stores and get a small collection of bar glassware. You must purchase some bar

3. Apply at a place that's just opening. I've done this five times. If you have a little experience with great eye contact, grooming, presence, and a killer-looking resume, then you're 99 percent guaranteed a bar position.

4. Know someone. Yep, some people get bartending jobs simply by knowing the right people and being in the right place at the right time. Pick out a bar that you like and get to know the manager. Work your magic and sell yourself. That's all we do anyway.

5. Learn all you can. Study books and other media, set up a practice bar at home, talk friends into having parties so you can practice tending bar, go to bars and absorb everything you can, then walk to the edge and jump. Fake it 'til you make it, baby.

tools because every profession has tools of the trade. You must know how to use them, and more important, get a good *feel* for them. And after you own them, you have the bonus of being ready to work any private party anytime, anywhere.

Don't feel overwhelmed—I've made building your own practice bar easy! Go to my Bar Store at www.charming.barstore.com and you'll find a Miss Charming's Hip Bartender and Wayout Wannabe Bartender Kit that I've put together for you to help get you started. You'll also be able to mix and match styles and colors to really personalize your new, cool tools. The only other thing you'll need is a large gym bag to store and tote your tools.

Teach yourself how to pour, strain, muddle, stir, build, rim, roll, chill, flame, float, layer, shake, everything. If you don't have a counter that's the height of a bar, use your ironing board. Go to bars and watch bartenders. What do they have on tap? Where is their wine kept? Where's the trash can? Are they running tabs? Are the beer glasses chilled? What kind of bottle opener are they using? Just be aware of everything they do. If you can find a bar where the bartender is slammed and you can hide in the corner at the end of the bar, this is great—you don't want them seeing you stare. Eye contact with a bartender should only be made if you need something or if they approach you.

3. Go out and find a job anywhere in the food and beverage industry, even if it's part-time. It's important that you understand the inner workings. Also, if you've never worked a POS system or cash register, I highly recommend that you pick up a shift somewhere where you have to so you can get some real hands-on experience with it.

4. Keep your eyes and ears open for any mention of any party of any kind. When you hear of someone throwing a party, tell them you'd like to bartend the party for free. If they say, "All we're serving is sangria," reply, "Ok! I'll serve the sangria!" If they're only serving beer and wine, it's a great chance for you to practice opening beer and wine bottles. The whole idea is repetition. Stop and think of something you're good at. Now, why are you good at it? Most times it's because you've had lots of practice.

5. Try to learn something new everyday. Learn how to cut garnishes, do bar tricks, spiral napkins, etc. Make flash cards, keep practicing, learn from books or any other media, and visit bars. When you finally apply at a bar, go there and hang out. Listen to the drink orders, and watch how they do things, and you'll be prepared for how that bar operates.

Feel free to email me if you have any questions or concerns and, of course, success stories.

Bartender License

You don't need a license, certificate, or any other paper to tend bar. Nurses, doctors, and architects need a license. Bartending is a blue-collar profession and even uses the basic application you filled out when applying for your first job at sixteen. However, some states and some establishments say that you have to be certified before you can work as a bartender. This just requires a food and beverage class that you and everyone else in the business must take. In these classes you learn basics like proper storage of food, safety, accepted forms of ID, etc. Establishments make you take these classes because they get a break on insurance. The most popular nationwide program is TIPS (www.gettips.com).

5 Bartend Like a Pro

Experienced bartenders can walk behind practically any bar and bartend: the only training required is the POS and to be shown where things are kept.

You got the job—congratulations! Now there's the small business of being good at it. Since you're working for tips, you have to be.

The Top Twenty Things That Will Make You Look Like a Pro

These are qualities bartenders pick up naturally with years of experience. If you're a new bartender, why not get a head start?

1. *Check your stock.* That's the first thing an experienced bartender does when they walk behind a bar. After all, you can't make anything if you don't have anything. Check the ice and juice levels; if they're low, fill them. Do you have backup garnishes? You don't want to stop in the middle of the night to cut fruit.

2. *Use both hands.* Experienced bartenders are practically ambidextrous. They use both hands at the same time *all the time*. Never have an arm dangling at your side while the other one is working.

3. *Have scratched up tools.* If you're an experienced bartender, your tools should look used. Scratch up your wine tool, bottle opener, lighter, and anything else in your pocket.

4. *Keep your head up* as much as possible, ears open, and eyes constantly scanning drink levels, servers, guests, suspicious activity, and so on. Bartenders tend to keep their heads down because they are always doing something. You have to be aware of everything going on around you, so get that head up as much as you can. If the bar has mirrors, use them to your advantage.

5. *Know how to make powdered sour mix properly.* Most bars use powdered sour mix, and the proper way to make it is to fill a gallon container halfway with hot water. Dump in the powder, screw the lid on, and shake it for about ten seconds. Next, add cold water very slowly (so it doesn't foam up), put the lid on again, and shake again. Refrigerate.

6. *Don't make one drink at a time* unless you have an order for only one drink. Let's say you have an order for a *Piña Colada, Cosmopolitan, Vodka Tonic, Screwdriver,*

Corona, Bud Draft, and a *Kahlúa & Coffee*. Set a Piña Colada glass, a Martini glass, two highball glasses, and a coffee mug on the bar. Add ice to the Martini glass so it can chill while you are making the other drinks. Make the Piña Colada and pour it in the glass, grab a shaker tin and make the Cosmo, then dump the ice out of the Martini glass and strain the Cosmo. Grab the well bottle of vodka in your left hand and a bottle of Kahlúa in your right; pour the Kahlúa in the coffee cup and the vodka in both of the highballs at the same time. Squirt the tonic, pour the OJ, and add the coffee (top with whip cream or let the server add it when she returns so that it doesn't melt too quickly). Now grab the Corona and pour the draft beer.

If you had poured the draft beer first, the head would've gone down by the time you finished making the order. If you had made the coffee first, it would've cooled. Also, when you set your glasses up like this, if you forget what you're making, nine times out of ten you can glance at the glasses and be reminded.

7. *Don't fill your drinks to the rim.* Inexperienced bartenders, lazy bartenders, and bartenders that have never learned properly do this. Always allow 1/4" to 1/2" breathing/travel/melting room at the top. If you are using real whipped cream you can fill to the top, and when you shake a drink with sour or juice the frothy part can go to the rim.

8. *Know how to handle money.* Experienced bartenders have excellent cash handling techniques. They handle money probably as much as a bank teller. Watch the way bank tellers shuffle the bills from hand to hand. One hand is pulling and the other is pushing. Practice counting, stacking, and arranging bills and coins until it feels natural.

9. *Behind you.* Behind. Behind. Behind you. Behind. Behind you. Experienced bartenders reading this are

The Top Ten Questions to Ask on Your First Day

If you ask these questions, the bartender you're working with will think that you've worked at a bar before. How else would you know to ask? (Besides reading this book.)

1. Start opening cabinets and coolers familiarizing yourself with where things are kept and ask questions like *Do we stock at the end of the night? Where are the kegs kept?* and anything else you think of as you are looking inside. All experienced bartenders will do this.

2. *Where are the restrooms for the guests?*

3. *What bottled beers do we serve?*

4. *Do we run tabs, and if we do, what's the procedure? Do we hold their credit card? Do you have many walkouts?*

5. *Where are the backup mixers kept?*

6. *Can you run me through the glassware?* Every bar uses different glassware so you have to go over it. You should ask something like, *What are we using for a highball?*

7. *What do we charge for a double?* Some places just double the price, however, many places just add $1.50 or $2.00. It's different everywhere.

8. If there is no coffee machine at the bar, ask where you get the coffee for a coffee drink.

9. *Do the servers cut the fruit or do we?*

10. *What liquor do we use for our house Cosmos? Sex on the Beaches? Long Islands? Are there any standard drinks we make differently? Are our Martinis two ounces?* I just want to be consistent with everybody because I know how different places can make drinks a little differently...blah, blah, blah.

Note: Bring a pocket-sized spiral notebook and write down everything you need to know. You'll be given a number. Write it down. You'll use the number to log into the POS system. The system only knows you as a number. Write down every step of the POS procedure—this will not seem weird or make you look inexperienced. It's actually smart. Experienced bartenders know that the cash register is the #1 thing behind the bar that will slow you down on a busy night. It will kick your butt. You

smiling because they know what this is. When working with another bartender and you step behind them to get something you always say softly, but loud enough for them to hear, *behind*. Anytime you get in a bartenders space you have to let them know. I've seen people get bloody noses, get knocked down, and even knocked out from an elbow because they didn't warn the other person that they were in their space. You can also lightly touch them on the shoulder. You must let them know you're there.

10. *Keep the half-and-half closed.* Experienced bartenders will keep the pour flap closed when pouring half-and-half. Open the half-and-half carton, then close the flap. This way, when you're making drinks with it, just squeeze the carton over the glass and you will have better control over its flow.

11. *Know how to do a reverse grip pour.* Once you get a good strong feel for holding spirit bottles, this is the next move you should learn to look like a pro.

12. *Know the common verbiage when doing inventory.* When you participate in inventory, all you need to know is that you measure the bottles in points. Each bottle has ten points. Look at the bottle as if it's divided up in ten parts. So if your manager asks you about the Bacardi bottle and it's half full, then it's called .5 (point five). If a bottle is full, however, don't say .10; just say it's one or a full bottle.

13. *Clean as you go.* All good bartenders clean as they go. If you make a mudslide Martini, then understand that cleaning the shaker is part of making that drink. Personally, I don't even take a guest's money until after I rinse the shakers because they need to see that it's part of what it takes to make the drink. The top priority is anything a guest can see.

14. *Know the proper way to rim a drink.* Most bartenders dunk the rim of a glass into the spongy section of a

rimmer, and then dunk into some sugar or salt. This is wrong; when the salt or sugar is on the rim, it falls into the drink. What you want is the salt or sugar to be on the outside edge of the rim, so you have to tilt the glass and rotate it around the rimmer.

15. *Know the brandy snifter tricks.* Lay a snifter on its side in the air then pour the spirit to the rim for a proper pour. If the guest requests the spirit to be heated and your bar doesn't carry a brandy warmer, preheat the brandy snifter by filling it 1/4 of the way with hot water (the kind at a coffee station) then fill a rocks glass half with hot water. Dump out the hot water in the snifter and pour in the Cognac and set the bowl inside the rocks glass. It's also nice to present it on a saucer with a cocktail napkin.

16. *Know the juice container trick.* You can make juice flow quickly out of a store-n-pour juice container by sticking a drinking straw into the spout to create an air hole. Can't argue with science.

17. *Know how to pronounce these words:*
    Apéritif (uh-pair-a-TEEF)
    Amaretto Disaronno (dee-sa-ROW-no)
    Angostura Bitters (ang-uh-STOOR-uh)
    Blue Curacao (CURE-uh-sow, sow rhymes with cow)
    Cabernet Sauvignon (cab-er-NAY soh-vihn-YAWN)
    Cachaca (ka-SHA-suh)
    Caipirinha (ki-pee-REEN-ya)
    Chambord (Sham-BOARD)
    Chardonnay (shar-doh-NAY)
    Cointreau (KWAN-trow)
    Courvoisier (core-VAH-see-A)
    Crème de cassis (ka-CEASE)
    Crème de cacao (ka-KAY-o, or ka-KAH-o)
    Crème de noyaux (noy-YOH)
    Dom Pérignon (dom pay-ree-NYON)
    Drambuie (dram-BOO-ee)

must master it. Memorize where the keys are so that you can whiz through. Find out where the *back-up* button or *delete* button is right away.

Also, let's say that a guest orders a beer and hands you a $20 bill. When it's handed to you, look at it, look back up at the guest, and say, "Out of twenty?" This confirms the amount given to you. If you don't say what the amount is, they can always say, "Hey, I gave you a $50." Trust me, people will try it. Every experienced bartender knows this. Also, if they give you a $100 to pay a tab that's something small like $22.50, always count back their change in front of them as opposed to laying the whole thing down, that way they can't yell at you a few minutes later that you shorted them $20.

Galliano (gall-lee-YAH-no)

Glenfiddich (gle-FID-ick)

Glenlivit (glen-LIVE-it)

Glenmorangie (glen-MORang-ee, rhymes with orangy)

Grand Marnier (GRAN mahr-nYAY)

Maraschino (mare-eh-SKEE-no, or mar-eh-SHE-no)

Mescal (mehs-KAL)

Mojito (mo-HEE-toe)

Pinot Noir (PEE-no NWAR)

Riesling (REEZ-ling)

Rumple Minze (ROOM-pull MINTS)

Sambuca (sam-BOO-ka)

Sommelier (sum-ul-YAY)

Worcestershire (WOOS-tuhr-sheer)

18. *Know how to bounce cut a bottle.* Let's say, for example, that you have glasses lined up with ice and several of them need the same spirit from the same bottle you are holding. When you finish pouring in one, bounce the bottle down then up, and the flow will stop, for one to two seconds. During this time aim the bottle over the next glass. So the order goes: pour, bounce, aim at the next glass, pour, bounce, aim at the next glass, etc. Try it at home first. It works the best when using a reverse grip.

19. *Know at least three ways to strain a drink.* Experienced bartenders know many ways to strain a drink.

20. *Know how to close the bar.* Any experienced bartender can walk into a bar the next day and know instantly if the bartender the night before has experience tending bar. A good sign is that many things are turned upside down. Basically, tools, juice containers, blender parts, draft beer trays, bar mats, soda gun nozzle and holder, fruit tray, and any other items should be washed, rinsed, and orderly turned upside down in a drain area. The juice containers are normally rinsed, then turned over at a draining angle in the well. Sometimes bars keep their fruit for two days, so they might be covered in the cooler. Personally, I throw all fruit away every night. Pourers that have been on liqueur bottles should be soaked overnight. The register area will be organized, and nothing anywhere behind or in front of the bar should feel sticky. Also, if you ran out of something, good bartenders will leave a note on the register for the next bartender letting them know.

Bartender Duties

Most bartender duties are the same no matter where you work. Some may have little quirky things unique to that bar, but here are the basics.

Paper Work
Spill Sheet

Most bars have a *spill sheet* that is kept behind the bar so that when a mistake is made the drink can be recorded. It's needed so the manager can add the missing drink to the inventory. The sheet will be simple like this:

Date	Drink	Alcohol & Amounts	Reason	Name of Bartender

Reasons could be that the guest changed his or her mind, you made the wrong drink, or the server spilled it.

Opening duties:
stocking your well with everything you need (juices, well bottles, tools, ice, etc.), getting and counting a bank, cutting fruit, stocking napkins and straws, making sure all glassware is clean and ready to go, making coffee and tea, preparing wine bottles, filling washing sinks, checking the levels of the kegs, getting back-up liquor bottles, and anything else your bar requires.

Working duties:
your cash drawer and all transactions with credit cards, tabs, and making correct change, smiling, changing kegs, making drinks for servers and guests, smiling, washing glasses, keeping mixers filled, checking IDs, replacing empty bottles, smiling, serving food, cleaning spills, dumping trash, smiling, handling many items while your hands are slippery and wet, dealing with many personality types from the guests to your coworkers, constantly evaluating your guests' intoxication levels, constantly checking drink levels, smiling, giving directions and advice, entertaining a little, and anything else the bar requires.

making sure the servers tip you out, cleaning every part of the bar, putting the juices away, melting the ice, cleaning all your tools, organizing and cleaning around the register, locking everything, stocking (if required), closing all your tabs, doing your paperwork, counting your money, turning in your bank, cleaning the floors, hauling the trash, and anything else your bar requires.

When working with another bartender, I prefer to set tabs in a rocks glass (or whatever) in front of the guest at the bar. This way, if I'm too busy to attend to them the other bartender can easily add drinks on the tab because they have the ticket to look it up in the computer. Also, if I get busy, guests can look at their tab and leave money in the glass and don't have to wait for me.

Comp Sheet

Some bars allow bartenders to comp (give away) a couple drinks a shift. They're mostly given to regulars or new guests for promotion, but the drinks have to be recorded for inventory as well. Sometimes bars will just use the spill sheet and then write *comp* in the reason category.

Tabs

Throughout your shift you're likely to be running tabs for guests. Some bars have strict policies on how they want this done. The strictest will want you to add drinks to tabs right away, then set the tab in plain sight in front of the guest at the bar. Others allow you to keep the tabs behind the bar (usually around your register). Some bars require that you get some sort of collateral to run a tab, such as a credit card. Many times bartenders will open a tab, lay it on the back bar, and put the credit card on top of it. Some will have paper clips to attach the two. When the guest orders another drink, a bartender who's busy will grab a pen and just mark on the tab to show that you need to add another drink later. Some bars don't allow you to do this. The main thing is to not lose any of your tabs, so keep them in a safe place.

When guests ask for their tabs, don't ever assume that they want to charge it to the credit card they gave you to hold the tab. Always ask, because sometimes they just want to pay cash. Lots of people share credits cards with others (spouses, Mom and Dad, companies, etc.), and they may not want cocktails from Joe's Bar & Grill to be on their statements.

If a guest walks out and accidentally leaves a credit card, the best thing to do is just hold on to it to see if he or she returns. If at closing the guest has not returned, you'll have to write *sig on file* (signature on file) in the place where he or she would have signed their name. Sadly, you *cannot* add a tip. There is one exception to that rule: some bars have a policy that parties of six to ten and more are automatically charged a percentage gratuity. Give the card to a manager to keep in lost and found.

Cash Out

Every bar has a different POS system and cash-out paperwork, but they all follow the same basic procedure.

1. You're given money to start your shift called your *bank*. It's usually around $200 to $300 in small change. Some places give you a safe and a key and you're responsible for keeping your own bank, then dropping the money you owe into another safe. Hotels and resorts often work this way. Also, when you are given a bank, count it. If it's short at the end you have to pay it out of your pocket.

2. At the end of the shift you print a reading/report on the POS that tells you what you owe. It will have all of your charge sales and cash sales. Use this to figure out how much money you made, then return your bank and the earnings.

Some places make you do a blind drop, which means that you don't know the exact amount of cash you're supposed to be giving them. You simply take out your $200 that you were given (if that's how much your bank was at the beginning of your shift) and put the rest of the money in a bag of sorts (or whatever they use). The bars that normally do this are the ones that have had trouble with bartenders stealing money in the past.

Cleaning
Closing Up

There's a lot of cleaning to do at the end of the night; pretty much everything has to be cleaned and locked up. To clean beer lines, pour the remaining hot coffee down the drains and follow with hot water. Clean the coffee pots with a mixture of kosher salt, your remaining lemons from the fruit tray, and soda water from the gun. Wipe lipstick off the glassware with a cocktail napkin or clean bar towel. When cleaning the bar at the end of the night, use a soapy wet bar towel to wipe and follow with a dry one. Clean any machines that hold a drink in bulk, like a margarita dispenser.

Railroad

A railroad is a list of cleaning duties divided up by day and shift. When you start your shift, look at the railroad to see what you are supposed to clean that day. This ensures that all the bar's sections get thoroughly cleaned at least once a week.

A Basic Railroad

	Opening Bartender	Closing Bartender
Monday	Clean beer cooler #1	Brass polish footrail
Tuesday	Clean beer cooler #2	Soak pourers overnight and cover bottles
Wednesday	Drain pourers and place on bottles	Sweep under everything
Thursday	Clean splash wall near trash can	Wipe all back bar bottles
Friday	Deep clean Island Oasis	Clean and polish stainless steel
Saturday	Clean back up coolers	Clean and organize cash register area
Sunday	Clean glass cooler	Wash all napkin caddies

Knowing Your Guests

As a bartender, you have about five to ten seconds to size a guest up and know how to deal with them (and make money from them). Here are few to look out for.

Intoxicated Guests

Handling intoxicated guests can be tricky. First of all, you should never let a guest get to this point, but sometimes it's hard because you don't know how many drinks (or anything else) they've had before coming to your bar. If you ever have to take food and beverage training classes, they more than likely will tell you about the green, yellow, and red light method:

Green light: Guests are sober.
Yellow light: Guests have a buzz, and they laugh, smile, and begin to talk a little louder.
Red light: Guests need to be cut off. They will fumble, stumble, their eyes are red, speech is slurred, and they talk very loud.

If you have a tab on a red light and have to cut them off, it gets trickier because you want to be tipped but now they may be mad and stiff you. All bars are different and attract different types of people, so the way you handle this has to match your venue. If you work a nightclub, it's easy because you just call over security or the bouncer and they're out of there. Hotels and resorts are tough because guests will repeat over and over, "But I'm not driving anywhere!"

The best thing is to do it in a way that makes you the middleman and takes the blame off you. One way is to get one of their friends to talk to them about slowing down. Another is to blame it on the manager. When you say, "I'm so sorry, but my manger says I have to wait a little bit before I can serve you anymore alcohol. Can I get you some water, juice, or coffee right now? It's on the house." Don't say the words *cut off* and say whatever you decide to say loud enough for only them to hear. If they don't want anything, set a glass of water next to them anyway, but put it in a high-ball glass with a lime so that it looks like a cocktail.

Rude and Mean Guests

You will meet many rude people, and the first mistake bartenders make is to take it personally. Let it roll off your back; it has nothing to do with you as a person. Guests can act anyway they chose. Generally, rude people just like having power over other people. Don't give them that power— you lose it the second you show that they're bothering you. I tend to start treating them extra nice, which generally confuses them and makes them drop the rude act, since it's not getting them anywhere.

Let's say that you have an extreme situation where the guest is yelling and cursing at you. Stay calm, in control, and say things like, "I'm so sorry you feel that way," or, "How can I make this situation better for you?" If they continue, get management and let them handle it.

Snobby Guests

Snobby people are different from mean or rude guests— these people actually believe that they're smarter and superior to you. They tend to treat you like a common servant. Don't get me wrong: these people aren't necessarily rich; they can be anyone. So how do you treat this kind of guest?

My personal approach is normally spiked with humor. At one bar I used to work at I bought the game Operation. I'd say, "Okay, I'll tell ya what—if you can get all these body parts out without the nose buzzer going off more than once, then I'll serve you another drink." It turned it into a lighthearted situation. Reinforcement from their friends always helps with this sort of tactic. No one ever won, but their drunken mind accepts the justice of it. Especially men. Men are great when it comes to challenges because, win or lose, they're going be a man and honor it.

Your relationship with management is very important. When you start at a new bar, you should always show tremendous responsibility and other commendable qualities because when a situation like this occurs you'll know that management will back you up. There's nothing worse than a boss who doesn't back you up when you've made a calm and intelligent decision.

Do guests ask bartenders for free drinks? Amazingly, yes they do. It's one of those mind-boggling things I haven't been able to figure out. Do people come to their job and ask for free things? Anyway, it will happen to you many times, and the best way to deal with it is to have some good comeback lines. The two most popular that I use all the time are: "Sure you can get a free drink! Just get one of your friends to buy it for you!" This works well when they are at the bar with some friends. They all laugh. The second one is a serious sincere one. "Hey, lemme tell ya, if it were up to me, I'd give ya a drink. But see all those bottles back there? I don't own them, I just sell it for someone else. But if I owned them, hell yeah, I'd give you a drink." This one is so logical that it stops them dead in their tracks.

The cousin of the free drink request is *make it a good one,* or *make it strong,* or *make it in a tall glass.* Geeeez, where do these people come from? Honestly, most of them have learned this from other bartenders who didn't know how to handle the situation, caved in, and gave the guest a strong drink to shut them up, so

What do they want? They want short, polite questions and to be fussed over as if they were royalty. One personal example is when a man I knew who fell into this category ordered a Cognac, and I nodded my head slowly, silently communicating, *your wish is my command.* Then as my head came back up I asked, "Would you prefer your Cognac warmed?" They seem to always go for the extra special choice you present to them because it gives them the special attention they crave. When they are leaving, say something like, "It was a pleasure seeing you today." The most important part of dealing with this type of guest is not sounding fake or condescending. Also, don't be surprised if you are left an average or below average tip.

The "I Wanna Be Your Best Friend" Guest

You'll know these guests from the first sentence that comes out of their mouths. They give you incredible eye contact, include you in their conversations with other guests, introduce themselves and ask your name, say something funny to get your attention, compliment you, or all of these at once. Some are cool, but others are irritating. Throw them a bone every once in a while because they desperately crave your attention (and this can lead to an excellent tip). Make sure you shake hands, introduce yourself, and say, "Nice to meet you." I tend to introduce them to other people at the bar so they have someone to talk to. Oh, and this type loves big smiles.

Presentation Is Everything

We live in a society that places a lot of value on presentation. Here are some techniques that will give you more style and make you look more professional behind the bar.

Making Drinks in Front of Guests

When guests order cocktails that are shaken or strained, why not make it in front of them? It's a much nicer presentation because it's like a mini-show. Making a Martini? Set the chilled Martini glass on the napkin in front of them, make the cocktail, then shake and/or strain right in front of them. They love it. Plus, you don't have to perform a balancing act of carrying it down the bar. This works great for shots and shooters too. When a cocktail server has an order for a round for a table, I send them out with a tray of shot glasses nicely arranged around a bottle full of the shot mixture. The server loves to pour the shots, and the guests love the presentation.

Napkin Spirals

Have you ever seen cocktail napkins on the bar fanned in a spiral? There are many ways to do this, but the easiest is to hold a four-inch stack of napkins in your hand, take a mixing glass or shaker, set it on top of the napkins, and push down and turn, while at the same time pushing up with the hand holding the napkins. Lift the glass off the napkins and turn again and you'll be able to see how the napkins are beginning to spiral. Just continue.

Drink Candles

Buy some birthday candles for special guest occasions. You can stick them into a drinking straw or garnish. Make a bar candle by sticking a drinking straw into another drinking straw (making a long straw) and sticking matches into the top. And if you don't have any matches or candles, just light the straw! You can also stock up on sparklers in July and December. Some bars won't let you use them, but sometimes you can get permission from your manager if you take full responsibility by carrying the drink to the special guest, waiting for the sparkler to die, removing it, then discarding it. Guests love sparklers.

they could just get a tip. But what this action does in the long run is hurt every other bartender that this guest visits. So please, I'm begging you to take control and stop doing this. All you have to do is smile and say, "Sure, no problem. Would you like a double?" Say it as if it's normal and that their request equates to you that they want a lot of alcohol in their drink and you're trying to accommodate them. Here's the fun part—they will look at you like a deer caught in the headlights for about three seconds while they digest what you've just nicely asked them. From here you will get a number of answers: *sure,* or *how much more money is a double,* or *no.* The bottom line is that you took control of the situation.

At the end of your shift, you should never think about anything that happened during that shift again. Don't even talk about it to another coworker to vent. You're clocked out, that part of you is over, and tomorrow is a new day.

Ladies First

I may get some flack on this one, but please serve ladies first. Trust me, they notice. If there are several ladies, then respectfully begin with the oldest and then work your way around clockwise, or down the bar. And of course, if it's a special occasion then start with the guest of honor.

Transporting Dirty Dishes

Unless you are working at a roadhouse or another bar that doesn't care, never stick your fingers into dirty glasses or beer bottles when clearing them away. It's very unattractive and unsanitary because you are touching places where your guests' mouths were. Always use trays and touch glassware by the outside. Hauling out a bus tub right in front of guests is unprofessional and inappropriate, so don't do it. This is only appropriate when a shift is over and no guests are present. When carrying a large tray of half-eaten food and dirty glassware, simply throw napkin linens over them. It helps stabilize the glassware and covers up the dirty parts.

Couples

There's an imaginary gender line that must be followed here: If you are female, always pay attention to the female before the man. And, if you are male, always connect with the man first. There is a weird dynamic when it comes to partners, dates, wives, husbands, boyfriends, and girlfriends. Alcohol can conjure up all kinds of feelings, and the last thing you want your coupled guests feeling is that you are hitting on or interested in their partner.

Cue Sticks

Some nice bars have ornate pool tables, and it's a great presentation to balance three cue sticks straight up to form a pyramid. It takes a little practice to get it to work, but when you've got it, it's easy. Now, to top it off, set the cue ball on top where the tips meet and watch guest's faces when they walk into the room.

Rainbow Shooters

One memorable way to present shooters to a group of guests is to put a drop of food coloring in the bottom of the shooter glasses. Wait until a guest orders a round of a shooter without much color, like a *Lemondrop* or *Kamikaze*. When you pour the shooters, each one is different color. Just make sure you get their attention before you pour so they can enjoy the show. In all the thousands of times I've done this no one has ever noticed the drop of food coloring in the bottom of the glass before the pour.

Bloody Mary Tray

Bloody Mary lovers go gaga when I pull out my little silver tray full of goodies and set it next to their drink. I fill it with hot sauces (I like to have at least two different kinds), salt and pepper, lemons, limes, celery, Worcestershire, olives, or anything else I have available at the bar in which I work. I line it with a few cocktail napkins and make it very presentable.

Chocolate Writing

If you buy a condiment squeeze container (like those ketchup and mustard containers) and fill it with chocolate syrup, you've created a tool whose uses are only limited by your imagination. On light-colored drinks you can draw hearts, stars, simple art, names, messages like *Happy Birthday*, anything at all. The chocolate works best when kept cold.

Dry Vermouth Mister

Yes, they sell canister misters for dry vermouth, but for something a little different why not buy a fancy perfume bottle that has a handheld pump attached to mist the top of a Martini connoisseur's cocktail?

Shooter Stack with One Hand

If you are carrying four shooters to a table and your hand is large enough to hold three rocks glasses, set the fourth one balanced on top for a cool presentation.

Food Service

If guests are eating food, glassware should be served on their right and taken from the right. Plates are served from the left and taken from the left (this keeps the plates from knocking over the glassware). You want to avoid reaching across the table, but if you must then all you have to say is, "May I clear this out of your way?" In a bar atmosphere these etiquette rules are sometimes very hard to follow. Just do your best.

If you serve food at your bar, forks go on the left of the plate and knives on the right. But most just have prepared rolls that can be laid across the plate at an angle. It's also a nice touch to lay out linen napkins with points facing you and the guest to serve as a placemat for a plate of food. Not only does it look nice, it's great for cleanup.

Champagne

When opening Champagne, always keep the bottle pointing up and away from anyone or anything fragile. Remove the foil around the top—there should be a little starter tab sticking out to help you. Next, unscrew and remove the wire cage. This moment can be critical because the wire cage is a safety net, so put your hand (or linen napkin) over the cork as soon as you can. Hold the bottle with your hand cupped around the bottom and twist.

You want the cork to make a quiet hiss and pop, not an explosion of the sort in an NFL locker room. Ha! That's funny! I love that NFL addition! Pour Champagne by holding the base of the bottle in one hand. Begin by pouring a little into each glass, allowing the Champagne to settle, then go around again and fill the glasses. A little Champagne poured into a glass and tasted before pouring all the glasses is *not* standard—this is the way wine is served, not Champagne. Also, most of the time, Champagne is ordered for a special occasion: birthday, job promotion, anniversary, and so on. You should try to find out that information when a guest orders it. Your face should light up and you should say something excited, like, "Champagne? what's the special occasion?"

When serving, it's customary to start with the guest of honor. If there's no guest of honor, ask who would like to taste first. At a large event where Champagne is used as a toast, such as a wedding or New Year's Eve party, the very best and easiest way to serve it is to make sure every guest is given a glass, then the servers/bartenders go to the guests. You can fill trays and trays and trays of glasses filled with Champagne, but it's extremely hard to carry this type of glass in volume. You can also have an area where the glasses are displayed and guests pick up filled glasses from a table, but this creates chaos in one area of the room. You could create many stations around the room, and of course, there's the very grand Champagne-glass pyramid that demands attention and grace.

Wine

If you are opening wine in front of guests, first show them the bottle, so they can verify it's what they ordered. In wine bars, this is critical: if the wrong bottle is opened it can cost a lot of money. If the cork of the bottle is covered with foil, flip open your knife and cut it off in a circular motion to expose the cork. (The knife part is referring to the little knife that is on every wine tool/waiter's corkscrew—it wouldn't make sense to have a pocket knife, put it away, and then get your wine tool. The knife and screw is an all-in-one thing.) Use your waiter's corkscrew and screw down the center of the cork three to four turns. To get started, it helps to press it into the cork until it grabs. Then flip the lever on the top edge of the bottle and pry up, letting the leverage do all the work for you. Of course, like anything, this takes practice before it starts looking good.

After you open the bottle, set the cork on the table and wipe the neck and opening with a linen napkin to remove any dust or cork particles. Now pour a little wine into the glass of the guest who ordered the wine. If it's to their satisfaction, then they will motion to you that it's good and then you can fill all the glasses, starting with the one you've already poured into. Don't fill the wine glasses to the top. A bottle of wine will yield four six-ounce glasses. So depending on how many guests are at the table, you'll have to guesstimate how much you should pour. If it's only two people, then simply pour each glass halfway up and set the bottle on the table if it's a red wine and into a bucket of ice if it's a white wine.

Fifty Miscellaneous Tips and Hints

1. If you cannot remember if a guest ordered salt for their margarita or not, simply rim half of the glass with salt, and they can drink from either side.

2. When guests with British accents order lemonade, they mean Sprite or 7-Up, but double check just to be sure.

3. When a guest with a British accent orders whiskey, he or she means Scotch whisky, but double check.

4. When serving beer to Europeans, know that they like more head than Americans.

5. Spotters/shoppers are hired to act like normal guests, then they report everything they see happening to management. Keep them in mind—they could be at your bar at any time.

6. Know that every bar you work at will teach you something new about the bar world. No one knows it all.

7. Pourers should only be kept on bottles that are used a lot. That's their purpose.

8. When stocking beer, an easy way to not have to pull all the current beer to the front of the cooler then stock the new beer behind it is to move the current beer to the left (or right) of the cooler and put the new beer on the empty side. If you use this method and everyone working the bar follows it then everyone always knows which side of the beer to grab first.

9. Don't bring nice pens to work because they'll be stolen, lost, or never returned.

10. Know that all Cognac is brandy but not all brandy is Cognac. Cognac can only be made from grapes grown in the Cognac region of France. Brandy can be made from grapes and other fruit anywhere in the world.

11. Know that sour mash means that part of the yeast mixture from one batch is used to start another batch. Like the way sourdough bread is made. People think Jack Daniel's tastes the way it does because it's a sour mash whiskey. Nope—many whiskeys are made using the sour mash procedure. Jack Daniel's tastes like it does because it drips through ten feet of sugar maple charcoal before it's put into charred barrels.

12. Know that Champagne can only be called Champagne when it's made in the Champagne region of France, and all other bubbly wines must be labeled and called sparkling wine.

13. Know that Tequila must be made from 51 percent of the *blue* agave plant and mescals can be made from any and many agave plants.

And now, what you really want to know about bartending—how to parlay these skills into cash.

1. Names. People love to hear their name, and people love knowing the bartender's name. When you shake someone's hand across the bar and say his or her name ("Nice to meet you, Joe"), you've made a regular for life. Don't do this for everyone who sits at the bar: you'll know when it's right. And you have to find ways to remember names. I always focus and ask something like, "How do you spell that?" Of course, you won't do that for all names, but you have to connect it in your brain somehow. Sometimes you can make a connection with the drink they order. Also, when a guest hands you a credit card, you have a golden opportunity to know their name. When you hand their card back, say, "Thank you, Mr. Smith."

2. Buy a bag of individually wrapped candy or mints and give your guests some when you give them their tab. Bar guests are surprised by this because it's more of a server gesture, but appreciate it because

14. When you have to tell the guest that you're out of something, it's much better to say, "I'm sorry, we're sold out of that." When you just say you're *out* of something it makes it sound like your manager is disorganized and doesn't know how to order properly, but saying you're *sold out* sounds like it's a popular item (and implies they have good taste!).

15. Know that while anyone in America can make Bourbon, Kentucky is the only state allowed to put the words Kentucky Bourbon on the bottle.

16. No matter what you are told, only one thing sobers up the human body, and that's *time*. Coffee makes a wide-awake drunk, food makes a full drunk, and a cold shower makes a wet drunk.

17. If your bar carries more than one Johnnie Walker Scotch, you'll have to ask guests which one they would like.

18. Bartenders more than likely won't be taking any breaks. Shifts can be six to twelve hours long. Many bartenders take a power nap before going to work.

19. When you start working a new bar, do not start moving things around or giving advice on where things should be or how things should be done until you settle in after several weeks. And you never want to say the words, "Well at the last bar I worked, we did it this way." No one wants to hear how you did it before, because it doesn't matter. You're going to do everything the way they want you to do it. And drop the attitude.

20. Cleaning up the tools you used to make a drink is part of making a drink, so you should always get into the habit of rinsing out the blender or shaker tins immediately afterwards.

21. Buy a tuxedo T-shirt to wear when working fun private parties.

22. When up-selling, one method to use is to ask if they want you to use their favorite spirit. "Would you like me to use your favorite vodka?"

96

23. The classic Martini is made with gin. Period. So, when someone asks you for a Martini and says nothing else, the best thing to do is smile and say, "Sure, would you want me to use your favorite gin?" This lets them know without preaching that a classic Martini is made with gin (even though these days vodka Martinis share the classic Martini spotlight).

24. Whenever you are slow, never just stand around. There's always something to clean or organize.

25. Know that you will burn out. Doing a job that is physically and mentally demanding catches up with you. You'll know when you begin to get snippy with guests and coworkers. It's okay; many professionals who deal with the public go through this (police officers, cab drivers, strippers, etc.). Just make sure you take a mini-vacation and recharge. Go out and let someone serve you.

26. When making drinks, you want to strive for only picking up a spirit bottle or mixer once during an order. While you have a bottle in your hand, pour it into all the glasses that require it.

27. The dryer a Martini is ordered, the less vermouth they want.

28. When guests spill something on the bar, a lot of bartenders get irritated. The guest is already embarrassed, so just look at them, smile, and say, "It's okay, it happens." Their facial expression will instantly change, and they'll probably leave you a bigger tip.

29. Breakage refers to your empty bottles at the end of the night.

30. If you are too busy to get to a guest at the moment, make sure you acknowledge them in some way. When guests are acknowledged, they don't mind waiting.

31. When you're slammed, don't get frustrated. Guests don't mind waiting in line, so just acknowledge the people you can't get to and give each person you are

their breath smells like alcohol. Guests like it when you give them little things.

3. Smile and have good eye contact. Attentive eye contact makes a person feel that they matter. Here's an actor's trick: if you have a hard time looking into someone's eyes, look at the space right in between their eyes, above the bridge of the nose. To a guest you are looking at them dead in the eyes, but you're not. The bar is a stage.

4. Guests will look at the total of their tab and tip accordingly. Isn't that what you do when you go out? So, your goal is to get that tab as high as you can. Maybe you can suggest some food or a new popular drink. Many times when a group of friends start to feel good you can suggest some new shooters...bam bam bam. Nothing bumps that tab up like a round of shots.

5. When you give back change, don't put it in their hand. Set it on the bar or in a check presenter or tip tray, anything but their hand. When they have it in their hand it's too easy for them to stick it in their pocket. When it's

on the bar they have to reach and pick it up and usually leave something because people are watching. Cocktail servers do this all the time. They set the change on their tray, forcing you to reach out and take your change. Also, make sure you break down their change so that they have something to tip you with.

6. There are three words you should never say: "I don't know." If you don't know, then say, "Hmm, that's a good question. Let me ask around for you." Most bar guests are shocked that you'd go through the trouble.

7. Bar guests like it when you clean their space. It makes them feel important and pampered. Just smile and say, "Let me clean this up for you a little."

8. Compliment them on something. Don't make up anything that sounds fake. There's always something to say about their great eyes, hair, shirt, tie, mannerisms, smile, dimples, the way they stand tall with their shoulders back, their handwriting, their choice in sports teams, their drink choice, etc.

dealing with direct attention. And never forget that if it weren't for these guests, you wouldn't have a job.

32. Pour tests are sometimes mandatory for bartenders who are allowed to free pour (don't have to use a jigger). It's a set of test tubes that have measurement lines on them called an Exacto Pour. Management will give you a liquor bottle filled with water and ask you to pour these measurements separately into a glass: ¼, ½, ¾, 1, 1 ¼, 1 ½, and 2 shots. Each pour is individually poured into the tubes to measure your accuracy.

33. Bartenders, when out at another bar, *do not ever* tell another bartender that they are a bartender too. There's only one exception, and it's when the bartender asks you first. It's the biggest joke between real bartenders. The joke is that when a guest says they are a bartender, what they're really saying is, *I'm a lousy tipper, but I'm going to pretend that we have a common bond so you will give me lots of attention.* Maybe they have been behind the bar, but not long enough to know not to say this. Bartenders show other bartenders that they are bartenders through action, not talk.

34. Hold spirit bottles firmly, and don't be careless with them. Most bottles are worth around $100 to $200 each. Most are bought for $20 to $50 and marked up four to five times to make a profit. So think about that when you go to grab one.

35. Yes, you will spill something. The worst is when you spill on a guest, but just apologize a lot and grab some napkins. And a free drink never made anyone more upset.

36. Yes, you will break something. And when a guest breaks a glass, the first thing they do is start grabbing for the big shards. Tell them right away not to touch anything and that you will take care of it for them. The last thing you want is to tell your boss that a guest with bloody hands wants to talk to them. For the extra tiny little

pieces of glass, simply wet a bar towel and lay on top the pieces then swipe up. The wetness picks them up.

37. Most bartenders do not like anyone to come behind the bar. They like their space, so if you're a server, always ask.

38. Not every bartender is into sports, but some guests get very upset when you don't know the ballgame score. If you are a sport agnostic bartender (like me) politely make it known that you're not the person to ask. Try playing dumb: "Oh, baseball? That's the one with the big orange ball, right?"

39. If you have to write down drink orders, use *bartender shorthand*. Instead of writing in longhand, for example, Bourbon and Coke, you would write B/C. Every spirit and mixer can be shortened. Back in the 1970s and '80s, cocktail servers actually wrote their orders this way and gave it to the bartender. Abbreviations for call and premium spirits are easy too: Crown = Cr, Bacardi = Bac, Southern Comfort = Soco, etc. Mixers are easy: DC = Diet Coke, T = tonic, OJ = orange juice, etc. Then there are the special ones like an X for *rocks,* and an upward arrow for *up*. Some abbreviations will differ: some people like to write *Marg* for margarita while others will write *Rita*. It's all up to what works best for you.

40. There are good and bad aspects to every job in the world. For example, in a hotel bar you might have to walk very far to pick up appetizers in the kitchen, but there's a cleaning crew that cleans your floor mats and mops your floor. Or you make killer money at a restaurant, but constantly transferring tabs to servers when guests' tables become available is a pain in the butt. Just make sure the pros/cons balance tips in your favor.

41. Have you ever been somewhere and overheard employees talking about their personal or work life? Better yet, did they continue their conversation in front of you?

9. When you have a slow moment, ask them something about their life. People love to talk about themselves. Let me say that again. People love to talk about themselves. And if you work somewhere where children are around, pay attention or do something for the kids—it's a gateway to a parent's wallet.

10. Entertain. Learn one bar trick, one magic trick, or one good short joke, and watch your tip jar skyrocket.

Don't do this! Guests should never hear you talking about private matters with others coworkers. As a matter of fact, if I ever own a bar this action will be grounds for termination.

42. If you are a female bartender I have something to say to you. You should be able to perform all bartender duties just like the guys. You need to change kegs, carry cases of beer, and haul trash. These are part of a bartender's duties, and if you can't do them you're not qualified to work behind the bar. Now, with that said, if you prove that you can do these heavy, dirty jobs in the beginning, when you are working with guys there's a natural progression that leaves you counting the money and cleaning the bar while they do the grunt work. But it's important for them to know that, if needed, you are a team player and are totally capable of doing anything that needs to be done.

43. Start your shift with the ice well filled as high as it can be filled. This way you don't have to run and get ice in the middle of your shift and you also save your back muscles from having to bend over so far.

44. When a guest orders a drink, try adding a little trivia they probably don't know. For example, if they order a *Tanqueray & Tonic*, mention while you are pouring that it's believed the shape of the bottle was inspired by a cocktail shaker. Guests love it. Other great ones are: the Cuervo 1800 bottle comes with it's own one-ounce measuring cap, Canada created Crown Royal for Queen Elizabeth's 1939 visit, Southern Comfort was created by a bartender in New Orleans during 1874, and Michelangelo probably drank the very same Amaretto Disaronno of today because he was fifty years old when it came out in 1525.

45. Some bottles are always next to each other on the back bar. Usually blackberry brandy and banana liqueur are together because of the *Rum Runner*. Baileys, Kahlua, and Grand Marnier sometimes get put next to one another, and the two crèmes de menthe and the two crèmes de cacao usually sit together as a family. And Southern Comfort should be with the liqueurs, not the whiskey.

46. When you get busy and simply don't have time to talk to guests, try to find out little tidbits of info about them like where they're from, where they grew up, what they do for a living, where they went to school, and so on. This way you can connect people at the bar and they start talking to each other and have a grand ol' time and think you are the best bartender around.

47. The proper way to keep the ice scoop is stuck into the ice with the handle up. This keeps your nasty hands from touching the ice.

48. When you make the wrong drink, and it's not carbonated, always strain it into a glass and set to the side. It'll be ready to use when it's ordered again. If no one orders that drink again, then you'll have to record it on the spill sheet.

49. You'll probably have many bar keys on a ring and will have to learn which go with what. Most bar keys are small and are used to lock cabinets. You may also have some coolers that use a padlock. Also, it's a very good habit from the beginning to never put the bar keys in your pocket—it's too easy for you to forget about them, and you'll end up taking them home. Buy a cheap little hook to put on a belt loop or something.

50. When you turn something over to dry, you must always have it propped slightly in a way that air can get under it.

6 Bar Tricks and Magic

Bar tricks entertain guests, and entertained guests stay longer. It's a win-win situation for everyone: owners sell more food and beverages and get repeat business, guests are happy, and bartenders get bigger tips. First, always ask if someone would like to see a bar trick. Good bartenders know how to feel people out and give them the exact service they desire. A guest at the bar reading a book with earphones on does not want to see a bar trick. They want a nice drink and a clean place to sit

No one knows where or when the very first bar trick was performed, but ancient tombs and wall paintings show us that tricks have been around since probably 5000 BC. The classic cup and ball trick was discovered in Egyptian scrolls, India had its snake charmers and carpet flyers, court jesters performed for English royalty, and throughout history, speculation is high that the average Jane or Julius witnessed a few shenanigans of this sort at local village drinking houses. In medieval times, tricks fell by the wayside due to their association with witchcraft, and it wasn't safe to play them again until the 1700s.

Bar magic tricks are a little different from standard bar tricks. A bar trick is more of a brain-teasing challenge that uses items found around the bar. When you perform a challenge, generally you can move around and still make drinks if you need to while the competitor thinks about it. With magic tricks, since they are a little more elaborate and involve slight of hand, they glue your feet to the floor. Never do magic tricks when you're busy.

Human behavior is an interesting thing indeed. For the most part, women will sit back, smile, and simply enjoy the entertaining experience of a trick. Most men, on the other hand, don't like to feel stupid, and they want to know if a prize is involved. Tell them the prize is that they get to learn a trick that they can use for the rest of their life. Encourage them to look at it as a positive learning experience. When it comes to magic tricks, with most men, it never ceases to amaze me how they simply can't sit back and enjoy it. You can see the wheels turning in their heads as they try to figure it out. Never do a trick twice in a row and never tell them how it's done. I've had many, many men offer to pay for an answer. Do I give it to them? Sure, but I get the money first.

Top Five Bar Tricks

Snifter and Olive

This is the one that started it all. I saw this trick performed by a guest the first year I tended bar and have passed it on to thousands upon thousands of people since.

What you need: Brandy snifter, olive, and any glass.

Challenge: The object is to get the olive into the glass by only touching the brandy snifter. The snifter must remain inverted at all times, and you cannot smash the olive on the rim of the snifter and try to shake it off into the glass. No other items are used.

How? Rotate the snifter round and round over the olive, and it will lift the olive up into the snifter by way of centrifugal force. Keeping the rotation going, carry it over your target, then stop and it will fall into the glass.

Tips: I like to use a Martini or wine glass for aesthetic reasons and because I think the trick works best using a tall glass—it's a little more impressive. You can replace the olive with a stemless cherry (or anything round; however, rinse cherries first because they are sticky).

Upside-Down Beer Bottle

This one is awesome because anywhere you go, you'll find a bottle and a bill. It can also be a big money maker.

What you need: Beer bottle (preferably longneck) placed upside down on a bill.

Challenge: To get the bill out from under the bottle. You can't touch the bottle, but you can touch the bill. However, you cannot jerk or shimmy the bill out.

How? You roll the bill and it pushes off the bottle.

Tips: There's usually a drop or two of beer left in a beer bottle when you turn it over on the bill, so the bill is a little wet. You want that dampness because it keeps the bill somewhat attached to the bar top, discouraging easy manipulation. If too much beer puddles, just grab a cocktail napkin and wipe it off. There are several variations on this trick. My favorites are to set a tall, full drink on top of the bill in place of the bottle. You can also set a pint glass on top of the bill and balance a quarter on the rim of the glass, then retrieve the bill without the quarter falling.

Elementary Sticks

There are so many puzzles involving sticks! I use this one all the time when I need to buy ten to fifteen minutes, because it usually takes someone that long to figure it out.

What you need: Ten cocktail straws, matches, or toothpicks set up to read 1 + 11+111 (1+2+3).

Challenge: To get the answer of this equation to equal four by only moving one stick. The stick picked up must be put back down in the equation.

How? Move one of the sticks in the middle and make a plus sign in the last group of sticks, so the equation reads 1+1+1+1.

Tips: When explaining the challenge, let them know that the answer will remain very elementary: there's no multiplication, division, Roman numerals, or funky-shaped numbers. Tell them it's something they would see in the first grade. Again, don't give them the answer right away. Hints that can be used are telling them to think about what would equal four and that the one you pick up is somewhere in the first four sticks.

The Eggtraordinary Egg

This is by far the simplest yet biggest crowd-pleasing bar trick ever. Never begin with this trick. It's important to use it as a climactic trick once you have a group of people at the bar because it will have the whole bar cheering.

What you need: Two shot glasses set side by side and a raw or hard-boiled egg placed in one of the glasses.

Challenge: Get the egg into the other shot glass without touching anything.

How? You blow down hard and quick into the air pocket of the shot glass with the egg, and the egg will flip over to the other glass.

Tips: All shot glasses will not work. You must have any kind that leaves a bit of breathing room at the top after the egg is inserted; glasses with thick glass bottoms work great. Two jiggers will work too. And unless you work somewhere that has a kitchen stocked with eggs, just bring some to the bar yourself. For less mess, just hard-boil them.

Paper Rose

Everyone should know how to make a rose from a cocktail napkin. It's easy!

What you need: One cocktail napkin.

How? 1. Open up the napkin completely.
    2. Roll into a big loose tube.
    3. Pinch where you want the rose bud to be.
    4. Twist the napkin underneath the bud, making the stem.
    5. Stop halfway and pull up the bottom corner to make a leaf.
    6. Pinch under the leaf and continue to twist down. You did it!
       Now just fluff and adjust the rose bud.

Flash Paper Roses

For a really attention-getting trick, use *flash paper*. This is that cool paper magicians use to make a big, bright flame. It burns quickly and completely, with no ashes. Make a paper rose from flash paper, light it, and while it bursts in flames pull up a real live rose. People's mouths will drop. You can buy flash paper at your local magic shop. When you buy it they will make you sign a waiver because it's very important that it's not left in hot places (like the dashboard of your car) because it will ignite. It costs about $20 for five large sheets, but you only need a little bit.

The Top Bar Magic Tricks

Before we start making magic, there are a few things you need to know. Two magic terms you should know are *patter* and *prep*. Patter is what you say while performing a trick, and prep is short for preparation and is what you do secretly before the trick begins. Distract the audience with your patter and have your prep in place for the perfect moment. Also, you'll learn that there's a method to the arrangement of your tricks. The first one must capture the audience's attention and set the stage for the following tricks. Perform a climactic trick once you have a group of people and always insert a humorous trick here and there to keep it interesting.

I Have You Figured Out

This first trick is the very *first* one I always perform because it blows people's minds and captures their attention immediately. If you only learn one magic trick in your whole entire life, this is the one to learn. The best thing about this trick is that you can do it anywhere with practically anything. It might sound confusing at first, but once it clicks, you'll be doing it all the time, and people will think you're so cool.

What Happens? You lay out four fruits from the fruit caddy, and place one fruit under a shaker tin in front of a guest. Don't let them see what kind of fruit it is. The guest chooses one of the fruits, then you lift the shaker tin and viola! It's the one they chose.

What you need: Shaker tin, two olives, one cherry, one lime, and one lemon. Understand that any other items can replace all of these items. You just must have one extra item to hide (in this case, the olive). You can also use any cup or glass that is not transparent in place of the shaker, or even someone's hand behind their back or in their pocket.

The Trick: First off, this type of trick is called a *force* in the magic world. Basically, you are *forcing* a person or persons to choose something that you want them to choose. Keep in mind that it doesn't matter what they say because you are in charge of guiding them to choose the fruit you have secretly hidden under the shaker tin. Now, with the four fruits and the extra olive under the shaker tin sitting on the bar top, ask someone to *say* out loud two fruits of their choice. Let's pretend that someone says the lime and olive. You then reach for the lemon and cherry (leaving the lime and olive) and say, "Okay, the lime and olive." Now, let's pause for a moment. What if they had said the lemon and the cherry? Ah, yes, this is where it sounds a little tricky…but it's not. Keep in mind that no matter what someone says, *you* control what is taken away and you are always going to leave the match of what you have hidden. In this case you've hidden the olive. So, again, what if they had said lemon and cherry? Well, then you reach and take the lemon and the cherry and say, "Okay, so that leaves the lime and olive." So either way, the olive remains (this is what you want).

Now you have the lime, olive, and the hidden olive under the shaker tin on the bar top and the lemon and cherry in your hand. You now ask someone to *pick up* either the lime or the olive. If they pick up the lime, reach out the hand that is holding the lemon and the cherry and say something like, "Now put the lime with its family." After they place the lime in your hand, point to the olive and say something like, "See what you left on the bar?" Then lift the shaker tin and say, "That's what I thought you'd leave."

Let's backup. What if they pick up the olive? Easy! Just reach over and pick up the lime to get it out of their vision and say something like, "See what you picked up?" Lift the shaker tin then say, "That's what I thought you'd pick."

Tips: The number one tip is not to forget what you hid. Secondly, don't hide your prediction on your body because people get suspicious. Also, notice the first time they choose you want them to *say* the two fruits because you need to control what is taken away. The most important thing is to say the words, *say two fruits* and not the words *pick two fruits*.

Unbreakable Stick

Here's another hands-on, mind-blowing trick that can be performed at the bar or at a dinner table.

What Happens? You place one toothpick, cocktail pic, or wooden match in the center of an open cloth napkin, fold it up, hand it to someone to break the stick, then when you open the napkin the stick is intact.

What You Need: Two sticks (toothpicks, cocktail pics, or wooden matches) and a cloth napkin with a hem.

The Trick: Prep the napkin by secretly shoving one of the sticks into the hem. Open the napkin, spread it on a table, and place the second stick in the center. Fold up the napkin, and pick it up in such a way that your hand is holding onto the secret stick.

Hand the napkin to someone, being sure to give them the hidden stick. After they confirm that they can feel it, have them break it. After they break it, reach out to take it back, lay it down, open it up fold by fold and watch their amazed faces when they see that the stick is not broken.

Tips: Make sure that you shove the stick deep in the hem, with at least one-fourth of an inch of empty space left on the end. If you don't, when they break it a little bit will stick out and bust you. If your stick is long enough, you can ask a second person to break it again. This really builds up the mystery.

By far the best bar magic tricks are the ones that fit in your pocket, and the following three tricks are absolutely the best to invest in. When you go to your local magic store to buy a trick they always have a magician that shows you how it works. That's part of the bargain when you buy magic. If you buy it online it will come with basic instructions and usage ideas, but the personal face-to-face method of learning is much nicer.

Thumb Tip

- This inexpensive ($5), flesh-colored fake thumb fits over your, uh…thumb. It has an unlimited amount of uses. You can make something disappear into thin air, and no one ever notices it. Common bar uses include: Pouring the contents of a sugar packet in your clenched hand and making it disappear, then reappear by pouring the sugar into a guest's hand. The thumb tip is in your clenched hand and catches the sugar as it's poured in. Then you have someone say some magic words while you slyly stick the thumb from your open hand into the thumb tip. This hides the sugar, so when you open your hands for inspection it appears that the sugar has disappeared, but it's really inside the thumb tip that is on your thumb. Get the idea?
- They also make steel-tipped thumb tips. I used one on a guy's black leather jacket once to put out a cigarette butt. He freaked out because it looked like I was putting it out on his leather jacket, but in reality it was being crammed into the thumb tip.
- You can also fold and unfold a $1 bill in one smooth motion, and as you unfold it, Wow! It has turned into a $100 bill.
- There's another variation of the thumb tip that is a must-have item. It's called D'lite and is a mesmerizing red, blue, green, or white light that you pass from your fingertip. Make sure that you buy a pair of them, and you'll be able to pass the light in your ear then out your mouth, from hand to hand, behind your back, through your clothes, etc. People's jaws drop. Anyone can learn it in five seconds. You can get a pair for around $20, and they are worth every penny.

Pen Through Anything

This pen, invented by John Cornelius in 1993, will penetrate anything without tearing it. Stick it through a bill, a bar tab, a business card, anything! It's pretty amazing and costs around $20.

Honorable Mention Trick

There's an awesome trick called Airbourne Glass that was invented in the 1960s by John Fabjance. Many magicians have performed it including Lance Burton, and Rickey Jay in the film *Boogie Nights*. You pour from a liquor bottle into a glass that is magically suspended midair. Its answer is in my first book, *Miss Charming's Book of Bar Amusements,* and also can be seen in Dean Serneels's *Practical Bar Magic* DVD at www.flairco.com. Or you can walk into any magic shop and buy it.

Flair Bartending

Modern dictionaries define the word *flair* as style, talent, and possessing a unique quality. For today's general public, the term *flair bartending* conjures up images of Tom Cruise juggling liquor bottles in the 1988 film *Cocktail*. There's no doubt that this film was the spark that ignited the flame for the recent explosion of this ever-growing, constantly evolving, flipping, spinning, mind-blowing world of performance bartending.

"Professor" Jerry Thomas is considered to be the first known and recorded flair bartender because of his showmanship while serving cocktails. He traveled with a custom-made set of solid silver bar tools and was considered a true performer behind the bar. His blue blazer drink was lit on fire and poured back and forth, creating quite a show. It was just one of his signature cocktails, but is the best example of his entertaining abilities. He is also credited with publishing the first known cocktail recipe book and bartender guide in 1862 and 1887.

Today, flair bartending is not about just juggling bottles. For the average bartender, flair just means a personal style, a cool way of making something ordinary into something extraordinary. Why not flip a shaker tin once before you put ice into it, then use both hands to pour in two liquors at once? It takes the same amount of time yet adds a certain showmanship. This is called *working flair,* and it spread in the late 1990s, when exhibition bartenders were forced to develop and perfect new moves that were low risk but had high impact and did not slow their speed of service to satisfy bar owners and managers. Flair can be the way you spin a cocktail napkin, tell a joke, pour a beer, handle a crowd, or stack shot glasses.

The Top Ten Flair Moves Anyone Can Do

1. Reverse Grip

If you choose to learn only one move for the rest of your life, this should be the one. The reverse grip is exactly what it sounds like. Instead of grabbing a bottle as you normally would, twist your wrist inward, and grab the neck of the bottle the other way. It makes you appear that you've been behind the bar a long time and know exactly what you are doing. Truthfully, it's a no-brainer move, but from the other side of the bar it impresses. The only thing that will feel awkward in the beginning is how to end the pour. The way you stop the flow of liquid is called a *cut*. You can slowly cut the bottle down or make a clean, quick cut. It's up to you. The most important thing is to make sure to allow plenty of room to swing the bottle back down to its right side up position because you don't want to break the bottle on anything. Your boss doesn't want you to either.

2. Impressive Pours & Clean Cuts

Anybody can pour one inch away from a shaker tin or glass of ice, so why not bump it up a notch and pour one, two, or three feet away? This is called a *long pour*, and it's very easy. Simply start your pour about an inch away from the glass or tin, and raise the bottle as high as you want to make an impressive, long liquid stream. If you are holding a glass or tin in your other hand then you can move it down and the bottle up to make the stream even longer. To really blow them away, try a move created by award-winning flair bartender Tony Cogburn: while long pouring, simply rotate your body in a complete 360-degree circle.

Long pours are great for double shots. You can raise the bottle up then down and up again for show. If you can, end with a quick, clean cut. Practice your cuts until they are smooth and clean so there is absolutely no alcohol spillage. For strained drinks, you can do a semihigh pour from the shaker tin into the glass. Make sure you snap a clean cut with the tin for more style.

3. Sex Pour

If you've mastered the first two moves, this easy, eye-catching move will be a natural progression from the others. Instead of taking the bottle straight to a glass of ice or shaker tin, swing the bottle around your head and then pour. So, first you reverse grip a bottle, then, while keeping the bottle vertical, swing it around your head (right-handed grips swing counterclockwise, and left-handed grips swing clockwise). Once around, flip the bottle over and pour. Just make sure no one or no thing is in your space so you don't break the bottle or hurt someone.

4. Tin Flip

There are a few ways to flip a tin, and this is a great beginning one. Start with the tin sitting upside down, then grab the tin at the top (really the bottom, because it's upside down), flip it up, and as it falls back down catch it on its side. The tin is now in your hand right side up and allows you to make one smooth and flowing motion straight into the ice bin. Don't be afraid of height. Height is good whenever you flip something in the air because it gives you more time to react and it looks impressive from the other side of the bar. Once you master one hand, start with the other, then try both at the same time.

5. Tin Spin

To spin a tin, rest it on your palm and spin. Start with a half spin and work your way up. You'll discover that this is one of those Karate Kid/Kung Fu moves—it's all about letting go. Your fingers simply provide the starting spin speed while your palm stretches completely open, even curved back at times, while the tin smoothly spins on the one-fourth-inch callus of your index finger. Once you get the feel of it you will be spinning every condiment bottle you touch. Mastered that hand? Now start with the other. Once you have the tin flip and spin mastered, you can combine them into a great, flowing beginner routine. Flip, spin, and then scoop the ice.

Let's combine the first five moves to make a flowing routine. Say someone orders a Sour Appletini. Try this: Grab a Martini glass, and set it in front of the guest, then drop in a cherry. Flip the shaker tin, spin it, then scoop some ice. Reverse grip a citrus vodka bottle, swing it around your head, and long pour into the shaker tin, then cut. Reverse grip the sour apple bottle, swing it around your head, long pour, cut, and then pour in the sweet-n-sour mix. Shake and strain the cocktail into the Martini glass. See how that works? Need to make two Sour Appletinis? Then flip two tins, hold both tins in one hand, and so on, then shake and strain both cocktails at the same time. Other variations include keeping the tins on the bar and using both hands to pour both bottles at the same time, or keeping both bottles in one hand while the other hand pours the sweet-n-sour mix.

6. Tin Split

The *tin split* is a clever and magical-looking move. One day you may see a competition bartender actually marry this move and the legendary cup and ball magic routine. A tin is inserted into another tin of the same size, then both are flipped up. While in midair they split from each other. You then catch each tin with each hand.

7. Stunning Glass Stacks

Glass stacks are used when more than one drink is ordered. Sure, anyone can line up glasses, but why do that when it takes the same amount of time to make an unforgettable presentation?

Two glasses

Easy: You'll need five glasses total. Three are turned over and used as a presentation lift for the two that will be used by the guests.

Challenge: Using solid-bottomed rocks glasses, balance one on the rim of the other. It'll feel very awkward at first, but with practice you'll become a whiz.

Three glasses

Easy: Build a pyramid using two glasses on the bottom and the third balanced on top.

Challenge: Build the two-glass challenge then balance another glass on top so that you have three stacked glasses. This is total physics. The secret is to balance the glasses on the rim at ten o'clock and two o'clock or visa versa.

See the illustrations for more glass stacks. Keep in mind that if you ever stack three levels or higher you must set up on a curve so that you can pour into all the glasses. Champagne glass fountains are always set up circular for this reason.

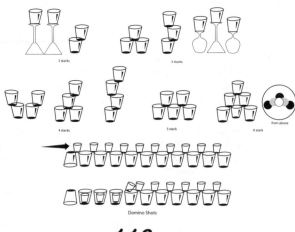

2 stacks   3 stacks

4 stacks   5 stack   6 stack   from above

Domino Shots

8. Waterfall Pour

The waterfall pour is an easy and entertaining way to serve multiple drinks or shots. Essentially, this trick involves pouring a stacked set of drinks across a line of glassware on the bar top. Start by arranging the glasses in a straight line on the bar top. Next, combine the ingredients in another set of glasses, which you will stack together before pouring. By default, the easiest glass to use is the Libbey's fourteen-ounce Gibraltar for the stacked glasses, as they fit together perfectly and are very durable. It's not recommended to try to stack more than five or six glasses together as the weight might break the glassware. You can also use shaker tins in place of the stacked glasses, but ice will need to be added to keep the proper spacing for the pours. Also, be sure to add one extra glass or tin to the top of the stack to give you something to hold while pouring out the drinks.

Once the ingredients for the drinks or shots have been added and the second set of glasses stacked together, grab the bottom glass with one hand and the top glass with the other. Starting with the bottom glass, aim your pour into the first glass lined up on the bar top. By slowly lowering the bottom glass as you pour it out and then raising the last stacked glass, you will get a waterfall effect as all of the drinks pour down from the stacked glasses into the glasses on the bar top.

9. Cool Beer Pour

Put a cocktail napkin in front of your guest. Open a beer with another napkin, then let your guest see you wipe the lip and neck of the bottle for sanitation's sake. Set the bottle onto the middle of the cocktail napkin you laid in front of them, then place a glass upside down over the upright beer. Grab the bottom of the beer bottle with a regular grip with one hand, then a reverse grip the glass with the other. Keeping the mouth of the bottle pressed against the bottom of the glass, turn it all upside down so that the glass is now upright and the bottle is upside down *inside* the glass. Keep

A super-easy yet mind-blowing variation to try is the *domino stack*. Let's say that a group of people at the bar orders ten *Jäger Bombs*. You'll need ten shot glasses and eleven rocks glasses. Set the rocks glasses up in a row leaving about a half-inch between each glass. Turn the first glass upside down. Place the shot glasses on top of the half-inch gaps. Pour the Red Bull into the rocks glasses then pour the Jägermeister into the shot glasses. Ready? Starting with the shot glass that is half on the upside down rocks glass, knock it over, and it will create a domino effect knocking every shot glass into every rocks glass. Bam! Bam! Bam! Make sure you practice this with water ahead of time. Minor setup adjustments due to different types of glassware can be ironed out at this time.

in mind that all of this sounds much more complicated than it actually is. Now, slowly raise the bottle keeping the lip of the bottle at the beer level all the way up.

10. Basic Bottle Flip

Here's a baby step towards becoming a novice flair bartender. Hold the neck of a bottle, then flip it up and slightly towards you. After the bottle makes one revolution, catch it by the neck in the same place where you let it go. After flipping the bottle take a small step backwards to meet the bottle. After learning this move you'll begin to discover that flair bartenders do not stand stiffly in place. They are bending and moving their bodies to work with nature and not against it. Also, don't flip a bottle that's more than a quarter full.

Drinking Fun and Facts

Bar Jokes

A guy walks into a bar and says, "Ouch!"

Two peanuts walk into a bar. One was a salted.

A dyslexic man walks into a bra.

A skeleton walks into a bar and says, "I'll have a beer and a mop."

A horse walks into a bar, and the bartender says, "Why the long face?"

A tissue walks into a bar, and the bartender asks he can pour him a drink. Tissue says, "Hell no, it'll go right through me!" The bartender says, "Well, you don't have to get all snotty about it."

A string walks into a bar and orders a drink. "Sorry, we don't serve strings," says the barman. "That's discrimination," says the string. So the string walks into the bathroom and ties himself in a knot and messes up his end. He comes back out and approaches the bar and again attempts to order a drink. "Aren't you that string I just refused to serve?" asks the barman. "No. I'm a frayed knot."

A mushroom walks into a bar and starts buying drinks for everyone. Eventually, someone leans over and says to the mushroom, "You're a fungi to have around."

A priest, a rabbi, a nun, a doctor, an engineer, and a blond walk into a bar. The bartender says, "Hey, what is this, some kind of a joke?"

Four fonts walk into a bar, and the barman says, "Get out! We don't want your type in here!"

A C, an E-flat, and a G go into a bar. The bartender says, "Sorry, but we don't serve minors."

The Dali Lama walks into a bar, and halfway through his drink the bartender asks, "How is everything?"

A pony walks into a bar and in a soft and raspy voice says to the bartender, "Gimme a beer." The bartender says, "Sure buddy, sounds like you got a cough." The pony replies, "I'm a little hoarse."

A willow tree walks into a bar, and a guy sitting next to the counter says to the bartender, "Who's the new guy?" And the bartender says, "I don't know, but I've heard he's a shady character!"

A guy walks into a bar and asks for ten shots of the finest single malt scotch. The bartender sets him up, and the guy takes the first shot in the row and pours it on the floor. He then takes the last shot and does the same. The bartender asks, "Why did you do that?" And the guy replies, "Well the first shot always tastes like crap, and the last one always makes me sick."

A guy walks into a bar with jumper cables and the bartender says, "You can come in, but don't start anything."

A man walks into a bar and says, "Give me a beer before problems start!" The man orders another beer, again saying, "Give me a beer before problems start!" The bartender looks confused. This goes on for a while, and after the fifth beer the bartender is totally confused and asks the man, "When are you going to pay for these beers?" The man answers, "Now the problems start!"

A neutron walks into a bar and orders a beer. The bartender sets the beer down and says, "For you, no charge!"

A pig goes into a bar and orders ten drinks. He finishes them up, and the bartender says, "Don't you need to know where the bathroom is?" The pig says, "No, I go wee wee all the way home."

A man walks into a bar with a slab of asphalt under his arm and says, "A beer please, and one for the road."

A kangaroo walks into a bar. He orders a beer. The bartender says, "That'll be $10." He adds, "You know, we don't get many kangaroos coming in here." The kangaroo says, "At $10 a beer, it's not hard to understand."

A man walks into a bar and sits down next to a lady and a dog. The man asks, "Does your dog bite?" The lady answers, "Never!" The man reaches out to pet the dog and the dog bites him. The man says, "I thought you said your dog doesn't bite!" The woman replies, "He doesn't. This isn't my dog."

A guy walks into a bar, and there is a horse behind the bar serving drinks. The guy is just staring at the horse, when the horse says, "What are you staring at? Haven't you ever seen a horse serving drinks before?" The guy says, "No, I never thought the parrot would sell the place."

A hamburger walks into a bar, and the bartender says, "Sorry, we don't serve food in here."

A dog with his leg wrapped in bandages hobbles into a saloon. He sidles up to the bar and announces, "I'm lookin' fer the man that shot my paw."

A guy walks into a bar, sits down and hears a small voice say, "You look nice today." A few minutes later he again hears a small voice, "That's a nice shirt." The guy asks the bartender, "Who is that?" The bartender says, "Those are the peanuts. They're complimentary!"

A baby seal walks into a bar. "What can I get you?" asks the bartender. "Anything but a Canadian club," replies the seal.

A grasshopper hops into a bar. The bartender says, "We have a drink named after you." The grasshopper says, "You've got a drink named Steve?"

Two five-dollar bills walk into a bar, and the bartender tells them that this is a singles' bar.

A duck walks in a bar and orders a beer then says, "Put it on my bill."

A snake crawls into a bar and orders a whiskey, but the bartender won't serve him because he can't hold his liquor.

A man walks into a bar and orders twelve shots of Tequila. As he slams the tenth one, the bartender says, "I don't think you should be drinking those so fast." "You would if you had what I have," the man says, throwing back number eleven. "Well, what is it you have?" The man throws back his last shot and says, "Fifty cents."

A businessman walks into a bar and orders a Martini. After he finishes the drink, he peeks inside his shirt pocket then he orders another Martini. After he finishes that one, he again peeks inside his shirt pocket and orders another Martini.

The bartender finally asks the man why he keeps looking inside his shirt before ordering a Martini. The man says, "I'm looking at a photo of my wife. When she starts to look good, then I know it's time to go home."

An Irishman, an Englishman, and a Scotsman walk into a pub and each order a pint of Guinness. Just as the bartender hands them over, three flies buzz down and one lands in each of the pints. The Englishman looks disgusted, pushes his pint away, and demands another pint. The Scotsman picks out the fly, shrugs, and takes a long swallow. The Irishman reaches in to the glass, pinches the fly between his fingers, shakes him, and yells, "Spit it out, ya bastard! Spit it out!"

An Irishman walks into a bar and orders Martini after Martini, each time removing the olives and placing them in a jar. When the jar is filled with olives the man starts to leave. The bartender asks him what that was all about, and he says, "My wife just sent me out for a jar of olives."

Charles Dickens: I'll have a Martini.
Bartender: Olive or twist?

What's the difference between a dog and a fox? About five beers.

Beauty is in the eye of the beer holder.

What would you call a drunk who works at an upholstery shop? A recovering alcoholic.

Three old ladies who were hard of hearing are walking down the street. First lady: Whew, it's windy today!
Second Lady: No. Today's Thursday!
Third lady: So am I! Let's go to a bar!

There was a guy who had at least four or five drinks of whiskey every day of his adult life. When he died, they cremated him, and it took two days to put out the fire.

How many Irish does it take to change a light bulb? Twenty-one. One to hold the bulb and twenty to drink until the room starts spinning.

This really drunk guy walks up to a parking meter and puts in a quarter. He stares at the needle that has stopped at sixty and exclaims, "I can't believe I lost a hundred pounds!"

Where does an Irish family go on vacation? A different bar.

What is the difference between an Irish wedding and an Irish funeral? One less drunk.

A doctor tells a man that the best thing to do is to give up drinking and smoking, get up early every morning, and go to bed early every night. The patient pauses and then asks, "What's the second best thing to do?"

A giraffe bellies up to the bar and says, "Hey guys, the highballs are on me!"

Two young Irishmen were getting ready to go on a camping trip. The first one said, "I'm taking along a gallon of whiskey just in case of rattlesnake bites. What are you taking?" The other one said, "Two rattlesnakes!"

A drunk stumbles out of a bar and runs right into two priests. He says, "I'm Jesus Christ." The first priest says, "No, son, you're not." So the drunk says it to the second priest. The second priest says, "No, son, you're not." The drunk says, "Look, I can prove it." He walks back into the bar with the two priests. The bartender takes one look at the drunk and exclaims, "Jesus Christ, you're here again?"

A man walks out of a bar and meets a policeman. "Hey," the policeman says, "Your eyes are bloodshot, have you been drinking Bloody Marys?" "Well," the man says, "Your eyes are glazed, have you been eating donuts?"

After the Great Britain Beer Festival in London, all the brewery presidents decided to go out for a beer. The guy from Corona sits down and says, "Hola, señor. I would like the world's best beer, a Corona." The bartender gives it to him. The guy from Budweiser says, "I'd like the best beer in the world. Give me the King of Beers, a Budweiser." The bartender gives him one. The guy from Coors says, "I'd like the only beer made with Rocky Mountain spring water; give me a Coors." He gets it. The guy from Guinness sits down and says, "Give me a Coke." The other brewery presidents look over at him and ask, "Why aren't you drinking a Guinness?" The Guinness president replies, "Well, if you guys aren't drinking beer, neither will I."

Pick-Up Lines

Most pick-up lines are used as an icebreaker to pick up women. After all, in most cases, to pick up a man all one needs to say is, "Let's go!" Distasteful pick-up lines can be found on the Internet by the millions. However, the type of woman you'd use them on is questionable.

A line that I use all the time to flirt, make someone feel good, or get them out of my well/service area is to say, "Excuse me, can you please move away from the bar? You're melting all the ice." It will take a good three seconds for this line to sink in their head, and that's when you give them a sexy smile. The line can be used by anyone on the other side of the bar as well and anywhere there is ice. It works like a charm.

Well, here I am. What were your other two wishes?

If I were Peter Pan, you'd be my happy thought.

Go up to someone, and check his or her shirt tag and say, Sorry, I was just checking to see if you were made in heaven.

Look at all those curves, and me with no brakes!

I know that milk does a body good, but gosh, how much have you been drinking?

Do you believe in love at first sight, or should I walk by again?

Are you lost ma'am? Because heaven's a long way from here.

Can I borrow your cell phone? I want to call your mom to thank her.

My friends voted you *The Most Beautiful Girl Here,* and the grand prize is me.

I'd say bless you when you sneeze, but I can see that God already has.

Hi, I'm a thief, and I'm here to steal your heart.

Is there a rainbow today? I just found the treasure I've been searching for!

You must be Jamaican because Jamaican me crazy.

If I said you had a great body, would you hold it against me?

Apart from being sexy, what do you do for a living?

Hi, I'm Mr. Right. Someone said you were looking for me.

You remind me of a magnet, because you sure are attracting me over here!

I think I'm in heaven because you look like an angel. Can you take off your shirt so that I can check for wings?

Girl, I'd drink your bath water.

What does it feel like ·to be the most beautiful girl in this room?

You must be a broom, cause you just swept me off my feet.

Damn girl, you have more curves than a racetrack.

I didn't know that angels could fly so low!

Do you have any raisins? No? How about a date?

I'm new in town and can't find my way around, could I have directions to your place?

I think you've got something in your eye. Oh, never mind, it's just a sparkle.

I was so enchanted by your beauty that I ran into that wall over there. So I am going to need your name and number for insurance purposes.

If I could rearrange the alphabet, I'd but U and I together.

Are you a parking ticket? Because you've got fine written all over you.

Hershey factories make millions of kisses a day, but I'm asking for only one.

If you were words on a page, you'd be what they call fine print!

Excuse me, I think it's time we met.

Do you have a map? I keep getting lost in your eyes.

Is there an airport near, or is that my heart taking off?

If life is a meat market, you're prime rib.

See my friend over there? He wants to know if you think I'm cute.

Did the sun come out, or did you just smile at me?

Do you have a Band-Aid? I skinned my knee when I fell for you over there.

Can you touch my hand? I just wanted to know what its like to be touched by an angel.

Shall we talk or continue flirting from a distance?

They say that beauty protects against all evil. With you around I feel really safe!

Are you from Tennessee? Because you're the only ten I see!

Can I take your picture? I want Santa to know exactly what I want for Christmas.

Famous Toasts & Their History

Here's mud in your eye
It's said that this toast came from World War II as a wish of good fortune to farmers. They also say that it came from the kick of mud thrown in your face from a winning horse at the horse track.

Here's looking at you, kid
Yes, Humphrey Bogart is responsible for making this toast famous in *Casablanca*, but it was first said in Old World pubs. It was commonplace for a person to start a fight when another person's view was blocked when drinking from a stein. Isn't this fighting dirty? Anyway, this led to the production of glass-bottomed steins so that one could see another coming at them.

Down the hatch!
When stocking a ship with supplies, which includes barrels of rum, wine, ale, water, etc., you load through and down the hatch. Hatch is a naval word for door.

Bottoms up!
Simply means that the bottom of the glass is up.

Cheers!
It's said that this was a lower class toast in England. The upper class would say, *To your health,* or *Good luck!*

Drinking Toasts

I drink to your health in public,
I drink to your health alone,
I've drunk to your health so many times,
I'm now worried about my own.

It's better to have a bottle in front of you,
Than a frontal lobotomy.

Here's to the men of all classes,
Who through lasses and glasses,
Will make themselves asses.

A toast to the cocktail party,
Where olives are speared,
And friends are stabbed.

I used to know a clever toast,
But now I can't think of it.
So fill your glass to anything,
And, bless your souls
I'll drink it!

Here's Champagne for our real friends,
And real pain for our sham friends.
Here's to living single and drinking double.
May your liquor be cold,
May your women be hot,
And may your troubles slide off of you,
Slicker than snot.

Champagne costs too much,
Whiskey's too rough,
Vodka puts big mouths in gear.
This little refrain,
Should help to explain,
Why it's better to order a beer!

Here's to cheating, stealing, fighting, and drinking.
If you cheat, may you cheat death,
If you steal, may you steal a woman's heart,
If you fight, may you fight for a brother,
And if you drink, may you drink with me.

May you never lie, steal, cheat, or drink,
But if you must lie, lie in each other's arms,
If you must steal, steal kisses,
If you must cheat, cheat death,
And if you must drink, drink with us, your friends.

In water one sees one's own face.
But in wine one beholds the heart of another.
Here's to you as good as you are,
Here's to me as bad as I am,
But as good as you are,

123

Denmark: Skaal

Egypt: Fee Sihetak

England: Cheers

Esperanto: Ja Zia Sano

Estonia: Tervist

Ethiopia: Letenatchie

Finland: Kippis

France: A Votre Sante

Germany: Prosit

Georgia Republic:
Gaumardjos

Greece: Iss Ighian
Greenland: Kasugta

Hawaii: Okele Maluna or
Hauoli Maoli Oe

Holland: Proost

Hungary: Kedves
Egeszsegere

Iceland: Samtaka Nu

India: Aancllld

Indonesia: Selamat

Ireland: Slainte

Israel: Le Chaim

Italy: Alla Tua Salute

Japan: Kampai

Korea: Ul Wi-Ha Yo

And as bad as I am,
I'm just as good as you are,
As bad as I am!

Another candle on your cake?
Well that's no cause to pout,
Be glad that you have strength enough,
To blow the darn things out!

Here's head first in a foaming glass,
Here's head first to a lovely lass,
Here's head first for a bit of kissing,
Here's to all others that don't know
The fun that they are missing!

There are good ships and wood ships,
The ships that sail the sea,
But the best ships are friendships,
And may they always be.

When I die don't bury me at all,
Just pickle my bones in alcohol,
Put a bottle of booze at my head and feet,
And then I'll know my bones will keep.
Drink to the girls and drink to their mothers,
Drink to their fathers and drink to their brothers,
Toast their health as long as you are able,
And dream of their charms while you're under the table!

Here's to us,
May we never drink worse.

Here's to the girl dressed in black,
When you whistle she never turns back,
And if she turns back,
She's such a treat,
She makes things stand,
That have no feet.

One bottle for four of us,
Thank God there's no more of us!
Here's to steak when you're hungry,
Whiskey when you're dry,
All the girls you ever want,
And heaven when you die.

Here's to good food, good fortune, and good whiskey!

The German likes his beer,
The Frenchman likes his wine,
The Scotsman likes his whisky,
And the Irishman likes his hot,
The Aussie has no national drink,
So he drinks the bloody lot!

Mother's in the kitchen washing out the jugs,
Sister's in the pantry bottling the suds,
Father's in the cellar mixin' up the hops,
Johnny's on the front porch watchin' for the cops.

Sudan: Sabatuk Fy

Swahili: Afya

Sweden: Skal

Syria: Kull Sana Wo or
Enta Salem

Tagalog: Mubuhcly

Tanzania: Kwa Afya Yako

Thailand: Sawasdi or
Chai-o

Tibet: Tashidelek or Phun
Tsun Tsok

Turkey: Sherefe

Ukraine: Budjmo or Na
Zdorovya

Wales: Lechyd da

Yugoslavia: Na Zdraviye

Zulu: Oogy Wawa or
Poo-zim-pee-La

He that buys land buys
many stones,
He that buys flesh buys
many bones,
He that buys eggs buys
many shells,
But he that buys good
beer buys nothing else.

There are several good
reasons for drinking,
And one has just entered
my head,
If a man can't drink when
he's living,
Then how the hell can he
drink when he's dead?

Old Mother Hubbard,
Went to the cupboard,
To get a big drink of gin,
When she got there,
The cupboard was bare,
And the old man was wip-
ing his chin.

Work like you don't need
the money,
Love like you've never
been hurt,
Dance like no one is
watching,
Make love like it's being
filmed,
And drink like a true
Irishman.
May the winds of fortune
sail you,
May you sail a gentle
sea,
May it always be the
other guy,
Who says, this drink's on
me.

Here's to the perfect girl,
I couldn't ask for more,
She's deaf, dumb, and oversexed,
And owns a liquor store.

Who'd care to be a bee and sip,
Sweet honey from the flower's lip,
When he might be a fly and steer,
Head first into a can of beer?

Here's to the girl on the hill
She won't,
But her sister will,
Here's to her sister!

Here's to the wine we love to drink,
And the food we like to eat,
Here's to our wives and sweethearts,
Let's pray they never meet.

Here's to the bride and mother-in-law,
Here's to the groom and father-in-law,
Here's to the sister and brother-in-law,
Here's to the friends and friends-in-law,
May none of them need an attorney-at-law.

Of all my favorite things to do,
The utmost is to have a brew.
My love grows for my foamy friend,
With each thirst-quenching elbow bend,

Beer's so frothy, smooth and cold,
It's paradise, pure liquid gold,
Yes, beer means many things to me,
That's all for now, I gotta pee!

Let's drink to California way out by the sea,
Where a woman's ass,
And a whiskey glass,
Made a horse's ass of me.

May your guardian angel be at your side to pick ya up off
the floor and hand ya another cold one from the store.

May all your joys be pure joys,
And all your pain Champagne.

I'll drink to the girls that will,
I'll drink to the girls that won't,
But I won't drink to the girls that say they will,
And then I find out they don't.

May your glasses be ever full,
May the roof over your heads be always strong,
And may you be in heaven half an hour,
Before the devil knows you're dead.

May the most you wish for be the least you get.

Merry met, and merry part,
I drink to thee with all my heart.

See that big white cloud
up there,
All white and fluffy at the
top,
Just like a jug of beer,
It's time to have a drink,
boys,
For if that cloud should
burst,
The beer would all run
out,
For it's just a cloud of
thirst.

May the saddest day of
your future be no worse
than the happiest day of
your past.

Here's to love,
The only fire against
which there is
no insurance.

May we kiss whom we
please,
And please whom we kiss.

Here's to health and
prosperity,
To you and all your
posterity,
And them that doesn't
drink with sincerity,
That they may be damned
for all eternity!

Wine comes in at the mouth,
And love comes in at the eye,
That's all that we will know for truth,
Before we grow old and die,
I lift the glass to my mouth,
I look at you and I sigh.

In heaven there is no beer,
That's why we drink it here.

Here's to holly and ivy hanging up,
And to something wet in every cup.

Here's to those who wish us well and those that don't may go to hell.

Here's to when I want it,
And if I don't get it,
It makes me mad,
And if I do get it,
It makes me frisky,
Now don't get me wrong,
'Cause I mean whiskey.

NASCAR was an offshoot from the drivers of moonshine during prohibition.

A raisin dropped in a fresh glass of soda will bounce up and down continually from the bottom of the glass to the top.

Here's to the women in the high-heeled shoes,
Who smoke men's fags and drink men's booze,
And when they kiss, they kiss so sweet,
They make things stand that have no feet!

Here's to women's kisses,
And to whiskey amber clear,
Not as sweet as a woman's kiss,
But a damn sight more sincere!

I have known many,
Liked a few,
Loved one,
Here's to you!

Here is to the fools of the world, for without them the rest of us could not succeed.

You guys came by to have some fun,
You'll come and stay all night, I fear,
But I know how to make you run,
I'll serve you all generic beer.

Pangrams

A pangram is another word for a holoalphabetic sentence: a sentence that uses every letter of the alphabet. The most popular one is "The quick brown fox jumped over the lazy dog." Here is a collection of bar and cocktail-related pangrams.

English

Pack my box with five dozen liquor jugs. (32 letters)

Quit beer, vows dizzy, puking, Michael J. Fox. (34 letters)

Amazingly few discotheques provide jukeboxes. (40 letters)

Five wine experts jokingly quizzed sample Chablis. (43 letters)

Zany Jacques French's pub mixed watery vodka gimlets. (44 letters)

Six plump boys guzzled cheap raw vodka quite joyfully. (45 letters)

Jacky amazed a few girls by dropping the antique VOX bottle! (49 letters)

The public was amazed to view the quickness and dexterity of the juggling bartender. (70 letters)

French

Portez ce vieux whisky au juge blond qui fume.

(Take this old whiskey to the blond judge who smokes.)

Moi, je veux quinze clubs de golf et whisky pur.

(Me, I want fifteen golf clubs and some pure whiskey.)

Spanish

Joven intoxicado por el whisky: ¡una qué figura usted esta exhibiendo!

(Whisky-intoxicated youngster, "What a figure you're showing!")

Queda gazpacho, fibra, látex, jamón, kiwi, y viñas.

(It is still gazpacho, fibre, latex, ham, kiwi, and vineyards.)

Whisky bueno: ¡excitad mi frágil pequeña vejez!

(Good whisky, you excite my frail, little old age!)

Italian

Quel vituperabile xenofobo zelante assaggia il whisky ed esclama: alleluja!

(That blameworthy and zealous xenophobe tastes his whisky and says, "Alleluja!")

Polish

Pójdê"e, kiƒ t´ chmurnoÊç w g∏àb flaszy

(Come on, drop your sadness into the depth of a bottle.)

Catalan

Jove xef, porti whisky amb quinze glaçons d'hidrogen, coi!

(Young chef, bring whisky with fifteen hydrogen ice cubes, damn!)

Bar- and Cocktail-Related Trivia and Lore

In English pubs, ale is ordered by pints and quarts. So in old England, when customers got unruly, the bartender would yell at them to mind their own pints and quarts and settle down. That's where we get the phrase mind your Ps and Qs.

Many years ago in England, pub frequenters had a whistle baked into the rim or handle of their ceramic cups. When they needed a refill, they used the whistle to get some service. "Wet your whistle" is the phrase inspired by this practice.

It was the accepted practice in Babylon four thousand years ago that for a month after the wedding, the bride's father would supply his son-in-law with all the mead he could drink. Mead is a honey beer, and because their calendar was lunar based, this period was called the "honey month" or what we know today as the "honeymoon."

Before thermometers were invented, brewers would dip a thumb or finger into the mix to find the right temperature for adding yeast. Too cold, and the yeast wouldn't grow. Too hot, and the yeast would die. This is one theory for where we get the phrase "rule of thumb."

If you stacked twelve billion Budweiser longneck bottles end to end it would reach 1.7 million miles, the distance it takes to travel to the moon and back three times.

In the 1800s, liquor was a beautician's secret! Yes, rum was considered an excellent product for cleaning hair and keeping it healthy, and brandy was believed to strengthen the hair roots.

No alcoholic beverage can be over 190 proof (95 percent alcohol). At any higher proof, the beverage will draw moisture from the air and self-dilute.

Old U.S. laws required that alcohol containers be concealed in public by being placed in paper bags or "packages" by liquor stores. This gave us the names "package stores" that sell "package goods."

English inns were once required to pay a tax known as a "scot." Customers who left town to drink in rural taverns were said to be drinking "scot free."

The oldest recipe for beer in Europe was found in the ruins of the Spanish village of Geno and dates back more than three thousand years.

Emperor Carlos V was the first beer importer and one of its most illustrious aficionados. It is said that, even in his retirement in Yuste, he kept a Flemish brewer in his reduced entourage.

In Kentucky, you are considered sober until you cannot hold onto the ground. (Can you imagine the DUI tests in that state?)

John Wagner, who had a small brewery in back of his house on St. John Street in Philadelphia, brewed the first lager in the United States. He brought the first lager yeast to the U.S. from a brewery in Bavaria.

Beer is great for controlling slugs in your garden! You can make a slug trap by pouring one or two cans of beer in plastic containers and placing them near plants prone to slug damage with the rims an inch above the surface of the soil. (No word on what brand of beer that slugs prefer though.)

Hippocrates recommended prescribing beer for its tranquilizing properties and because it quenches thirst, eases speech, and strengthens the heart and gums. (At least, he thought so!)

In the mid 1970s, Australians were the third biggest per capita beer drinkers, after Germans and Belgians. In the 1990s, though, they weren't even in the top ten!

In medieval times, an alcoholic beverage was often served with the English's breakfast.

The tune of "The Star Spangled Banner" was derived from "To Anacreon in Heaven," a British drinking song.

Nine people die every week on UK roads in drink-related accidents, half of them innocent victims.

Alcohol is believed to feature as reason behind 25 percent of school expulsions in the UK.

Each year, $200 million is spent on alcohol advertising.

Alcohol-related absenteeism and poor work performance costs British industry more than £2 billion a year.

Researchers have determined that one acre of potatoes can yield twelve hundred gallons of ethyl alcohol in a year.

Recent reports suggest that almost 50 percent of all British teenagers know how to buy alcohol that has been smuggled into the country.

In olden times, saloons offered free lunches, most of which were overly salted, forcing the thirsty diner to buy an alcoholic drink. Many bars now offer peanuts and salty snacks for the same reason.

Thirty-four percent of men drink and drive compared with 23 percent of women.

Of pedestrians who were killed in traffic accidents, 39 percent of the drivers had drunk more than the legal limit for driving.

Belgium has more brands of beer than any other nation on Earth. They have four hundred different brands.

The average number of grapes it takes to make a bottle of wine is six hundred.

Worldwide, approximately 20,000 brands of beer are brewed in 180 styles.

In the 1600s, thermometers were filled with brandy instead of mercury.

Both red wine and dark beer are rich in flavonoids, which are believed to have a positive effect on blood pressure and cholesterol levels. Here's to your health!

We already know red wine may protect your heart. But a recent study by a Harvard pathologist showed that resveratrol, an antioxidant in red wine, may increase the life span of yeast cells. It significantly lengthens the lives of fruit flies too. Will it work in humans?

Beer glasses are by far the most common weapon of assault in Britain according to Jonathan Shepherd, a surgeon at University of Wales College of Medicine and an expert on alcohol-related assault.

A traditional drink found throughout Andean countries is *Chicha*, made from fermented maize or rice. The fermentation process is augmented by human saliva. Chicha makers chew the ingredients and spit them back in the pot to brew.

In the 1500s, lead cups were used to drink ale. The combination would sometimes knock a person out for a couple of days, and people would take them for dead then prepare them for burial. They were laid out on the kitchen table for a couple of days, and the family would gather around to eat and drink and wait and see if they would wake up; hence the custom of *holding a wake*. People realized they had been burying people alive when some coffins were dug up and scratch marks were found inside, so they tied a string on the wrist of the corpse, led it through the coffin, up through the ground, and tied it to a bell. It was actually someone's job to sit out in the graveyard all night on the *graveyard shift* to listen for the bell. Thus, someone could be *saved by the bell* or was considered a *dead ringer*.

Celebrity Drinking Quotes

You can't be a real country unless you have a beer and an airline—it helps if you have some kind of a football team, or some nuclear weapons, but at the very least you need a beer.
—Frank Zappa

Always do sober what you said you'd do drunk. That will teach you to keep your mouth shut.
—Ernest Hemingway

They'll talk about me showing cleavage and my belly, but they don't say anything about the artists who accept an award and can't even talk because they're so drugged out. After the awards show, I go home, drink, and go to bed.
—Britney Spears

People who drink light "beer" don't like the taste of beer; they just like to pee a lot.
—Capital Brewery, Middleton, WI

Look, sweetheart, I can drink you under any goddamn table you want, so don't worry about me.
—Elizabeth Taylor, from *Who's Afraid of Virginia Woolf?*

I drink because she nags, she said I nag because he drinks. But if the truth be known to you, he's a lush and she's a shrew.
—Ogden Nash

The hard part about being a bartender is figuring out who is drunk and who is just stupid.
—Richard Braunstein

Twenty-four hours in a day, twenty-four beers in a case. Coincidence?
—Stephen Wright

Drink to me.
—Pablo Picasso's last words

He was a wise man who invented beer.
—Plato

If God had intended us to drink beer, He would have given us stomachs.
—David Daye

I'd rather have a bottle in front of me, than a frontal lobotomy.
—Tom Waits

Why is American beer served cold? So you can tell it from urine.
—David Moulton

Give me a woman who loves beer, and I will conquer the world.
—Kaiser Wilhelm

Time is never wasted when you're wasted all the time.
—Catherine Zandonella

133

I drink to make other people interesting.
—George Jean Nathan

They who drink beer will think beer.
—Washington Irving

We drink and we die and continue to drink.
—Dennis Leary

One can drink too much, but one never drinks enough.
—Edward Burke

The telephone is a good way to talk to people without having to offer them a drink.
—Fran Lebowitz

One Martini is alright, two is too many, three is not enough.
—James Thurber

Why don't you get out of that wet coat and into a dry Martini?
—Robert Benchley

Drinking provides a beautiful excuse to pursue the one activity that truly gives me pleasure, hooking up with fat, hairy girls.
—Ross Levy

If the headache would only precede the intoxication, alcoholism would be a virtue.
—Samuel Butler

"I suppose I'll be able to get a drink there." "I told the stewardess liquor for three." "Who are the other two?" "Oh, there are no other two."
—Sean Connery & Cec Linder, from *Goldfinger*

Time don't let it slip away,
Raise your drinking glass
Here's to yesterday
—Aerosmith, from *Full Circle*

Do not allow children to mix drinks. It is unseemly and they use too much vermouth.
—Steve Allen

And wine can of their wits the wise beguile / Make the sage frolic, and the serious smile.
—Alexander Pope

Adhere to the Schweinheitsgebot. Don't put anything in your beer that a pig wouldn't eat.
—David Geary

Let schoolmasters puzzle their brains
With grammar, and nonsense, and learning,
Good liquor, I stoutly maintain,
Gives genius a better discerning
—Oliver Goldsmith

A "good" beer is one that sells! You may think it sucks, but if the market embraces it, so be it. Now a "great" beer or world-class beer is another matter...
—Jim Busch

Fill with mingled cream and amber,
I will drain that glass again.
Such hilarious visions clamber
Through the chamber of my brain.
Quaintest thoughts, queerest fancies
Come to life and fade away.
What I care how time advances;
I am drinking ale today.
—Edgar Allen Poe

I have a total irreverence for anything connected with society, except that which makes the road safer, the beer stronger, old men and women warmer in the winter, and happier in the summer.
—Irish novelist Brendan Behan

Three be the things I shall never attain:
Envy, content, and sufficient Champagne.
—Dorothy Parker

I would give all of my fame for a pot of ale and safety.
—William Shakespeare, from *King Henry V*

I envy people who drink; at least they know what to blame everything on.
—Oscar Levant

I don't drink. I don't like it. It makes me feel good.
—Oscar Levant

I can't die until the government finds a safe place to bury my liver.
—Phil Harris

I am drinking the stars!
—Dom Pérignon

Wine gives strength to weary men.
—Homer

Give a man a beer, waste an hour. Teach a man to brew, and waste a lifetime!
—Bill Owen

Why is there so much wine left at the end of my money?
—Milan Maximovich

I drink no more than a sponge.
—Francis Rabelais

Now is the time for drinking, now the time to beat the earth with unfettered foot.
—Horace

Beer is made by men, wine by God!
—Martin Luther

A tavern is a place where madness is sold by the bottle.
—Jonathan Swift

I drink when I have occasion, and sometimes when I have no occasion.
—Miguel de Cervantes, from Don Quixote

A little bit of beer is divine medicine.
—Paracelsus

I'm Catholic and I can't commit suicide, but I plan to drink myself to death.
—Jack Kerouac

Come, come, good wine is a good familiar creature if it be well used; exclaim no more against it.
—Shakespeare

Cover a war in a place where you can't drink beer or talk to a woman? Hell no!
—Hunter S. Thompson, on the Gulf War

You can always retake a class, but you can never relive a party.
—Drew Navikas

W.C. Fields:
I never drink anything stronger than gin before breakfast.
Now don't say you can't swear off drinking; it's easy. I've done it a thousand times.
Reminds me of my safari in Africa. Somebody forgot the corkscrew, and for several days we had to live on nothing but food and water.
Back in my rummy days, I would tremble and shake for hours upon arising. It was the only exercise I got.
I've been asked if I ever get the DTs. I don't know. It's hard to tell where Hollywood ends and the DTs begin.
How well I remember my first encounter with the Devil's Brew. I happened to stumble across a case of Bourbon—and went right on stumbling for several days thereafter.
I always keep a supply of liquor handy in case I see a snake— which I also keep handy.
My illness is due to my doctor's insistence that I drink milk, a whitish fluid they force down helpless babies.
If I had to live my life over, I'd live over a saloon.
I never drink water; that is the stuff that rusts pipes.
What contemptible scoundrel has stolen the cork to my lunch?
A woman drove me to drink and I didn't even have the decency to thank her.
I never eat breakfast on an empty stomach.

Humphrey Bogart:
Of all the gin joints in all the towns in all the world, she walks into mine.
I never should have switched from scotch to Martinis.
The whole world is about three drinks behind.

Benjamin Franklin:
Beer is proof that God loves us and wants us to be happy.
He that drinks fast, pays slow.
There can't be good living where there is not good drinking.

Rodney Dangerfield:
I drink too much. Last time I gave a urine sample there was an olive in it.
My doctor told me to watch my drinking. Now I drink in front of a mirror.
I drink too much, way too much. When my doctor drew blood he ran a tab!
I'm a bad drinker. I got loaded one night and the next day they picked me up. In court, the judge said, "You're here for drinking," and I said, "Okay, Your Honor, let's get started."

Joe E. Lewis:
I distrust camels and anyone else who can go a week without a drink.
I went on a diet, swore off eating and heavy drinking, and in fourteen days I lost two weeks.
I drink to forget I drink.
Whenever someone asks me if I want water with my scotch, I say, "I'm thirsty, not dirty."

Favorite Celebrity Cocktails
What do the stars drink? Well, I asked my bartender friends all over the world and here's what they told me.

Oprah Winfrey: Pomegranate Martini and Lemondrop Martini.

Queen Elizabeth II: Gordon's gin and tonic with three slices of lemon, while visiting Australia.

Johnny Depp: Blueberry and ginger Bourbon sour at the Buddha Bar in Paris.

Vanessa Paradis: Strawberry Mojito at the Buddha Bar in Paris.

Kylie Minogue: Lychee Martinis at the Opium in Belfast.

George Lucas: Old-Fashioned.

Kelly Ripa: Heineken.

Mark Consuelos: Heineken.

Alan Jackson: Bushwhackers on his private yacht.

A young Barbra Streisand: Champagne cocktail at the Playboy Mansion.

John Travolta: Bombay Sapphire Martini.

Hal Nederham: Absolut Citron on the rocks with twist of lemon.

Buddy Hackett: Gin Ricky.

P. J. O'Rourke:

A fruit is a vegetable with looks and money. Plus, if you let fruit rot, it turns into wine, something Brussels sprouts never do.

I like to do my principal research in bars, where people are more likely to tell the truth or, at least, lie less convincingly than they do in briefings and books.

Anyway, no drug, not even alcohol, causes the fundamental ills of society. If we're looking for the source of our troubles, we shouldn't test people for drugs, we should test them for stupidity, ignorance, greed, and love of power.

It is better to spend money like there's no tomorrow then to spend tonight like there's no money.

Dave Barry:

I've never been into wine. I'm a beer man. What I like about beer is you basically just drink it and order more. You don't sniff at it, or hold it up to the light and slosh it around, or drone on and on about it, the way people do with wine. Your beer drinker tends to be a straightforward, decent, friendly, down-to-earth person, whereas your serious wine fancier tends to be an insufferable snot.

I like beer. On occasion, I will even drink beer to celebrate a major event such as the fall of communism or the fact that the refrigerator is still working.

Without question, the greatest invention in the history of mankind is beer. Oh, I grant you that the wheel was also a fine invention, but the wheel does not go nearly as well with pizza.

Not all chemicals are bad. Without chemicals such as hydrogen and oxygen, for example, there would be no way to make water, a vital ingredient in beer.

Ernest Hemingway:
It was as natural as eating and to me as necessary, and I would not have thought of eating a meal without drinking beer.
An intelligent man is sometimes forced to be drunk to spend time with his fools.
This beer is good for you. This is draft beer. Stick with the beer. Let's go and beat this guy up and come back and drink some more beer.

Winston Churchill:
Most people hate the taste of beer—to begin with. It is, however, a prejudice.
Always remember that I have taken more out of alcohol than alcohol has taken out of me.
"Sir, if you were my husband, I would poison your drink."
—Lady Astor to Winston Churchill
"Madam, if you were my wife, I would drink it."
—His reply

Oscar Wilde:
I can resist everything except temptation.
Work is the curse of the drinking class.
Moderation is a fatal thing—nothing succeeds like excess.
We are all of us in the gutter. But some of us are looking at the stars.

Dean Martin:
I once shook hands with Pat Boone and my whole right side sobered up.
You're not drunk if you can lie on the floor without holding on.
If you drink, don't drive. Don't even putt.

Mike Ditka: Cape Cod.

Jim Belushi: Grappa, red wine, and Rémy Martin XO.

Courtney Thorne-Smith: Rosé wine.

Whitney Houston: Belvedere Martini.

President Gerald Ford: Gin & Tonic.

Andy McDowell: Midori Sour.

Jeff Gordon: White wine spritzer.

Johnny Halliday: Woodford Reserve Old-Fashioned.

David Bowie: Bombay Sapphire Martini.

Julia Roberts: Scorpino (2 oz. premium vodka, 1 oz. Cointreau, 2 oz. cream, 1 big scoop lemon Italian ice, then blend and serve).

Queen Elizabeth: Yellow Chartreuse after a fish and chip lunch at Claridges.

Elizabeth Montgomery: Sidecar, Sazarac, white wine, Smirnoff Bloody Mary, and Smirnoff Screwdriver at the Playboy Mansion.

President Herbert Hoover: Martini.

Jack Benny: Gin Martini.

Bing Crosby:
Bourbon neat.

The Smithereens, The
London Suede, Morning 40
Federation, and Bon Jovi:
Chartreuse on the rocks.

Dean Martin:
Pinch Scotch & soda,
Dewar's Scotch & soda,
and ginger ale on the
rocks with a little scotch
on the rim so that it looked
and smelled like a drink at
the Playboy Mansion.

Frank Sinatra:
Bourbon & water and
scotch & water.

Peter Lawford:
Rob Roy, Grants & water,
and Pink Lady at the
Playboy Mansion.

Janis Joplin:
100 proof Southern
Comfort neat and Tiger's
Paw (2 oz. of 100 proof
Southern Comfort, double
dash of Rose's Lime
Cordial, topped with soda).

Sally Field:
Grasshoppers made with
vanilla ice cream.

Tony Curtis:
100 proof Smirnoff on the
rocks with a twist.

Sammy Hagar:
Cabo Wabo margarita.

A young Goldie Hawn:
Miller High Life at the
Playboy Mansion.

Homer Simpson:
To alcohol! The cause of—and solution to—
all of life's problems.
I would kill everyone in this room for a drop of sweet beer.
All right, brain, I don't like you and you don't like me—so
let's just do this and I'll get back to killing you with beer.

Jack Handy:
Is there anything more beautiful than a beautiful, beautiful
flamingo, flying in front of a beautiful sunset? And he's carrying a beautiful rose in his beak, and also he's carrying a
very beautiful painting with his feet. And also, you're drunk.

Deep Thought: Sometimes when I reflect back on all the
beer I drink I feel ashamed. Then I look into the glass and
think about the workers in the brewery and all of their
hopes and dreams. If I didn't drink this beer, they might be
out of work and their dreams would be shattered. Then I say
to myself, "It is better that I drink this beer and let their
dreams come true than be selfish and worry about my liver."
If you ever reach total enlightenment while drinking beer, I
bet it makes beer shoot out your nose.

Drew Carey:
Oh, you hate your job? Why didn't you say so?
There's a support group for that. It's called EVERYBODY,
and they meet at the bar.
Things don't make me nearly as happy as talking and having a
beer with my friends. And that's something everyone can do.

Henny Youngman:
My grandmother is eighty and still doesn't need glasses.
Drinks right out of the bottle.

140

Appendixes

Bar Mat A bar mat is a long, thin rubber mat that drinks are prepared on. It's also called a spill mat. It's designed to catch liquids while making drinks. Some home bars just use folded bar towels as a workspace. Some crazy nightclubs pour whatever's in the bar mat into a glass and call it a "matador." Believe it or not, I've seen people actually drink it on a dare.

Bar Towels Bar towels are essential. Keep some damp and dry ones around the bar. A wet one placed under the rimmer will catch errant sugar and salt grains, making clean up easier. Another wet towel laid flat under a cutting board keeps the board from slipping around while you're cutting limes or oranges. Grab a dry one to pull off a pourer stuck in a bottle. Just whatever you do, don't refer to them as "rags"—your customers and friends see the towels near their drinks and will surely be put off by that term.

Beer Bucket Some bars sell buckets of beer. They are normally galvanized metal buckets filled with ice and beer bottles. They are great for large groups.

Beer Tap Handle Beer tap handles are normally supplied by the beer distributor. They are pricey, and distributors don't like it when you lose them. To operate, just pull them towards you. They're attached to the keg and will pour the beer out quickly. Some bars make you unscrew them and lock them up when the night is over. When a keg blows (runs out of beer), quickly stick a glass (plastic is best) on top of the handle or remove the handle. This is the universal signal for being temporarily out of that beer and will keep people from asking for it.

Bench-Mounted Wine Opener A bench-mounted wine opener allows you to open a bottle of wine in two seconds. To operate, start with the handle upright. Insert the neck of the bottle into the chute, hold it firmly with one hand, and pull the handle down then up. Most will pop the cork out for you once the handle makes its way to the full upright position again. Also, it works better if you cut the foil off the bottle first.

Blender You know what a blender is. Commercial blenders behind bars are built heavy duty and used for making blended frozen drinks by the pitcher or more. Some have great timers on them so you can multitask while it's blending. Most bars unscrew the bottom part of the blender to clean at the end of the day. The main four pieces are the blades, collar ring, retaining ring, and gasket. You need all four to work properly. If your blender is leaking, always check the gaskets first.

The blended drink is probably the biggest waste of mixer. Experienced bartenders can make a frozen drink and fill up a glass with nothing left over, and when they do so they always feel a small spark of accomplishment. The number one thing to keep in mind while making a blended drink is that you always need less mixer and ice than you think. Control your ice because you can always add more: you start to mess up when it's too thick (too much ice), and you have to add more mixer to compensate. When you're finished you've made enough for two or three drinks with only 1/3 shot of alcohol in each. It can be frustrating. You simply have to practice a few times so you can get a feel for it. And if you plan to practice at home, forget using the big hunkin' chunks of ice. You need small ice for the blender.

Sometimes, making a little too much can work financially in your favor. I always pour the extra in a shorter or plastic glass and give it to them, apologizing for making too much. They always joke around with a no-problem-you-can-do-that-anytime attitude and tip you extra. But in reality, they paid for the alcohol in that leftover drink, so rightfully they should get it.

Bottle Opener There are many different types of bottle openers to choose from. You can use a fancy wall-mounted opener or the simple one on your wine tool, but most modern bartenders use speed openers. They come in all colors and styles with retractable reels, belt hooks, and so much more. My favorite is a chrome ring bottle opener. You'll find a huge, fun selection at the Bar Store on my website.

Brandy Warmer Some guests will request their brandy or Cognac warmed. Select bars carry brandy warmers that hold a tea light; however, don't fret if yours doesn't—you can make one with items found around most bars. All you need is a rocks glass and hot water. Preheat the brandy snifter by filling it one-fourth of the way with hot water (the kind at a coffee station), then fill a rocks glass halfway full of hot water. Dump the hot water out of the snifter and pour in the Cognac, then set it angled in the rocks glass. It's also nice to present it on a saucer. You may have to experiment with the glassware at your bar to test which glass the snifter fits in best.

Can Opener/Church Key The most common punch can opener is called is also called a church key. It useful for opening cans and doubles as a bottle opener.

Cash Caddy Cash caddies attach to cocktail servers' trays. It holds their money, change, tabs, mints, lipstick, or whatever they want to put in there. Sometimes a cocktail server will slip it off their tray and hand it to you for safekeeping while they run to the restroom or something.

Champagne Stopper This helps keep the carbonation from escaping an opened bottle of Champagne. Start with the wings out, place the rubber part on the mouth of the bottle, push down, and fold the wings down to catch the lip of the bottle.

Champagne/Wine Bucket A Champagne bucket holds and keeps Champagne or wine cold. It's best to use them with a stand. They also make great tip buckets.

Check Presenter Check presenters are padded leather-like folders that are used to present a tab, check, or bill. It's a nice touch to hand a guest a check presenter rather than a small piece of paper.

Cigar Cutter A cigar cutter cuts the ends of a cigar. It was a very popular item for bartenders in the 1990s, but with all the smoking bans of the twenty-first century, they are slowly fading away. However, you will still have guests ask for one, then smoke their cigar outside.

Citrus Reamer A citrus reamer is a manual tool used to extract juice from fruit. They're mostly found at handmade cocktail bars.

Citrus Squeezer A citrus squeezer squeezes juice from, well, citrus. There are electric, manual, and handheld squeezers.

Cocktail Napkins Cocktail napkins are the social papyrus of the bar, used to collect phone numbers, addresses, directions, inspirational ideas, artwork, and more.

Cocktail Picks Picks are used to spear fruit. There are many styles, from novelty to frilled to sophisticated.

Corkscrew Many types of corkscrews are available, but real bartenders and wine stewards use a waiter's corkscrew. The very best to buy is a double lever waiter's corkscrew.

These come with a knife to cut the foil off a wine bottle; you'll find that you use that knife for things that you never imagined you would, like opening boxes, punching a hole in the top of cherry and olive jars to release the pressure, and opening beer bottles, packaging, and the protective plastic on new spirit bottles.

Using a waiter's corkscrew can feel awkward at first, but with a little practice it will begin to feel natural. Remove the foil from the bottle with the knife, fold the knife back in place, then use the screw to screw down the center of the cork about three to four turns. (By the way, the screw part is called the *worm*.) Next, flip the lever on the top edge of the bottle and pry up, letting the leverage do all the work for you.

Also, for some weird reason, white zinfandel bottle corks are the longest corks in the world; you'll have to screw a little bit deeper. Old and fine bottles of wine have long corks as well.

Corkscrews a real bartender wouldn't be seen dead with are:

Winged Corkscrew: They're the ones that look like they have a body with two arms, a head, and a one-screw leg.

Screw Pull: I know you've seen these big, pricey, bulky contraptions that come with an attractive case. The most popular brand is called the Rabbit. Basically, there are three long handles. The two lower ones are held tight to steady the bottle and the top lever is pulled down then up, extracting the cork from the bottle. These are just extravagant ways of performing what should be a simple task.

Prong Puller: This one has a handle and two thin prongs that you slide down the sides of the cork, which you then pull and turn. It looks and feels weird.

Lever Pull: This is absolutely the worst corkscrew ever. It's just a worm and a handle, and you pull with all your might without any leverage help. Watching someone try to use one will make you laugh.

Cutting Board Cutting boards are used for cutting fruit—don't use one that's been used for cutting meat! Bar cutting boards are smallish so they can be cleaned easily in a bar sink.

Dump Sink A dump sink is where you dump the remains of used drinks. The sink should always have netting or some sort of filter so that straws and fruit don't clog up the drain. Some bars actually use the trashcans to dump, but the ice melts into water and can make the trash too heavy to handle.

Fruit Tray A fruit tray has plastic compartments that fit together to hold your standard bar fruits: lemons, limes, oranges, cherries, etc. It's also called a condiment tray or holder.

Foil Cutter A foil cutter cuts the foil off a wine bottle to expose the cork. Simply set it on the rim, apply pressure, and twist in a circular motion to cut.

Funnel Of course you know what a funnel is, but what you might not know is how many times you'll wish you had one. They especially come in handy when you're working private parties and combining half-empty bottles of mixers and spirits.

Grater A grater is used mostly to grate fresh spices (for instance, nutmeg is popular in *Brandy Alexanders*). Just hold the small, stainless steel, curved grater over the drink and grate.

Glass Washer There are generally three ways glasses are washed behind a bar. The first one calls for five stainless steel areas and at least three sinks. You need an area for the dirty glasses, a sink with three electric bristle brushes to dip dirty glasses on, a rinse sink, a sanitizer sink, and finally an area for the clean glasses to drain. The second type of glass washer is automatic: you simply set the glasses in, and they rotate through a wash, rinse, and sanitizing cycle. The third is when a bar is close to a kitchen and you put the glasses in racks, then simply let the dishwasher run them through the kitchen dishwasher.

Guinness Spoon When a distributor puts a Guinness tap on your bar, it comes with a spoon that fits on the edge of the glass to help layer Guinness on top of ale to make a black and tan. Normally it comes with a metal beaded cord so you can hang it from the tap. Don't forget to clean it at the end of the night!

Gun A bartender's "gun" is the little spout you use to add soda and other such mixers into drinks. The soda gun will have buttons with letters on the buttons. Generally, S = soda water, C = cola, W = water, L = Sprite or 7-Up (L stands for lemon-lime soda), Q or T = tonic water (Q stands for quinine, which is in tonic water), and D = diet cola.

Soda guns either use a post-mix or a pre-mix system. Post-mix has bags of syrup housed in boxes that mix with a water line and a CO_2 line (CO_2 gives the carbonation). When you press a button on the soda gun, all three mix together and come out of the gun. Most modern bars use a post-mix system because the boxes are very easy to deal with. You know it's time to go change the box when your cola, for example, comes out clear (carbonated water).

Ice Bucket Word to the wise: if you're planning on having more than a few people to a party (or a few people are planning on having more than a few drinks), you're going to need more ice that what will fit in a bucket—buy bags. And of course, any commercial bar needs a big ice well.

Ice Crusher These are usually found in high-end bars, tropical bars, pool and beach bars and at home bars.

Ice Scoop You should be able to ice down at least three glasses with one scoop for maximum efficiency, which calls for a scoop of no less than twenty-four ounces. You should never ever dip a glass into the ice: If a glass chips or breaks even a little, you run the risk of a guest cutting their mouth and suing. Also, experienced bartenders always leave the ice scoop sticking handle up so that your hands never touch the ice.

Ice Tongs Unless you're entertaining a party of two in your living room, bedroom, or hotel room, these aren't the most useful bar tool.

Insulated Thermos Carafe Keeping carafes of regular coffee, decaf, and hot water behind the bar can make for quick and hot service.

Jigger A two-sided measurement tool used to measure the alcohol in cocktails. They come in about five different sizes, but the most common are 3/4 and 1 1/4, and 3/4 and 1 1/2. To keep from spilling (and just looking kind of dumb in general), steady the jigger on the edge of the glass rim, fill it with the liquor of your choice, then dump.

Keg System A keg is a large stainless steel container that holds beer and a CO_2 tank (the carbon dioxide gives the beer carbonation). To get the best beer out of a keg, the temperature of the beer and psi pressure (pound per square inch) of the tank need to work together to avoid foamy or flat beer. In most cases, the CO_2 lines for a beer keg need to be pressured between 12 and 14 psi. Over 14 psi and the beer will be too foamy, and below 12 psi the beer will be flat. And the beer keg temperature needs to be between 36 and 38 degrees F; below that the beer will be flat, and above it will be foamy.

Some words of wisdom: whatever you do, when you're putting the tap on a full keg, don't push down, or you will get sprayed with beer. Find the groove on top of the keg where the tap will twist in cleanly.

Knife You need a good sharp knife to cut fruit and garnishes. I prefer a serrated edge—clean-edged knives have to be sharpened too much.

Mixing Glass A mixing glass looks just like a pint glass and can be used with a shaker tin to shake drinks; use a julep strainer when you pour the drink into its serving glass to remove the ice (see "strainer" for a definition of a julep strainer). Use it to stir a classic *Martini* or *Manhattan*.

Muddler A muddler looks like a small wooden bat and basically acts like the pestle in science class. Use the flat end to crush and mash fruits, sugar cubes, herbs, and more for drinks like a *Mojito* or *Mint Julep*. Never use a varnished or lacquered muddler because those poisons will get into the drink. Make sure it's unvarnished and oiled.

Napkin Caddy A napkin caddy sits on the bar top and holds beverage menus, drinking straws, and cocktail straws. Some have extra compartments for cocktail picks and matches.

Olive Stuffer An olive stuffer is exactly what it sounds like—it's used to stuff olives. This weird-looking plastic tool simply loads your stuffing, then as you squeeze, it stuffs. Take the pimento *out* beforehand. The most popular stuffing is blue cheese, but some bars use almonds, pine nuts, and anchovies as well.

Pourer A pourer is a spout that is placed in a liquor bottle to make it easier to pour. They come in many different sizes for different speeds, and some have a ball bearing inside that helps you measure the right amount as you pour. When a pourer is stuck in a bottle, try letting the bottle hang and wiggling it back and forth. It usually loosens it up for you, but if it still won't come out, it'll have to be soaked.

Rimmer This holds your salt, sugar, juice, and anything else you want to use to rim glasses. It's popularly used to rim *Margaritas* with salt or *Lemondrops* with sugar. The proper way to rim is around the outside of the glass so that extra salt or sugar doesn't fall into the drink. Most bartenders put lime cordial in the spongy part of the rimmer to get the salt or sugar damp so it'll stick to the glass, but you can wet the rim with a lemon or lime slice as well.

Shaker A shaker is used to shake a drink (think *shaken, not stirred*). You can find many novelty shakers in just about any shape or form, but they are all broken down into two types: Cobbler and Boston. Cobbler shakers consist of three pieces, and a real bartender would not be caught dead with one. It's a sure sign of an amateur in a lot of bartenders' eyes because it's considered a home enthusiast cocktail shaker. A Boston shaker has two-pieces, usually a 16-ounce mixing glass or stainless 16- to 18-ounce tin and a 28-ounce shaker tin. You shake the drink, and then break the seal that has formed by tapping them against the bar or with your hand where they meet.

Strainer A strainer allows you to serve a cold cocktail without ice—simply shake the ice and drink together until cold, then strain the drink into a glass. There are two types of strainers: Hawthorne and Julep. A Hawthorne strainer has a metal coil on it and is used with a shaker. A Julep strainer is used on the mixing glass—it fits into the glass curved-side up

Straws There are normally two types of straws in a bar, drinking and cocktail. Drinking straws are tall straws for tall drinks, and cocktail straws are short straws for short drinks. Nightclubs buy big fat straws so that people drink faster, and then end up ordering more. You may not want to employ that strategy if you're having a party and paid for the booze!

Vacuum Pump and Wine Stoppers If you serve and/or drink a lot of wine, you'll need a rubber wine stopper to place into each bottle once it's opened. Place the vacuum over the stopper and pump until all the air has been pumped out to preserves the wine longer.

Well The well is where you make drinks. It contains your ice, liquor, juices, soda gun, bar mats, shakers, strainers, jigger, rimmer, and anything else you need to make drinks. Most everything you need should be no more than one step away from the well.

Zester/Channel Knife This cuts fruit rinds into curly, fancy twists for special drinks.

Home Party Tools

When you're throwing a home party or are asked to help with the bar at one, here are some extra tools you probably want to have on hand.

Dixie Cups These little paper cups are essential when making homemade shot glasses.

Duct Tape There are too many uses for duct tape to mention them all. Here are a few: to make homemade shot glasses of ice, secure any cords around the bar, secure any lights you have around the bar, and secure your specialty menu to the bar.

Fifth Bottles When people throw home parties, they tend to try to cut corners by buying in bulk. They pick up liter spirit bottles, which are a bad choice: first, they're not attractive. Every drink you pour all night will come out glug-glug-glug. Second, it's murder on your hands and wrists.
There are two better options. Find empty fifth bottles of the same spirit to pour the liters into. It's a much more manageable size. The second option is to invest in some large-neck or oversized pourers. These will fit into the liter bottles.

Funnel Use this to transfer bulk items to smaller and more manageable sizes.

Gallon Jugs Clean, empty gallon jugs are essential for premaking cocktails in bulk. They are also great to fill with water and freeze: place one inside a tall, insulated drink cooler that's filled with premixed cocktail, and you'll avoid overdiluting the drink with melting ice.

Half Gallon Paper Cartons These paper milk and juice cartons are excellent for freezing a block of ice around a spirit bottle. And it's fun to watch your guests' faces!

Ice Cube Trays All kinds of creative things can be frozen into a cube of ice. Flower petals, coffee beans, cherries, olives, pieces of fruit, candy, anything! Try serving Martinis on the rocks with olives frozen in the ice cubes, or freeze half water, half dry vermouth cubes with an olive inside and drop them into straight-up Martinis. Maybe try half water, half orange juice cubes for a *Sex on the Beach*, or half water, half melon liqueur cubes for a *Melon Ball*, or half water, half Blue Curacao for a raspberry vodka & Sprite. Use your imagination!

Insulated Coolers Insulated coolers are a must for backup ice and large batches of drinks.

Measuring Cups When making large batches of mixers, Jell-O, or many other things, measuring cups will come in handy.

Pitchers These can be used to mass-produce drinks, or as a container for juices and mixes.

Portion Cups Portion cups can be used to make chocolate shot glasses and are great for Jell-O shots.

Sno Cone Cups These are used to make homemade shot glasses of ice.

Glassware

When a guest orders a drink, the first thing you do is grab a glass. And you'll need to know which glass to grab. There are, of course, the basics, such as wine glasses, Martini glasses, and brandy snifters, but a lot of bars today use all-purpose glassware. I'm sure you've been at your favorite chain restaurant with your friends, and the server brings your table a draft beer, a Long Beach tea, a specialty drink on the menu, a Piña Colada, a water with a lemon, and a sweet tea, and they're all in the same pint glass. These all-purpose glasses cut down on a bartender's time but can make drinking specialty drinks a little less fun.

Most bartenders prefer Libbey glassware and pint glasses (www.libbey.com) because they are very durable and stackable. It always cracks me up when I see someone new to the business open up a bar and stock it with oh-so-pretty, wisp-thin glassware. It lasts about two months, and then the cases of Libbey's or other durable glassware shows up.

Sturdy Glassware

Collins (also called Chimney) 10 ounces. It's tall and thin, and an authentic Collins glass is frosted. They even make tall, skinny Collins straws that look like tall cocktail straws.

Double Old-Fashioned (also called Bucket) 12- to 15-ounce short sturdy glass a little bigger than an Old-Fashioned. People that don't like the awkwardness of a tall glass like these.

Highball 7–9 ounces. Most bars don't stock real highball glasses and use short Old-Fashioned glasses instead.

Mug 16-ounce beer mug with a handle that's sometimes kept in a cooler and served cold.

Old-Fashioned 10- to 12-ounce short, sturdy glass perfect for a Highball such as a Scotch & water or gin & tonic.

Pilsner 12-ounce curved beer glass that fits a bottled beer perfectly.

Pint 16-ounce beer glass sometimes kept in the cooler; however this is the all-purpose glass that gets used for many drinks.

Rocks Around 5–9 ounces and used for shooters for one spirit on the rocks, such as a Bourbon on the rocks. Sometimes people call it a Lowball glass.

Shot 1 1/2- to 2-ounce short glass designed for shots of liquor.

Stemmed Glasses

Brandy Snifter Can be found in 5–24 ounces. Used for brandy and Cognac, however many liqueurs can be served in a snifter, Sambuca (don't forget the three coffee beans), Grand Marnier, a fine Tequila, a single malt Scotch, etc. An easy way to pour is to hold the glass on its side and pour to the rim, then set upright.

Champagne Flute 6-ounce glass for Champagne and Champagne drinks.

Champagne Saucer 6-ounce glass for Champagne and Champagne drinks. The original bowl-type Champagne glass.

Champagne Trumpet 6-ounce trumpet-shaped glass for Champagne and Champagne drinks.

Champagne Tulip 6-ounce curvy glass for Champagne and Champagne drinks.

Hurricane 12–16 ounces and used for a lot of tropical drinks.

Irish Coffee Mug 7- to 8-ounce glass footed mug used for all coffee drinks.

Margarita Glass (Coupette) 7- to 10-ounce wide brimmed glass. Makes you think of a Mexican sombrero. There's also another glass called a Fiesta Grande that is 15 ounces.

Martini Glass (also called Cocktail Glass) 5- to 9-ounce glass that is also known as a cocktail glass. Used for Martinis, manhattans, and straight-up drinks.

Poco Grande Around 13 ounces. Bars will use a poco grande glass as an all-purpose tropical glass. I've seen just about every juice drink come out in this glass as well. Some people call it a tulip glass.

Pony 1-ounce curvy glass can be used for shots or cordials.

Sherry 3-ounce glass used for Sherry and Ports. Proper servings are 2 1/2–3 ounces. You also serve Port in this glass.

Wine Glasses

Most bars carry one all-purpose wine glass for red and white wines. Wine bars, of course, use the proper glassware and have a bunch of different sizes. The bowls of white wine glasses are more slender than red wine glasses, which have big, balloon-type bowls. A proper serving of wine is 5 to 6 ounces, which means you generally don't fill it to the top (it's sometimes hard to convince guests who don't know anything about wine that this is correct). The extra room is for swirling and for capturing the bouquet. Also, carry wine glasses by the stem.

Novelty

Coconut The best way to make coconut cups for glassware is to use a band saw. Saw off the top fourth of the coconut and leave in the coconut meat. Make a small slice on the bottom so that you can stand them up; don't slice too far, or it won't hold liquid!

Pineapple Buy a pineapple corer (not cutter). Corers will cut and slice, leaving just the pineapple shell.

Tiki Tiki glasses look like totem pole carvings and come in 12–24 ounce sizes.

Yard Yards are long, novelty beer glasses that come with a wooden stand to hold it upright on the table. Originally, they hung on the wall.

Rare and Historical Glassware

You'll sometimes come across glassware that was once commonly used in bars, but is rarely found in the twenty-first century or only in the most high-end bars. Here are some of those.

Absinthe Glass An absinthe glass is ornate with a short sturdy stem and a tall V-shaped bowl. The wide mouth is necessary to lay an ornate absinthe spoon across it.

Irish Coffee Glass This stemmed glass is about 7–8 ounces and does not have a handle.

Pousse Café This is a small stemmed 3- to 4-ounce glass used for making layered Pousse Cafés.

Punch Cup A 6- to 8-ounce cup that is most commonly sold with big punch bowls. You see them all the time in vintage black and white films.

Sour Glass (also called Delmonico) A sour glass looks like an overgrown Sherry glass that's 4–6 ounces.

Whiskey Tasting A whiskey tasting glass looks like a wine glass with a short stem or like a miniature poco grande tulip-shaped glass.

Zombie A Zombie glass is like an overgrown chimney/Collins-type glass that is around 12–20 ounces.

Quick Reference Charts

B

Density/Weight

All alcohols have different weights. Usually, the higher the alcohol content, the lighter it will be, but sometimes if other ingredients are mixed with it then the weight can change. This chart works best if you try not to layer spirits five to ten weights from each other.

NAME	COLOR	FLAVOR	WEIGHT
Cream	White	Milky	Very Light
151 Rum	Light Amber	Fire	Light
Maker's Mark Bourbon	Dark Amber	Bourbon	0.941
Hiram Walker Kirschwasser	Clear	Cherry	0.941
Dekuyper Kirschwasser	Clear	Cherry	0.941
Sauza Silver Tequila	Clear	Tequila	0.945
Jameson's Irish Whiskey	Amber	Irish Whiskey	0.948
Rain Vodka	Clear	Vodka	0.9498
Sauza Gold Tequila	Gold	Tequila	0.95
Skyy Citrus Vodka	Clear	Lemon Vodka	0.9555
Pernod	Clear	Anise/Licorice	0.985
Ouzo	Clear/Cloudy	Licorice	0.984
Southern Comfort	Dark Amber	Peach Apricot Whiskey	0.99337
Hiram Walker Ginger Brandy	Light Amber	Ginger Brandy	0.995
Tuaca	Amber	Vanilla Orange Caramel Brandy	1.0157
B&B	Amber	Sweet Herbal Cognac	1.0245
Dekuyper Sloe Gin	Dark Red	Sloe Berries	1.0261
Hiram Walker Peppermint Schnapps	Clear	Peppermint	1.027
Grand Marnier	Amber	Orange Cognac	1.03
Malibu	Clear	Coconut Rum	1.03

Hiram Walker Root Beer Schnapps	Brown	Root Beer	1.037
Cointreau	Clear	Orange	1.0385
Dekuyper Apricot Brandy	Dark Orange	Apricot	1.0437
Dekuyper Triple Sec	Clear	Orange	1.05
Chambord	Maroon	Black Raspberry	1.05
Lady Godiva White Chocolate Liqueur	White	White Chocolate	1.05
Baileys Irish Cream	Tan	Creamy Spiced Irish Whiskey	1.05
Irish Mist	Dark Amber	Honey Herb Whiskey	1.05
Dekuyper Blackberry Brandy	Dark Purple	Blackberry	1.0552
Campari	Red	Bitters	1.06
Benedictine	Light Amber	Herbal	1.07
Dekuyper Blue Curacao	Blue	Orange	1.0704
Dekuyper Root Beer Schnapps	Brown	Root Beer	1.0705
Drambuie	Light Amber	Heather Honey Scotch	1.08
Amaretto Di Saronno	Dark Amber	Almond	1.08
Sambuca	Clear	Licorice	1.08
Frangelico	Clear	Hazelnut	1.08
Tia Maria	Brown	Coffee	1.09
Dekuyper Anisette	Clear	Anise	1.0921
Dekuyper Melon Liqueur	Bright Green	Honeydew Melon	1.0924
Dekuyper Wildberry Schnapps	Clear	Berry	1.0894
Dekuyper Green Menthe	Dark Green	Mint	1.0885
Dekuyper Bluesberry	Clear	Blueberry	1.0863
Dekuyper Grape Pucker	Purple	Grape	1.0864
Dekuyper Banana	Yellow	Banana	1.0822

Marie Brizard Blue Curacao	Blue	Orange	1.0999
Dekuyper Coffee Liqueur	Brown	Chocolate Coffee	1.189
Hiram Walker Crème de Noyaux	Bright Red	Almond	1.148
Marie Brizard Coffee Liqueur	Brown	Chocolate Coffee	1.142
Hiram Walker Crème de Banana	Yellow	Banana	1.142
Midori	Bright Green	Honeydew Melon	1.15
Kahlua	Brown	Chocolate Coffee	1.152
Marie Brizard White Crème de Cacao	Clear	Chocolate	1.1602
Marie Brizard Dark Crème de Cacao	Brown	Chocolate	1.1602
Hiram Walker Crème de Cassis	Dark Red	Black Currant	1.179
DeKuyper Razzmatazz	Red	Raspberry	1.139
Marie Brizard Anisette	Clear	Anise	1.1371
Hiram Walker Dark Crème de Cacao	Brown	Chocolate	1.136
Dekuyper Buttershots Schnapps	Amber	Butterscotch	1.1225
Dekuyper White Cocoa	Clear	Chocolate	1.1204
Marie Brizard Green Crème de Menthe	Dark Green	Mint	1.1204
Marie Brizard White Crème de Menthe	Clear	Mint	1.1204

Dekuyper Cassis	Dark Red	Black Currant	1.1211
Hiram Walker Butterscotch Schnapps	Amber	Butterscotch	1.126
Galliano	Golden Yellow	Vanilla Licorice	1.11
Dekuyper Thrilla Vanilla	Clear	French Vanilla	1.1193
Dekuyper Hot Damn	Red	Cinnamon	1.1191
Jägermeister	Black/Green	Herbal Bitter	1.118
Marie Brizard Parfait Amour	Purple	Vanilla Orange Almond	1.1163
Goldschlager	Clear w/ Gold Flakes	Cinnamon	1.1111
Dekuyper Strawberry Liqueur	Red	Strawberry	1.1005
Dekuyper Watermelon Pucker	Red	Watermelon	1.1051
Dekuyper Peachtree	Clear	Peach	1.1037
Dekuyper Mad Melon	Red	Watermelon	1.0971
Dekuyper Island Blue	Light Blue	Fruity	1.095
Dekuyper Apple Pucker	Lime Green	Sour Apple	1.0944
Dekuyper Cheri Beri Pucker	Red	Cherry	1.0937
Dekuyper Coconut Amaretto	Clear	Coconut Almond	1.0925
Grenadine	Red	Cherry Pomegranate	Heavy

Alcohol Freezing Point

How many times have you asked yourself, *I wonder if I can put this bottle in the freezer?* Here are your answers.

PERCENTAGE	PROOF	FAHRENHEIT	CELSIUS
12	24	20	-6.7
20	40	10	-12.2
27	54	0	-17.78
32	64	-10	-23.33
38	76	-20	-28.89
42	84	-30	-34.44

Champagne Bottle Sizes

NAME OF BOTTLE	MEASURE	EQUIVALENT SIZE	SERVINGS
Split	187ml	Quarter bottle	1
Half	375ml	Half bottle	2
Fifth	750ml	Bottle	4
Magnum	1.5L	2 Bottles	8
Jeroboam	3L	4 Bottles	17
Rehoboam	4.5L	6 Bottles	24
Methuselah	6L	8 Bottles	34
Salmanazar	9L	12 Bottles	50
Balthazar	12L	16 Bottles	68
Nebuchadnezzar	15L	20 Bottles	112

Wine Bottle Sizes

SIZE	OUNCES	5-OUNCE SERVINGS
187ml	6.3	1
375ml	12.7	2
750ml	25.4	5
1L	33.8	6
1.5L	50.7	10
3L	101.4	20
5L	169	34

Spirit Bottle Sizes

BOTTLE	SIZE	OUNCES
Miniature/Airplane	50ml	1.6
Half-Pint	200ml	8
Pint	500ml	16
Fifth	750ml	25.6
Quart	1L	32
Half-Gallon	1.75L	64

Beer Keg Sizes

TYPE	BARREL	GALLONS	NUMBER OF 16 OUNCE CUPS	BOTTLE/CAN EQUIVALENT
Keg	1/2 Barrel	15.5	124	6.9 cases
Half Keg	1/4 Barrel	7.75	62	3.45 cases
Quarter Keg	1/8 Barrel	3.88	31	1.72 cases
Party Ball		5	40	2.2 cases

Bar Measurements

TERM	USA	METRIC
Dash	1/8 barspoon	0.625ml
Splash	1/4 ounce	7.5ml
Lace	1/2 ounce	15ml
Sprinkle	1/2 teaspoon	2.5ml
Floater	3/4 ounce	22.5ml
Pony	1 ounce	30ml
Shot	1 1/2 ounces	45ml
Cup	8 ounces	230ml
Pint	16 ounces/2 cups	460ml
Quart	32 ounces/4 cups/2 pints	920ml
Gallon	128 ounces/4 quarts/16 cups	3.68L
Olives in a Martini	1 dropped or 2 speared	1 dropped or 2 speared
Coffee Beans in Sambuca	3	3
Sprig of Mint	3 leaves	3 leaves

ALCOHOL	CALORIES	CARBS in grams
Beer		
Most Light Pilsner Beer (12 ounces)	95-110	3.2-6.9
Most Regular Pilsner Beer	130-145	8.7-11.7
George Killian's Irish Red	163	13.8
Guinness	170	20
O'Doul's	70	13.3
Red Hook	188	12.6
Sam Adams	160	18
Sierra Nevada	200	12.3
Wine		
Red Wine (5 ounces)	95-105	1.7
White Wine	90-100	1.1
Rose/White Zin	90-100	1.1
Champagne	100-105	2
Dessert Wine	225	20
Port	170-180	13
Sherry	112	4
Vermouth (dry)	120	6
Vermouth (sweet)	150	8
Liquor		
Bourbon/Whiskey/ Scotch/Brandy (1 ounce)	65-83 (low to high proof)	Trace
Vodka/Gin/ Rum/Tequila (includes flavored)	65-83 (low to high proof)	0
Liqueur		
Advocaat (1 ounce)	167	30
Anisette	75	7
B & B	95	3
Bailey's	121	10
Coffee Liqueur	117	5
Crème de Banana	145	8
Crème de Cassis	120	7
Crème de Cocoa	150	10
Crème de Menthe	185	9
Curacao	155	8
Drambuie	165	3
Fruit Flavored Brandy	130	5

Calorie and Carbs

Calorie and Carbs

Peppermint Schnapps	125	7
Pernod	120	4.3
Sloe Gin	125	5
Southern Comfort	180	4
Tia Maria	138	3
Cocktails		
Apple Martini	148 3.	5
Bloody Mary	116	7
Brandy Alexander	300	11
Black Russian	117	5
Bourbon & Soda	105	0
Classic Martini	155	1
Daiquiri	110	5
Gin Rickey	115	3
Gin & Tonic	80	14
Gin & Diet Tonic	80	0
Irish Coffee	210	8
Mai Tai	310	17
Long Island Iced Tea	180	15
Manhattan	140	3
Margarita	170	4
Mint Julep	215	8
Old Fashioned	180	5
Piña Colada	270	32
Rum & Coke	80	14
Rum & Diet Coke	80	0
Screwdriver	175	15
Sloe Gin Fizz	230	11
Tequila Sunrise	200	14
Tom Collins	120	9
Whiskey Sour	170	6
White Russian	280	17

Online Resources

The hippest bar-related sites on the World Wide Web

Bar & Drink Supplies

Miss Charming's Bar Store
www.charming.barstore.com
You'll find anything and everything a bartender needs at my Bar Store, even my *Miss Charming Hip Bartender and Wayout Wannabe Bartending Kit,* containing everything a beginner bartender should own. You'll also find commercial bar supplies, flair bartender supplies, modern mixology supplies, books, videos, and all the hippest and hottest tools that the coolest bartenders are using worldwide. If you forget the address, then you can always get there at www.misscharming.com. Shipping is worldwide.

Spirit Brands
www.spir-it.com
Are you looking for a novelty cocktail pick, straw, stir stick, napkin, or other goodies for your drinks? Then this is the place. These are the people that mass-produce drink novelties for Disney,

Bacardi, Marriot, and more. They have a PDF catalog that you can download.

Oriental Trading
www.orientaltrading.com
This company has been around a long time. They have bulk items at low prices that are perfect for theme parties.

Drink Recipe Sites

Webtender
www.webtender.com
Webtender is the granddaddy of the drink databases. As a matter of fact, it was one of the first websites on the Web (1995) and still sports the default gray layout. It also has a great forum of bartenders from all over the world discussing all things related to the bar industry. You can find an answer to any bartender subject by using the search feature.

Drinkalizer
www.drinkalizer.com
Awesome eye candy drink database. The recipes are metric.

163

TGI Friday's Mixology

www.tgifridays.com/mixology.html
Fun, interactive site with lots of ways to search for recipes.

Bols

www.bolscocktails.com
Another great, interactive recipe site that lets you find cocktails according to sweet, weak, sour, and strong.

Cocktail, Bar, and Bartending Sites

Cocktail Times

www.cocktailtimes.com
Cocktail Times helps you become a great home bartender with everything you need to know about cocktails and distilled spirits, from the classic concoctions to the new inventions. Filled with great photos of cocktails. Established in 1998.

That's the Spirit!

www.thatsthespirit.com
A site filled with entertaining and drink ideas with lots of resources.

The Orbit Bar

www.theorbitbar.com
The Orbit Bar is a mobile bartending service in the UK that stays on top of bar and cocktail trends. You should check out their site to see what they have done and plan to do for inspirational ideas. Currently they

hold the Guinness world record for making the most cocktails in an hour.

Alconomics

www.alconomics.com
Alconomics is the science of spirits, the business of pleasure, and the art of the bartender. It teaches bartenders the mechanics of their jobs and the passion of their profession. Master bartender Angus Winchester writes about his travels to bars around the world.

New York City Bartenders and Patrons

www.nycbp.com

Cocktail

www.cocktail.com
Cocktail.com's mission is simple: to bring the drink aficionados and bartenders of the world the best cocktail recipes and advice. Founded in 1995.

Just for Fun

Miss Charming

www.misscharming.com
Click on over and check out my fun website! It's filled to the brim with everything relating to the bar and cocktail industry. I have a fun newsletter too!

Ultra Lounge

www.ultralounge.com

The ultra-hip site is for the Ultra Lounge music collection. Check out the "Hey, Bartender" section.

The Bartender's Joke of the Day

www.thebartend.net

This was the Internet's first bartender joke site. It's been around since 1995.

Great Big Stuff

www.greatbigstuff.com

Great big stuff has great big stuff! You'll find a twenty-five-inch-tall wine glass, ten-inch-tall Martini glass, twenty-inch Champagne glass, two-foot-tall Corona bottle, two-foot-tall Bud bottle, and so much more!

Minister of Martinis

http://007.atomicMartinis.com

The Minister watches all James Bond films, reads all the novels, and counts all the drinks. Did you know that 007 had 102 drinks in his films and 317 drinks in his novels? The breakdown is all here.

Airquee

www.airquee.co.uk

Need an inflatable pub or bar? Airquee designs and builds them!

Bar Menus

www.barmenus.com

Bar Menus is an online cocktail menu maker. Simply log on, choose from over forty stylish backgrounds, select from over one hundred of the most popular cocktails or add your own, enter your own prices and or logos, and simply print it out!

That Guy Game

www.thatguygame.com

The object is simple: Hit the town and find real-life guys who match the cartoon characters on the cards that you've been dealt. The game has gained A-list celebrity fans such as Julia Roberts, Drew Barrymore, Charlize Theron, and Minnie Driver.

Mixilator

www.mixilator.com

Let the Mixilator mix you up a cocktail with just a few clicks of your mouse.

Entertainment

Napkin Rose

www.napkinrose.com

Michael Mode, a magician who toured with Copperfield, presents the world's only custom-printed origami napkin roses. They come in several colors with an optional instructional DVD. You can also get the instructions from his website. These are great for bartenders!

165

Doc Eason

www.doceason.com

In 2005, The Academy of Magical Arts Awards, which has been held at the world-famous Magic Castle in Hollywood, California, since 1963, added a new category: Bar Magician. Doc Eason is the first to win this award.

Cocktail Connoisseurs and Modern Mixologists

King Cocktail

www.kingcocktail.com

Dale "King Cocktail" Degroff revived the classic cocktail in 1987 at the Rainbow Room in NYC. He is America's foremost mixologist and has also created award-winning cocktail menus and has pioneered a gourmet approach to mixing drinks. Dale is the president and founder of the Museum of the American Cocktail and the author of *The Craft of the Cocktail.*

Ardent Spirits

www.ardentspirits.com

Gary and Mardee Regan are very highly regarded cocktail connoisseurs, spirit experts, and authors, as well as bartending and restaurant consultants. They have published many books, such as *The Joy of Mixology, The Bartender's Best Friend,* and *The Martini Companion.*

Drinkboy

www.drinkboy.com

DrinkBoy.com is a website that, since 1998, has been dedicated to providing clear and concise information about the art of the cocktail. Robert Hess truly appreciates and respects the culinary potential of the cocktail and tells us that it's critical to understand its origins and its history. He also has a great forum for the enthusiast.

CocktailDB

www.cocktaildb.com

Ted "Dr. Cocktail" Haigh has been called the premiere cocktail historian in America. He's the author of *Vintage Spirits and Forgotten Cocktails.* He is also the curator for the American Museum of the Cocktail.

The Modern Mixologist

www.themodernmixologist.com

Anybody who starts their website with Sinatra singing about booze is okay in my book! Tony Abou-Ganim is currently featured demonstrating the art of the cocktail preparation on the Fine Living Network program *Raising the Bar.* His specialty drinks have been featured in *Vanity Fair, Fortune, Playboy,* the *New York Times Magazine,* and so many more. He also created the cocktail program at the Bellagio in Las Vegas and runs his own beverage consulting firm.

Mister Mojito

www.mistermojito.com

David Neprove is considered one of the country's top bar chefs. He's muddled his way into the Mojito world. He's the recent winner of the prestigious cocktail competition, The Barcardi Martini Gran Prix in Italy. He currently resides in San Francisco and runs the catering company Mr. Mojito.

IP Bartenders

www.ipbartenders.com

IP Bartenders are London's best-known mixologists. At the top of the heap is Ben Reed, thanks to his TV show *Shaker Maker.* He has written many beautifully photographed books including, *Cool Cocktails, The Cocktail Hour, The Martini, The Margarita and Other Tequila Cocktails, The Art of the Cocktail, Sunshine Cocktails,* and *Hollywood Cocktails.*

Events

Nightclub and Bar

www.nightclub.com

Nightclub & Bar hosts the world's largest food and beverage (F&B) conventions. The largest one is in Las Vegas around March.

The Drinks Show

www.drinksshow.com

Toronto's drink show is located in the historic distillery district and is usually held in June. You can sample hundreds of exquisite cocktails mixed by Toronto's hottest mixologists.

The Bar Show

www.newyorkbarshow.com

Bar convention held in New York City, usually in June.

The Beer and Cocktail Show

www.thebeerandcocktailshow.com

Toronto's Beer and Cocktail Show is a nightlife atmosphere pouring the latest trends in beer, cocktails, and everything that goes with it. It's usually around May.

Publications

Esquire

www.esquire.com/foodanddrink/database/frame_main1.html

David Wondrich is the cocktail writer for *Esquire's* mixology section. I love the way this man writes. It's so enjoyable. He is also the author of *Esquire Drinks: An Opinionated & Irreverent Guide to Drinking With 250 Drink Recipes* and *Killer Cocktails: An Intoxicating Guide to Sophisticated Drinking.*

167

Mixology

www.mixology.com

Hip and fun online cocktail culture e-zine.

Syrup Magazine

www.syrupmagazine.com

Reader-friendly online and offline mag offering alcohol-related information.

Nightclub and Bar Magazine

www.nightclub.com

An online and offline cocktail industry mag that hosts the largest F&B shows in the world.

Drinks International

www.drinksint.com

An online and offline drinks mag for people that want to keep up-to-date with the latest developments, technologies, and drink trends.

The Modern Drunkard

www.moderndrunkardmagazine.com

A funny, clever, and often dark view of the cocktail culture.

Tiki News

www.tikinews.com

Established in 1995, *Tiki News* is a printed magazine containing pages packed full of historic and current Tiki information. The first magazine to solely cover Tiki!

Instructional

Beverage Alcohol Resource, LLC Institute for the Appreciation, Understanding, and Service of Adult Beverages

www.beveragealcoholresource.com

Beverage Alcohol Resource (BAR) in New York City is the very first culinary mixology course. Its graduates are able to mix a balanced Sidecar, distinguish a Speyside malt from a Lowland malt, explain in detail the difference between Bourbon whiskey and Irish whiskey, recognize when a Tequila is overpriced, identify a potato vodka by its nose alone, explain the origin of the *Manhattan* cocktail and why the bitters are an integral part of the drink, draw up a cocktail list that matches the elegance of the establishment it's created for, and, in short, do everything that one expects from an educated professional.

Gary Regan's Weekend Cocktails in the Country Bartending Classes

www.ardentspirits.com

Log on to check out the latest bartender classes from Gary Regan. His latest series, Cocktails in the Country, is aimed specifically at professional bar, restaurant, and hotel employees.

BarSim

www.barsim.com

BarSim (tm) recreates the entire drink-making process in a fun, interactive, and educational bartending simulation. Pour, blend, shake, and garnish with software that allows you to realistically simulate making 150 of the most up-to-date drinks while learning liquor knowledge, interesting facts, proper technique, and fun bar tricks.

Flairco Bartending Institute—Mixology Plus

www.flairco.com

This finishing school for bartenders provides innovative and progressive training to working bartenders who wish advanced study in the arts and sciences of the professional craft of bartending. The Flairco Bartending Institute's programs have seamlessly brought together the schools of classic mixology, modern hospitality, and performance bartending.

Bartender PhD

www.bartenderphd.com

High-energy site put out by bartender Geebz. He has tons of streaming video for you to keep up with what's new and hot in local club venues.

BarTV

www.bartv.com

This site teaches you how to mix drinks with streaming video. Some information

is incorrect, but overall it's good for a home enthusiast bartender.

Bols Academy

www.bolsacademy.com

The Bols site offers lot of bartender info to click through.

TIPS

www.gettips.com

TIPS (Training for Intervention Procedures) is a dynamic, skills-based training program designed to prevent intoxication, drunk driving, and under-age drinking by enhancing the fundamental people skills of servers, sellers, and consumers of alcohol. TIPS gives individuals the knowledge and confidence they need to recognize potential alcohol-related problems and intervene to prevent alcohol-related tragedies.

Associations

The American Museum of the Cocktail

www.museumoftheamericancocktail.org

The Museum of the American Cocktail is a nonprofit organization that seeks to celebrate a true American cultural icon, the American cocktail. It welcomes a global network of the most passionate and talented bartenders, collectors, historians, and writers on the subject of drink.

The U.S. Bartenders Guild

www.usbg.org

The USBG's purpose is to improve customer-bartender relations, increase the prestige and status of practicing bartenders, and perform valuable public relations for the entire alcoholic beverage industry.

FBA (Flair Bartenders Association)

www.barflair.org.com

Since 1997, it has been the goal of the FBA to help teach the art of flair, grow the sport of freestyle or extreme bartending, and support all styles of performance bartending in a safe and fun manner worldwide.

The National Alcohol Beverage Control Association

www.Nabca.org

The NABCA's mission is to support and benefit alcohol control systems by providing research, fostering relationships, and managing resources for the responsible sale and consumption of alcohol beverages.

The Century Council

www.centurycouncil.org

The Century Council is a not-for-profit organization dedicated to fighting drunk driving and underage drinking. The Council develops and implements innovative programs and public awareness campaigns. Some of their efforts include the interactive virtual bar at www.baecdrom.org, the interactive CD "Alcohol 101 for High School Seniors" at www.alc101forhsseniors.com, and prom-night tips for parents at www.promtips.com.

American Beverage Institute

www.abionline.org

The American Beverage Institute is a restaurant trade association dedicated to protecting the on-premise dining experience—which often includes the responsible consumption of adult beverages and is the only organization in the nation that unites the wine, beer, and spirits producers with distributors and on-premise retailers in this important mission.

Distilled Spirits Council of the United States

www.discus.org

Industry Sites

BarMedia

www.barmedia.com

BarMedia is the brainchild of Robert Plotkin, and his mission is to serve the needs of aspiring professionals as well as enlighten the social host on the nuances of creative mixology.

Nightclub and Bar Magazine

www.nightclub.com

Keeping up with all related industry news. They also host the largest F&B shows in the world.

Adams Beverage Group

www.beveragenet.net
Keeps you updated on all the industry news.

Performance Bartending

FBA (Flair Bartenders Association)

www.barflair.org
Toby Ellis and Alan Mays established the FBA in 1997. Today it has almost ten thousand passionate and like-minded members in 131 countries that govern the sport of flair bartending worldwide. As a member you get to interact with other flair bartenders in the exclusive message board, receive discounts, view Flair Bar archives, have access to streaming video, and more.

Flair Bar

www.flairbar.com
Flair Bar is the number one flair online e-zine. An absolute must for anyone wanting to know what's up with current flair bartending trends. Longtime flair competition winners Rick Barcode and Rob Husted head it up. All articles change every month, but FBA members can view the archives.

Flairco

www.flairco.com
Dean Serneels is the inventor of the plas-tic practice flair bottle and bar unit that folds up into a suitcase. Check out his cool splash page. He also has a set of hip MTV-type training DVDs available.

Bar Magic

www.barmagic.com
This was the very first flair website. The old site is no longer there, but Toby Ellis still owns it. He has changed it to a unique drink design agency. If you want to keep your finger on the pulse of the cocktail culture then clicking through his eye candy pages will give you a good idea.

Bottles Up

www.bottlesup.com
Chuck Rohm is one of the grandfathers of flair. This was one of the first flair sites and Chuck sold the very first flair video on the Internet. It's always great to see the pioneers going strong.

Flair Bartending

www.flairbartending.com
Love to flair but can't make it to a competition? This quickly growing site allows you to send in a video and vote in an online competition!

Flair Devils

www.flairdevils.com
The site is HOT. Awesome graphics! The Flair Devils travel the world, teach classes, consult, and perform. Christian Delpech, ten-time World Flair Bartender Champion, is part of the team.

Stars of the Bars

www.starsofthebars.com

This is a slick-looking site that brings you worldwide flair bartender streaming video.

Bottleslinger

www.bottleslinger.com

Chuck McIntosh is considered the bad boy of flair. He produces *Jackass*-type bartending videos.

Extreme Bartending

www.extremebartending.com

Scott Young was the first to provide a video flair series in 1998. Today the series can be purchased in DVD format.

Flair Moves

www.flairmoves.com

This site is filled with video clips of flair instruction.

The Flair School

www.theflairschool.com

The Flair School offers basic online flair training and flair tutorials for those interested in starting out in this art form.

Extreme Flair Wear

www.extremeflairwear.com

The name says it all.

Bar- and Cocktail- Related Contests

International Bartenders Association

www.iba-world.com

Log on to view the current events and cocktail contests.

Mattoni Grand Drink

www. mattonigranddrink.com

Mattoni Grand Drink cocktail competition takes place in stunningly beautiful locations and is broadcasted online via Internet on their international cocktail portal.

Legends of Bartending

www.legendsofbartending.com

Legends is a world flair bartenders international competition organized by Ken Hall. It takes place around March in Las Vegas and is the largest, most prestigious competition in the world.

Iron Bar Chef

www.ironbartenders.com

The Iron Bar Chef competition has been created to inspire all cocktail chefs from the professional bartender to the home spirit connoisseur. All mixologists interested in gourmet handcrafted cocktails are invited to create and submit their unique cocktails.

Bar and Club Finder

World's Best Bars
www.worldsbestbars.com
Slick and hip site that lists bars and clubs worldwide with images.

Murph Guide
www.murphguide.com
This site, run by Sean Murphy, has been keeping up on almost every bar in New York City since 1997. Complete with photos of the bartenders in the bars and lots more!

Happy-Hour.Com
www.happy-hour.com
Find a restaurant, bar, or club near you that offers happy hour specials. See each establishment's discounted drink and food specials and happy hour times.

Happy-Hour.Net
www.happy-hour.net
Find college-type bars near you or enter a bar near you.

Podcasts

Tikibartv.com
Martiniplace.com

Blogs

All About Bartending
www.allaboutbartending.blogspot.com

The Art of Drink
www.theartofdrink.com/blog

The Shaken Not Stirred Blog
www.martiniplace.com

The Bar Mix Master Has Spoken...
www.barmixmaster.com

DC Drinks
www.dcdrinks.blogspot.com

Days That End in Y
www.daysthatendiny.com

Glossary

2 Fingers A type of measurement. Take a glass and wrap 2 fingers near the bottom to measure out how much spirit to pour into the glass. In most glasses it will measure out to two shots of spirit (unless you have really big fingers). There's even a Tequila named Two Fingers.

3-Deep Term that means that there are three layers of people surrounding the bar waiting to get a drink. You can also say 2-deep, 4-deep, 5-deep, and so on. Some bars have a line, but the ones where you can get a drink at any part of the bar use the *deep* term as in, *Wow, we were 3-deep all night long.*

86ed Slang term for a guest being banned from coming into that bar, or when something is out of stock.

A

Absinthe (AB-sinth) A pale green spirit with high alcohol content and an anise flavor. Its nickname is The Green Fairy. It's controversial because it was banned in Switzerland in 1907, The Netherlands in 1909, America in 1912, and in France in 1915. It contains wormwood, which has hallucinatory qualities. It's served by pouring the absinthe in the glass then laying a absinthe spoon across the top. A sugar cube is then placed on the ornately slotted spoon (serves as a strainer), and cold water is poured on the sugar cube until it dissolves. When mixed with the water it turns whitish.

Absolut Swedish vodka. Flavored versions include Peppar, Citron, Kurant, Mandrin, and Apeach. Absolut Citron is believed to have started the flavored Martini craze with the Cosmopolitan.

Advocaat (ad-vo-KAHT) Liqueur from the Netherlands made of grape brandy, egg yolks, vanilla, and sugar and with a custard texture. People say that it tastes like eggnog.

After Shock American liqueur produced by Jim Beam Brands. Hot & Cool Cinnamon was the first flavor, and it now comes in black (cranberry), cool citrus, silver (apples & Red Bull), and thermal bite (green hot & spicy).

Agave (ah-gahv-EE) The plant Tequila and mezcal is made from. They take the sap/juice of the hearts of the plant. By Mexican law, Tequila must be made from at least 51 percent of the blue agave plant, and the best Tequilas are made from 100 percent blue agave plants. Mezcal can be made from any agave plant.

Alcohol In chemistry, the most common alcohol comes in ethanol and methanol form. The main thing to know is that ethanol is potable (drinkable) and methanol is not.

Ale Beer made from top fermenting yeast.

Alizé (AH-lee-zay) Owned by the Kobrand Corporation that produces Cognac and Cognac-based liqueurs. To date they make Alizé Red Passion, Alizé Gold Passion, Alizé Wild Passion, Bleu, VS, and VSOP.

Amaretto Almond-flavored liqueur.

Amaretto Disaronno (dee-sa-ROW-no) The most famous Italian almond flavored liqueur first produced in 1525. The company says that the recipe hasn't changed since. It's interesting to ponder whether the famous artist Michelangelo drank this very same liqueur. He was fifty years old in 1525 and lived to be eighty-nine. I betcha he did!

Angel's Share Refers to the evaporation of spirits that are aging in barrels. Also called the Angel's Portion.

Angostura Bitters (ang-uh-STOOR-uh) Brand of aromatic bitters invented around 1825 in Venezuela by German scientist Johann Siegert. The company is now in Trinidad.

Anisette Clear anise-flavored liqueur.

Apéritif (uh-pair-a-TEEF) A drink that you have before dinner. It's meant to stimulate your appetite. Examples are fortified wines like vermouths, Sherry, Port, Dubonnet, and Lillet. Bitter aperitif examples are Campari, Amer

Picon, and Fernet Branca. And these days an aperitif can be a liqueur as well, like Ouzo, Sambuca, Pernod, Irish cream, or coffee liqueur.

Applejack American apple brandy first made in American colonial times. The term *applejack* comes from *jacking,* a term for freeze distillation. The Laird family first produced it in 1698 and remain the oldest producer of applejack to this day.

Appleton Jamaican Rum Jamaican rum produced since 1749. Comes in Light, Gold, Dark, Rare, and Estate Extra.

Aquavit (AHK-wuh-veet) Also called *Akvavit.* Scandinavian liquor distilled from grain or potatoes and flavored with caraway seeds. Drunk as icy cold shots.

Aqua Vitae (AHK-wuh VEE-tee) Latin term that means *water of life.* Sometimes it means the *spirit of wine,* which means that it describes brandy.

Ardent Water One of the very first *water of life* terms used to describe distilled spirits. Ardent means *to burn.*

Armagnac (ar-mahn-YAK) Fine French brandy from Gascony. Cognac's only real rival. Comes in Three Star, V.S.O.P, Napoleon, Extra, and Hors d' Age.

B

B & B A liqueur that's a combination between of brandy and Benedictine D.O.M. Benedictine monks first created Benedictine in the 1500s, and in the 1930s a barman working the famous 21 Club in Manhattan combined brandy and Benedictine. The rest is history.

BAC Blood Alcohol Content. It is also called Breath Alcohol Content or Blood Alcohol Concentration.

Bacardi World's most popular rum. Don Facundo Bacardi first produced it in Cuba. Then due to the Cuban Revolution in the 1960s, he moved to Puerto Rico. It comes in Carta Blanca, Limon, 8, Solera, Gold, Amber, Black, Select, Añejo, Reserva, O, Breezer, Rigo, and 151. There's a bat on every bottle because bats are good luck in Cuba.

Back Water or other drink served with another cocktail; most times it's water. A typical guest request is, *Can I have a whiskey on the rocks with a water back?* High-end bars will automatically serve you water with your cocktail to keep you hydrated.

Back Bar The back of the bar. The call, premium, and liqueur bottles are usually displayed on the back bar.

Baileys Irish Cream The brain behind this beige Irish creamy liqueur made with imported vanilla from Madagascar, cocoa from West Africa, and cream from Irish cows was David Dand. It was introduced in 1974 and is ranked in the top ten of the best selling spirits in the world. The company says that it took four years of research to keep it from curdling and that a bottle will last two years without refrigeration. Diageo now owns it.

Bank The money given to you to work with for your shift. It's usually kept in a cash register drawer.

Bar Die The name for the structural front part of the bar.

Barfly Someone that hangs out at a bar all the time.

Bar Log Many bars keep a log/journal behind the bar simply because many bartenders don't see each other due to schedules, yet they are all working the same bar. This way you can check the log for any important information you might need to know.

Bar Mat Long, thin rubber mat that drinks are prepared on. Catches small spills made throughout a shift.

Bar Spoon Spoon that has a long, spiraled handle. You can stir drinks like a classic *Martini* or *Manhattan* in a mixing glass, guide a thick frozen/blended drink from the blender pitcher into a glass, or layer a drink with it.

Bar Time Bar time is usually set around ten minutes faster than normal time. This helps at closing time.

Bar Towels Cloth towels that are essential behind a bar.

Beaujolais (boh-zhuh-LAY) A light red table wine made from the gamay grape. Beaujolais is also a wine region in East Central France.

Beefeater A dry London dry gin that has been produced since the 1800s.

Beer Alcohol brewed from malted barley, sugar, hops, and water.

Beer Bucket Galvanized metal buckets with handles that you fill with ice and beer bottles.

Belgium Lace A term that means when beer foam sticks to the insides of the glass as it decreases. It's a sign that the glass has been properly cleaned. It's also called *brussels lace*.

Bellini (beh-LEE-nee) Cocktail invented in Harry's Bar in Venice, Italy, in 1945 and named in 1949 by Giuseppe Cipriani. A true *Bellini* is made with Prosecco (praw-SAY-co, Italian sparkling wine) and white peach purée, not Champagne and peach nectar.

Bench-Mounted Wine Opener Wine opener mounted to the bar for opening wine bottles quickly.

Benedictine D.O.M French liqueur made from herbs, plants, peels, and secrets by Benedictine monks since 1510. The D.O.M. stands for *Deo Optimo Maximo*, meaning, *To God, Most Good, Most Great.*

Bitters Distillation of herbs, barks, roots, seeds, flowers, etc., making a very aromatic alcohol. Used to flavor cocktails and food dishes.

Black Velvet A cocktail made from stout beer (usually Guinness) and Champagne. You float the Champagne slowly on top of the stout to create a layer. It was invented in 1861 in London in honor of Prince Albert when he died at age forty-two of typhoid fever.

Black Velvet Whisky Canadian blended whisky produced by Gilbey's in Toronto.

Blavod American black vodka first introduced in 2003. It was invented by Mark Dorman, and its color comes from a herb from Burma called a black catechu. However, to blindfolded drinkers, it tastes like vodka.

Blender Electric equipment that makes blended/frozen drinks.

Bloody Mary It's said that Paris bartender Pete Petiot mixed up some vodka and tomato juice. He took his Bloody Mary to the King Cole Bar in New York City and embellished it with pepper, Worcestershire sauce, Tabasco, lemon, lime and raw horseradish and sold it as a hangover cure. The name changed to *Red Snapper*, then *Morning Glory*, and then back to *Bloody Mary*.

Blue Blazer The flaming drink that the grandfather of bartending, Jerry Thomas, created. The drink is like a hot toddy using warm blended Scotch whisky, hot water, and honey. He would heat two mugs and put the warm whisky in one and the water and honey into the other then light the whisky and pour it into the other mug. He then would constantly pour the mugs back into one another, creating a long blue flame.

Blue Curacao (CURE-uh-sow, sow rhymes with cow) Orange-flavored liqueur that is colored blue. It's like a blue triple sec, only a tiny bit sweeter.

Boilermaker The original *Boilermaker* was a shot of whiskey dropped into a pilsner beer. Many kinds of Boilermakers have developed over the years such as an *Irish Car Bomb, Flaming Dr. Pepper,* and *Jäger Bomb.*

Bollinger Champagne (bowl-ahn-JAY) The Champagne choice of James Bond.

Bomb Refers to dropping a shot of spirit into something such as a Jäger Bomb. It's a spin-off from a *Boilermaker.*

Bombay A dry London gin bottled from a recipe dating back to 1761. It also comes as a super premium brand called *Bombay Sapphire* that sports a beautiful translucent sapphire-colored bottle.

Bootleg The practice of making illegal alcohol. Bootleggers would sometimes hide the alcohol in their boots.

Booze Slang word for alcohol. It comes from the Dutch word *bulzer,* which means *to drink to excess.*

Bordeaux (boar-DOH) A region in southwest France considered the largest fine-wine district in the world.

Bourbon American whiskey that is made from a mash between 51 to 79 percent corn and aged at least two years in charred oak barrels. Anyone in America can make Bourbon, and only Kentucky can put the words *Kentucky Bourbon* on the label.

Branch If a guest asks for *Bourbon & Branch,* it means that they want Bourbon mixed with spring water (bottled water).

Brandy A spirit distilled from grapes and/or other fruits.

Brandy Warmer Some guests will request their brandy or Cognac to be warmed. Select bars carry brandy warmers that hold a tea light; however don't fret if yours doesn't because you can make one with items found around most bars. All you need is a rocks glass and hot water. Preheat the brandy snifter by filling it 1/4 of the way with hot water (the kind at a coffee station) then fill a rocks glass half with hot water as well. Dump out the hot water in the snifter and pour in the Cognac and set the bowl inside the rocks glass.

Breakage Your empty bottles at the end of the night. Some bars require you to break the empty bottles. If they don't, the empty bottles are still called breakage. There will be a designated place to keep the empty bottles behind every bar.

Bronfman Brothers Harry and Samuel Bronfman were Russian Jewish immigrants living in Canada. During prohibition, they made moonshine, fudged some labels, and sent it across the border in America. They worked the border laws in their favor. In 1928 they bought a distillery called *Joseph E. Seagram and Sons,* kept the name and became the largest producers of spirits in the world. By the 1970s they owned all the Seagram's brands, Crown Royal, Chivas Regal, Glenlivet, Gordon's Gin and Vodka, Captain Morgan, Myers's Rum, Jameson, and hundreds of wine labels.

Brown-Forman Owns Jack Daniel's Tennessee Whiskey, Jack Daniel's Ready-to-Drinks, Jack Daniel's Single Barrel, Southern Comfort, Gentleman Jack, Finlandia, Early Times, Canadian Mist, Korbel, Tuaca, Woodford reserve, Appleton, Old Forester, Sonoma Wines, Fetzer Wines, and much more.

Brut A dry style of Champagne.

Build Fill glass with ice and pour in the ingredients.

Burn the Ice A bartender term that means *melt the ice.*

Bushmill's Irish whiskey that has been produced since 1606.

C

Cabernet Sauvignon (ca-ber-NAY soh-vihn-YAWN) By far the most popular red wine in the world. The grapes are hearty, small, and thick, and the wine it produces is deep in color and texture.

Cachaça (ka-SHA-suh) A Brazilian spirit made from sugarcane. There are four thousand brands of cachaça in Brazil.

Calling Order Calling order is the way a server should *call out* their drinks. If they say, "I need a Coke, Bud, Screwdriver, Piña Colada, Sam Adams, and a Diet Coke," that's wrong. You need to group the order and call out the Piña Colada first because it takes longer to make. So the calling order for this order would be: Piña Colada, Screwdriver, Sam, Bud, Coke, Diet Coke.

Calvados (KAL-vah-dohs) French apple brandy from the Normandy region.

Campari (kahm-PAH-ree) Red Italian bitter red aperitif created in Milan, Italy, by Gaspare Campari.

Canadian Club Canadian blended whisky produced by Hiram Walker in Ontario since the late 1800s. Its nickname is *CC.*

Canadian Mist Canadian blended whisky often used in America as a well whisky.

Candy Lightner Founding president of Mothers Against Drunk Driving (MADD).

Call To call is to say the brand of spirit you want your drink made with.

Carding When you check someone's identification (ID) so see if they are old enough to consume alcohol by law.

Captain Morgan Captain Henry Morgan was a drunken Welsh pirate captain who was hired by the English monarchy to attack Spanish ships in the Caribbean. He torched cities, raped, tortured, looted, robbed, and murdered anyone in his way in a fearless barbaric fashion. He died at fifty-three in 1688 from alcoholism. Interestingly enough, his stolen treasure, which could probably fill a football stadium, has never been found. All we know is that he had a fondness for Jamaica and his sunken ship, *Merchant Jamaica,* was discovered in 1999 off the coast of Haiti. No treasure was found on the ship.

Captain Morgan's Spiced Rum Spiced Rum produced first in 1943 and purchased by Seagram's in 1983. Diageo now owns it. The rum produced for America is made in Puerto Rico. The rest of the rum is produced in Jamaica. As of 2006, there are five Captain Morgan rums: Silver Spiced, Original Spiced, Black Label, Private Stock, Parrot Bay, and Tattoo.

Cash Bar Usually refers to bar used for an event like a wedding where the guests have to pay for their drinks.

Carafe A glass container with a flared end that used to be used for wine, though not much any more. Bartenders used them for tip jars. However, a lot of bartenders now use buckets behind the bar due to theft of the tip jar/carafes.

Cash Caddy Cash caddies attach to cocktail servers' trays. It holds their money, change, tabs, mints, lipstick, or whatever they want to put in the caddy.

Cashed Out A term used when you have cleared all your tabs and turned in your money at the end of your shift.

Cava (KAH-va) Spanish for sparkling wine.

Ceasar A cocktail invented by Canadian Walter Chell. He entered it into a Calgary Westin Hotel contest and won in 1969. Basically, it's like a Bloody Mary, but he replaced the Mary mix with Clamato juice, which is a combination of clam and tomato juice.

Champagne Bubbly sparkling wine that is made in the Champagne region of France

Champagne/Wine Bucket A Champagne bucket holds and keeps the Champagne or wine cold. It's best to use them with a stand rather than set it on the table. And if set on the table, then folded linen must be under it to absorb the condensation. At parties it can be used for a tip jar.

Chambord (SHAM-board) French black raspberry liqueur made with honey, vanilla, and other herbs that are steeped in Cognac. It's called the *Liqueur Royale de France* and has been made in the Loire valley in France by one family since 1685. Its unique bottle is round with gold banding. It was drunk by royalty, and it is interesting to ponder if Marie Antoinette drank this very same liqueur at Versailles.

Charcoal Filtering In 1876, Andrew Albanov, a chemist, discovered that charcoal absorbs impurities. Charcoal is just wood that has been burned to carbon. As wood burns, its gasses and volatile compounds leave the wood as smoke, and the end result is charcoal. After distillation, a spirit is poured through charcoal because impurities will be absorbed by the carbon. Smirnoff became the first to use charcoal for vodka filtration.

Chardonnay (shar-doh-NAY) The most popular white wine in the world.

Charred Oak Barrel A Baptist minister named Elijah Craig was the first to discover that aging whiskey in charred barrels changed the flavor, giving it an amber color. His accidental discovery started when he could only afford used herring barrels, so to get the fish smell out he would burn the inside of the barrel.

Chaser Something drunk immediately after drinking something else; you are "chasing" the first drink.

Check A guest's bill. Can also be called tab.

Chill To chill a glass, add ice then water to the glass and allow it to chill while you are making the drink. When ready, pour out the ice and water, and your glass is chilled. A lot of bars keep Martini glasses in coolers, so you don't have hand chill.

Church Key Refers to the large punch-style can opener that also has a bottle opener on the other end.

Citrus Reamer A citrus reamer is used to extract juice. You'll find them at handmade cocktail bars and in homes.

Citrus Squeezer A citrus squeezer squeezes the juice of lemons and limes into drinks so you don't have to use your hands.

Clamato Juice A combination of tomato and clam juice.

Claret (CLAIR-it) Common name given to the red wines of the Bordeaux wine region in France.

Cobbler A tall type of cocktail from the 1800s that was made with a spirit and a liqueur served crushed with fruits packed in to the ice.

Coco Lopez A coconut cream invented in Puerto Rico.

Cocktail Glass Martini glass.

Cognac (CONE-yak) Distilled wine from the grapes grown in the Cognac region of France.

Cointreau (KWAN-trow) French orange liqueur made from Mediterranean and tropical orange peels. Its first name was Triple Sec White Curacao.

Comp Sheet A sheet behind the bar where you write down drinks that have been comped (given away) at the bar. Some bars allow you a couple comps a night to make regulars happy. You just have to write it down for inventory purposes.

Congener (CON-gen-er) In alcohol beverage terms, congeners are a poison found naturally in all fermented drinks that contribute to a hangover. They say that dark drinks like red wine, whiskey, scotch, and brandy have more congeners than light drinks like white wine, vodka, gin, and rum. They also say to keep in mind that the quality of the alcohol you choose to drink can supercede the dark/light issue.

Cooler White wine and Sprite or 7-Up over ice. A *spritzer* is white wine and club soda over ice.

Cordial Sweet-flavored liqueur.

Cork Fee The fee you pay to bring your own bottle of wine into an establishment.

Cosmopolitan The *Cosmopolitan* was probably the most popular cocktail of the late twentieth century. It's said that Cheryl Cook from Florida first served it, and Toby Cecchini tweaked it when Absolut Citron hit the market. Just when the drink was beginning to die off, the hit TV show *Sex in the City* skyrocketed its fame worldwide. In its basic form it's just a *Cape Codder* that got married to a *Kamikaze*.

Count When you free pour, you count in your head to measure the spirit you are pouring. Generally, a one-count is 1/4 ounce, two-count is 1/2 ounce, and so on. Some bartenders do a 3-count in their heads to pour 1 1/2 ounces. The timing between the count is one Mississippi, two Mississippi, three Mississippi.

Courvoisier (core-VAH-see-a) Famous brand of Cognac. It was Napoleon's favorite.

Coyote Ugly Slang bar term that means you wake up next to someone so ugly that you you'd rather gnaw off your arm to get away than wake them.

Crème de Cacao (ca-KAY-o, ca KAH-o) Chocolate liqueur. Comes in dark/brown and white/clear.

Crème de Banana A yellow, banana-flavored liqueur.

Crème de Cassis (ca-CEASE) A maroon, black currant–flavored liqueur.

Crème de Menthe Mint flavored liqueur. Comes in dark green and white/clear.

Crème de Noyaux (noy-YOH) Reddish brown, almond-flavored liqueur. Noyaux is French for *fruit pits.*

Crown Royal Canadian whisky made by Seagram's especially for Queen Elizabeth's visit in 1939.

Crusta A type of cocktail from the1800s that has a sugared rim and a long, thin lemon twist.

Cuarenta Y Tres (kwah-RAIN-tah-ee-TRACE) Yellow Spanish liqueur with a vanilla flavor also called Licor 43 because it's supposed to be made with 43 ingredients. It has a long history dating back to Phoenician times.

Cuba Libre (KOO-buh LEE-bray) While the Rough Riders were in Cuba fighting the Spanish in 1898, this drink was invented and named after the battle cry, *Free Cuba.*

Curacao (CURE-uh-sow, sow rhymes with cow) Orange-flavored liqueur made from the orange peels grown on the island of Curacao in the Dutch West Indies.

Cut Off A guest can no longer be served any more alcohol. *You've been cut off.*

Cutty Sark Blended Scotch whisky. It has an image of a clipper ship on the label.

D

Daiquiri A *Daiquiri* is made with light rum, fresh lime juice, and sugar. It's shaken and strained. This confuses many Americans. When they think of a *Daiquiri* they have an image of a frozen flavored Daiquiri in their heads, with strawberry being the top flavor. The name comes from the name of a beach in Cuba.

Daisy A type of cocktail from the 1800s served over crushed ice and made with grenadine or another fruit syrup and a sour mix of sorts.

Dead Soldier Refers to an empty bottle. The spirit has left the bottle, so it's dead.

Diageo Owns Smirnoff, Guinness, Johnnie Walker, Baileys, J&B, Jose Cuervo, Captain Morgan, Tanqueray, Dom Pérignon, Crown Royal, Goldschlager, Myers's Rum, Guinness, Pimm's, Red Stripe, Rumple Minze, Haig, Harp, Hennessy, Archers, Bell's, Bertrams VO Brandy, Black & White, Black Haus, Buchanan's, Bulleit Bourbon, Don Julio, Gilbey's Gin, Bundaberg Rum, Cacique, CARDHU, Dimple, Beaulieu Vineyard, Baron Phillipe Wines, Barton & Guestier Wines, Blossom Hill Wines, Castillo Wines, Sterling Vineyards wines, and a lot more.

Display Drinks (sometimes called *Dummy Drinks*) These are fake drinks you make for display purposes. Put some plastic wrap (like saran wrap) in the glass then fill the glass with a nonalcoholic mix that looks like the real drink. The plastic wrap will look like ice. A dummy drink can also mean a fake-looking drink to set at a table or chair so that it look occupied. It's a way of reserving a table when you can't put out a reserve sign.

Distillation Vaporizing a liquid then cooling the condensation and collecting the resulting liquid.

Dom Pérignon (dom-pay-ree-NYON) Popular expensive Champagne and also the name of the blind Benedictine monk who invented it.

Don Facundo Bacardi Masso Was the founder of the most popular rum in the world. Looking for adventure and fortune at age sixteen, he and his brother set sail for Cuba from Spain. They opened a store selling liquor, beer, and wine. He heard that the Royal Spanish Development Board was looking for someone to create new ways to make quality rum. He worked developing new rum for ten years, and Bacardi Rum was born. Don's wife saw bats hanging from the distillery's rafters and suggested that, in order to stand out from all the other rums, they put a bat on every label, as they were considered good luck.

Don Jose Antonio de Cuervo A Spanish settler who the king of Spain gave Mexican land to in 1758 in order to cultivate the agave plant. He made the most famous Tequila known worldwide. Today it's one of the oldest family-controlled spirit businesses in the world.

Drambuie (dram-BOO-ee) A heather honey and herbal Scotch whisky liqueur produced in Scotland by the Mackinnon family. The recipe was brought to them by Prince Charles in gratitude of keeping him safe during the Battle of the Culloden Moor. Drambuie comes from a Scottish Gaelic term *an dram buidheach* that translates to *the drink that satisfies.*

Draw Beer on draft. Also called *tap* and *draught.*

Dry Sack Popular brand of Sherry.

Dump Sink The sink behind the bar where you dump the remains of a used drink. It normally has some sort of meshy filter in the bottom of it to keep straws and fruit from clogging the drain.

E

Eau-de-vie (oh-duh-VEE) French for the *water of life*. It's the most popular term to describe distilled spirits.

F

Fernet Branca A bitters made of herbs, with a strong medicinal flavor. Produced in France and Italy.

Fermentation The conversion of sugar to alcohol with the use of yeast.

Fifth A measurement for a fifth of a gallon. It's used all the time when talking about bar bottles that are 750ml.

Finlandia Vodka from Finland.

Fino (FEE-no) Type of Sherry that's light and dry.

Fix A type of cocktail from the 1800s that uses lemon juice and crushed ice.

Flash Blender This piece of equipment was standard up until the 1990s, then they started dying off. It looks like a

milkshake machine made to make one milkshake. You would pour the drink into a shaker tin, and it would mix it, leaving a frothy top. It was used for sours and juice drinks mostly. Bartenders used this method over shaking sours.

Foil Cutter A foil cutter cuts the foil off a wine bottle to expose the cork. Simply set it on the rim, squeeze, and twist to cut.

Flag A flag is a cherry-speared orange slice; if you speared a pineapple slice with a cherry it would be called a pineapple flag.

Flip A type of cocktail from the 1800s that contains egg yolk.

Float To slowly pour on top.

Free Pour To free pour means that you are making drinks by freely pouring out of the bottle without using a measuring device. This way of pouring is fast and allows the bartender to be create with all types of showmanship pours. However, it also makes it too easy to over pour and can make drinks inconsistent.

Fortified Wine Wines that have had alcohol added (usually brandy) like Sherry, Port, vermouth, and Madeira. They can also have herbs and spices added as well.

Framboise (frahm-BWAHZ) French raspberry brandy.

Frangelico An Italian hazelnut liqueur made from hazelnuts, berries, herbs, coffee, vanilla, and caramel for coloring. The bottle is often said to resemble an Aunt Jemima Pancake Syrup bottle. It is supposed to resemble a monk's habit.

Froufrou Drink This is a sweet, usually colorful, pain-in-the-butt drink to make because you either have to blend it or pick up seven to ten bottles and mixers to make it. They are also called *girly drinks* and *chick drinks.*

Full Bar A full bar means that the bar is stocked fully to make pretty much any drink.

G

Galliano (gall-LEEY-AH-no) Yellow Italian liqueur that is made with many herbs and spices and tastes a little like licorice. It comes in a very tall, slender bottle.

Gibson A cocktail that's really a classic gin Martini garnished with cocktail pearl onions instead of olives. There are several stories to who invented it. One is that a man named Charles Dana Gibson asked a bartender named Charles Connolly at the private Player's Club in NYC to make a new cocktail. Another is when a man with the last name Gibson would have a bartender fill his Martini glass with water, so it appeared he could drink a lot. To know which one the water Martini was, the bartender used cocktail onions in place of olives. And another is that is was created after the popular Gibson Girl.

Gin Spirit made from grains, then distilled a second time with herbs and botanicals.

Gin Lane Gin Lane refers to a time in England's history when gin was cheaper than beer and became almost equivalent to the crack cocaine epidemic of the late 1900s. Artist William Hogarth depicts the time in a 1750 engraving plate showing poverty and misery. The engraving shows slummy London streets with a gin cellar with the inscription, *Drunk for a Penny, Dead Drunk for Two Pence, Clean Straw for Nothing.* An exposed room shows that a man has hung himself, a carpenter is trying to sell his tools, a housewife tries to sell her pots, people are fighting, laughing, and drinking, and a woman who was breastfeeding drops her baby.

Ginger Beer Nonalcoholic ginger-flavored soda.

Glenfiddich (gle-FID-ick) Popular single malt Scotch whisky produced since 1887. Glenfiddich means *valley of the deer.*

Glenlivit (glen-LIVE-it) Popular Highland single malt Scotch produced since 1825. It was Scotland's first registered legal stillery.

Glenmorangie (glen-MORang-ee, rhymes with orangy) Popular Highland single malt Scotch whisky first established in 1845.

Goldschlager A Swiss clear cinnamon schnapps with gold flakes added.

Grand Marnier (GRAN mahr-nYAY) French Cognac-based orange liqueur invented in 1880 by Louis Alexandre Marnier-Lapostolle.

Grenadine Nonalcoholic cherry and pomegranate syrup.

Grog A warm concoction of rum, lemon juice, sugar, cloves, cinnamon, and water. It was named after British Admiral Edward Vernon who earned the nickname Old Grog because of his grogram coat. His intent was to water down the rum rations with this yummy disguise.

Guinness Spoon When a distributor puts a Guinness tap on your bar, it's accompanied by a spoon that fits on the edge of the glass to help layer Guinness on top of ale to make a black & tan.

Guinness Stout A stout from Ireland.

H

Hand-Washing Sink The health department requires a hand-washing sink behind every bar. Legally you're supposed to use it for hand washing only.

Harvey's Bristol Cream Popular brand of Sherry.

Heaven Hill Owns Hpnotiq, Two Fingers, Pama, Evan Williams, Dubonnet, Whalers, Burnett's, and more.

Highball Originally, when a guest walked up to the bar and asked for a highball, the bartender grabbed a bottle of rye whiskey and mixed it with ginger ale. Today a highball just means a drink containing a spirit mixed with a carbonated mixer.

Hooch Hooch is a slang word for illegal alcohol. Alaska is responsible for giving this word to the English language in the late 1800s. When America purchased Alaska in 1987 they prohibited the sale of alcoholic beverages, so local Indians living in the Xutsnuuwu village (Hoochinoo in English) made their own alcohol. Soon it was shortened to hooch.

Horse's Neck Refers to the rind of a whole lemon cut into a spiral and used in a cocktail.

Hpnotiq French liqueur packaged in an aqua-colored bottle that is made from Cognac, vodka, and tropical fruit juice.

I

In & Out Refers to pouring *in* a little dry vermouth into a Martini glass, swirling it around, and dumping *out* the rest before pouring in the gin or vodka when making a Martini.

Infusion To soak fruit, herbs, botanicals, etc., in alcohol for a long period of time to infuse the flavors with alcohol. After the infusion, the mix is strained and rebottled.

In the Weeds Bartender term for being extremely busy with stock running low, making you feel like you can't keep up with the demand.

Inventory Inventory is taken weekly or monthly depending on where you work. Everything wet and dry used for the bar must be counted. It is then compared with store sales.

Irish Mist An Irish whiskey-based honey liqueur. Scotland has a honey liqueur called Drambuie.

J

Jack Daniel Jasper Newton "Jack" Daniel was born around the 1840s or 1850s. No one really knows exactly when because he sort of slipped through the cracks, being the tenth of thirteen children. At nine years old little Jack Daniel was taught how to make whiskey from a reverend's slave named Nearest Green. When Jack was thirteen years old, the church folk came down on the reverend for making whiskey, so he sold the business to Jack. At nineteen, Jack discovered a cave filled with cool spring water that fed sugar maple trees. Jack was the first to register his distillery, and it remains the oldest registered distillery in

America. His nephew Lem Motlow took over and moved the distillery to Alabama, then St. Louis, due to early prohibition in Tennessee. In 1938, he rebuilt the distillery in the original Cave Spring Hollow. In 1956, it was sold to Brown-Forman.

Jack Daniel's Whiskey Tennessee sour mash whiskey that was invented by Jack Daniel. He developed the taste of his whiskey by taking sugar maple wood and burning it to a perfected stage. After the wood is cooled, it is ground down and packed into cisterns ten feet high. The whiskey is then poured on top and the time-consuming process of white whiskey traveling through the ten feet of sugar maple charcoal begins. Drop by drop it's collected at the bottom and aged in new oak barrels for a minimum of four years. No one knows what the No. 7 on the bottle means.

Jigger A two-sided measurement tool to measure alcohol for cocktails. They come in about five different sizes but the most common sizes are 3/4 by 1 1/4 and 3/4 by 1 1/2.

Jim Beam Brands Owns Jim Beam, Sauza, Courvosier, Canadian Club, Laphroaig, Maker's Mark, DeKuyper, Clos du Bois, After Shock, Basil Hayden's, Booker's, Calvert, Kamora, Knob Creek, Mount Vernon, Old Grand Dad, Starbucks Coffee Liqueur, Vox, Teacher's, Geyser Peak, Harvey's Bristol Cream, and so much more.

Johnnie Walker Was a man from Kilmarnock, Scotland, who first blended scotches. In 1820, at age fifteen, he took his father's life insurance money and opened a little store. He sold sundries of sorts, tea, and whisky. He began thinking about how the teas he sold were blended, so he started blending whisky, making Walker's Kilmarnock Whisky. It became very popular in his little area, but exploded when his son, Alexander Walker, dreamed up a tall square bottle and bottled it with the name Old Highland Whisky in 1867. His sons made more Scotch whiskies and added the striding man image on the bottles. By 1920, Johnnie Walker was on every bar's back shelf. Today it comes in Red, Black, Gold, Blue, Green, Pure Malt, and Swing. The Swing bottle actually rocks back and forth.

Jose Cuervo The most popular Tequila in the world started by Don Jose Antonio de Cuervo, a Spanish settler to Mexico in 1795. The words written on the ribbon of every Jose Cuervo bottle are *Abolengo, Prestigo, Tradicion,* which translates to, Heritage, Prestige, and Tradition. Today, it produces Especial (called Cuervo Gold), Clasico, Traditional, Black, Reserva da la Familia, and flavored Tequilas such as Citrico, Oranjo, and Tropiña.

Julep A type of cocktail from the 1800s made with mint.

Jägermeister (YAY-ger-mice-ter) German herbal liqueur first introduced in 1935. It means *master of the hunt.* The Mast family says that it's made with fifty-six herbs, roots, and spices. Behind the bar, it's kept in the cooler and some bars have Jägermeister on tap machines that sit on the back bar, dispensing the liqueur at a cool five degrees.

K

Kahlúa Mexican coffee liqueur. It is the most popular coffee liqueur in the world.

Kirsch (KEERSH) German cherry brandy.

Kosher Salt The coarse salt used to rim the glass of a margarita.

L

Lager Beer made from bottom-fermenting yeast.

Laphroaig (la-FROY-g) Popular single malt Scotch made in Tormore, Scotland.

Last Call A term said in a bar to let guests know that it's time to order a last drink because the bar will be closing.

Layered Because alcohols are different weights/densities it allows them to layer on top of one another. Most people say that all layered drinks are types of Pousse Cafés, which is a layered after-drink with seven layers served in a cordial glass.

Legs When you swirl alcohol around while in a glass it coats the upper part of the glass and then drizzles down, forming what the booze world calls *legs.* The thicker the legs, the better. Mostly reserved for fine wine and whiskies.

Limoncello (lee-moan-CHEH-low) Italian lemon liqueur. It can come in a cream form as well.

Licor 43 A Spanish vanilla liqueur. See *Cuarenta Y Tres.*

Lillet (lee-LAY) A French fortified aperitif wine produced since 1872. Made very popular when James Bond ordered a Martini with this instead of vermouth.

Liquor A distilled spirit.

Liquor Room Where all the backup stock of liquor is kept. In most cases, only managers have keys. There is usually a clipboard inside so that whatever is taken is marked down. Some bars have a bottle-for-bottle policy, meaning that you can only get a full bottle in exchange for an empty bottle of the spirit.

Liqueur Sweet-flavored cordial.

Limousin and Troncais Forest The wood from these forests are located in the Cognac region of France. Their wood is used for making Cognac casks to age Cognac.

M

Madame Clicquot Invented pink Champagne, the mushroom-shaped cork, and a way of removing sediment from bottles called *riddling* in 1804.

Madeira (muh-DEER-uh) Madeira is fortified wine produced from grapes grown on the southern coast of Madeira Island, which is about 360 miles west of Morocco in Northern Africa and 540 miles southwest from Portugal. Portugal has owned it since only 1974. It was used to toast the signing of the Declaration of Independence. To reach the New World, ships had to pass through the tropics and the heat literally baked the Madeira, giving it a soft, deep, burnt taste. Soon pipes filled with Madeira were installed with ship ballasts and sent on tropical voyages. The heat mixed with the constant rocking made this wine last for years without spoiling.

Mai Tai (MY tie) Mai tai means *out of this world* in Tahitian. Vic Bergeron, also known as Trader Vic, claims to have invented the Mai Tai in 1944; Don Beach says the same thing. Evidence seems to lean towards Trader Vic. His original recipe uses Jamaican light and gold rum, fresh lime juice, a few dashes of orange Curacao syrup, French orgeat, and rock candy syrup. The gold rum is saved to float on top of the drink. Most modern bars don't carry orgeat (OAR-zhat) or Curacao syrup, but amaretto replaced the orgeat, triple sec replaced the Curacao, and the fresh lime juice and rock candy syrup was replaced by sweet-n-sour mix. The gold rum was even replaced by dark rum.

Mahogany A slang term meaning the bar top.

Manhattan A true classic cocktail made with rye whiskey, sweet vermouth, and two dashes of bitters with a cherry garnish. There are many stories of people claiming to have invented the Manhattan, but all agree on the location in which it was invented, Manhattan. One is that Churchill's mother had a bartender at the Manhattan Club invent it. Another is that a Supreme Court judge had a Manhattan club invent it. And another, it was invented by a NYC bartender that simply named it after the city in which he worked.

Margarita Tequila, orange liqueur, and lime. This is Mexico's national drink. As a bartender you will make thousands upon thousands of these. There are several stories of who invented it: a bartender who named it after a girl named Margarita; a bartender named Daniel Negrete; Pancho Morales, who worked at Tommy's Place in Juarez; and a woman named Margarita Sames in Acapulco.

Martini Without a doubt, the most popular cocktail in history. There are several stories of who invented it, and whole books have been written about it. Its glass shape is the icon for the bar world. A classic Martini is gin and dry vermouth, with a vodka Martini sharing some of the classic spotlight as well. It can be garnished with olives or a lemon twist, shaken or stirred, and served on the rocks or straight up.

Marry Pouring the contents of one bottle into another, thus two bottles are *married*. It's illegal. The law is that you can't pour anything into any bottle, not even if it's identical. It started when bar owners would water down their liquor to make more money. With that said, behind closed doors or out of eyesight, it's been known that bartenders working a two-well bar may marry identical bottles in order to consolidate.

Mead An ancient alcoholic beverage made with honey, flowers, and spices. A popular drink for Robin Hood and his Merry Men.

Mescal (mehs-KAL) Made from any agave plant. Tequila must be made from at least 51 percent blue agave plant.

Midori (mih-DOOR-ee) A green Japanese honeydew melon liqueur introduced by Suntory in 1978. Midori means *green* in Japanese.

Mint Julep The official drink of the Kentucky Derby, made with Bourbon, muddled mint leaves, and sugar.

Mist A type of drink from the 1800s where one spirit was served over crushed ice. Also called a *Frappe*.

Mixing Glass A mixing glass looks just like a pint glass and is used with a shaker tin to shake drinks. It's also used to muddle and to stir a classic *Martini* or *Manhattan*. You use a julep strainer with a mixing glass.

Mocktail A *Mocktail* is a nonalcoholic cocktail. It's also called a virgin drink or smoothie.

Moonshine Homemade alcohol that gets its name from being made illegally by the light of the moon.

Moscow Mule The drink that introduced vodka to America. Smirnoff vodka, lime juice, and ginger beer served in a copper cup.

Mount Gay Eclipse Rum from Barbados named after an eclipse in 1703. Started by two British sailors named William Gay and Ensign Abel Gay. They weren't brothers, so why they have the same name, I don't know.

Muddler A muddler looks like a small wooden bat. You use the flat end to crush and mash fruits, sugar cubes, herbs, and more to make drinks like a *Mojito* or a *Mint Julep*. Never use a varnished or lacquered muddler because poisons go into the drink. Make sure it's unvarnished and oiled.

Mull A type of warm wine drink with spices added; dates from the 1800s.

Myers's Jamaican dark rum known as the *Planter's Punch Rum*. For many years the planter's punch recipe was on the bottle.

Napkin Caddy A napkin caddy sits on the bar top holding napkins, drinking straws, and cocktail straws. Some have compartments to hold cocktail picks and matches.

NAVAN Vanilla Cognac from Courvoisier.

Neat A spirit poured and served at room temperature straight from the bottle.

Noble Experiment Another name for prohibition in America.

Noilly Prat (Noy-ee praht) A French vermouth.

Oban (O-bin) Popular single malt Scotch whisky made in Glasgow, Scotland.

Old School of American Bartending The time between 1897 and 1919 when drink making was appreciated and bartending was an art form. These classic drinks are found in *The Old Waldorf-Astoria Bar Book*. Isn't it interesting that a turn towards this style of bartending has returned one hundred years later?

Oloroso (O-lo-ROW-so) Type of Sherry that is dark and full-bodied.

On the Fly I need it *now*. I need it ASAP.

On the House This drink is free because the bar is buying it for you.

On the Rocks Over ice.

Open Bar Means that the bar is free. Found many times at big events and weddings. People who have been to an event before will always ask in anticipation, *Is it an open bar?*

Orange Flower Water Nonalcoholic water distilled from orange blossoms that tastes like perfumed oranges. Used in a *Ramos Fizz*.

Orgeat (OAR-zhat) Nonalcoholic almond syrup.

Ouzo (OO-zoh) Greek aperitif with a strong anise flavor.

Parfait Amour (PAR-fay uh-MORE) Purple liqueur flavored with roses, violets, vanilla, and spices.

Pat O'Brien's Popular bar in the French Quarter in New Orleans known for inventing the hurricane.

Pernod (purr-NO) French Anise-flavored liqueur that is considered an absinthe substitute. Henri-Louis Pernod first produced it in 1797. In the beginning, it was made with wormwood and it was absinthe.

Pernod Ricard Bought out Allied Domecq in 2005 and now owns Ricard, Ballantine's, Pernod, Chivas Regal, Kahlúa, Malibu, Beefeater, Havana Club, Stolichnaya, Jameson, Wild Turkey, Martell, The Glenlivet, Jacob's Creek, Montana, Mumm, Perrier-Jouët, and so much more.

Perrier (PAIR-e-A) French sparkling mineral water that comes from a natural spring. In 1898, Louis Perrier bought the estate that the spring was on. It's interesting to think that when you drink Perrier, you are drinking from an ancient natural spring that many have drunk from before. Julius Caesar was the first to build a stone basin near the refreshing bubbly spring in 58 BC.

Perfect Means to use half sweet and half dry vermouth as in a perfect Manhattan.

Peychaud's Bitters (PAY-showds) Bitters was invented by Antoine Peychaud in 1793 while operating a New Orleans's French Quarter pharmacy. He invented the cocktail called the sazerac, which included this bitters.

Pilsner (PILLS-ner) A beer first brewed in Pilsen (now in the Czech republic), in 1842 by Josef Groll. Before this, beers were cloudy and dark. In modern times it just means a pale yellow lager, with the most popular being Budweiser. There's even a beer glass named after it.

Piña Colada Puerto Rico's national drink. It means *strained pineapple*. It's said to be invented on August 15, 1954, at the Caribe Hilton's Beachcomber Bar in San Juan, Puerto Rico, by bartender Ramon "Monchito" Marrero Perez. He served it strained into coconuts and pineapples. Later, when the coconut cream called Coco Lopez made its way to the Beachcomber Bar, it was made frozen. A *Piña Colada* contains rum, pineapple juice, and coconut cream. Use vodka instead of rum and it's called a *Chi Chi*.

Pisco (PIECE-koh) A South American brandy that dates back to the Inca Empire (1400 to 1500). The Spanish brought grapes to the Peru area and made brandy that was aged briefly in earthen jars. Due to political and geographical challenges, pisco didn't hit the mainstream until the 1940s.

Poco Grande An all-purpose tropical drink glass for most bars. Shaped like a tulip and usually around 13 ounces.

Poire (PWAHR) A clear Swiss pear brandy with a whole pear in the bottle giving a ship-in-a-bottle illusion. Bottles are placed over a budding pear then attached to the tree and the pear grows inside. Later the bottled is filled with brandy made from the same orchard of trees. It's full name is Poire William.

Pomace (PUH-muss) After grapes have been pressed, brandy is made from its remains: seeds, skins, pulp, etc. This is called *pomace*. The most popular pomace brandy is Grappa from Italy.

Pony Glass One ounce curvy stemmed glass. When the measurement *pony* is asked for it means 1 ounce.

Port Fortified wine from Portugal. Most American bars, if they offer Port, will have a ruby or a tawny type. Ruby is sweeter than tawny. The most popular brands are Sandeman, Lindemans, and Noval.

POS Point of sale. In a bar, the POS systems are the computers used to make transactions. Most POS systems are kept on the back bar so they are out of public reach.

Pourer A pourer is placed in a liquor bottle to make it easier to pour. They come in different sizes for different speeds.

Pousse Café (poose ka-FA, rhymes with loose) An after-dinner layered drink. It has seven layers (some say nine), but don't worry, no one will ever ask you to make one. It's just important to know that all layered drinks like this are considered *types* of pousse cafés. And just for the sake of useless information, pousse café means *push coffee* in French.

Presbyterian Means that the mixer is half ginger ale and half soda water. It's called *press* for short like, *Can I have a whiskey press?*

Proof The strength of alcohol. If a bottle is labeled 43 percent, then you double it to get the proof. In this case it's 86 proof.

Prohibition (in America) The time between January 16, 1920, at one minute past midnight and December 5, 1933, at 3:32 p.m., when it was prohibited to manufacture, import, export, or sell alcoholic beverages, except for medical and religious reasons. It was also called the Noble Experiment. By many people (mostly women), it was believed that the high crime rate, general laziness, deadbeat dads, poverty, etc. from the late 1800s to the early 1900s was due to alcohol. But prohibition created organized crime, bootlegging, and many deaths due to people trying to make their own alcohol. It's agreed that it was a failure.

Prosecco (praw-SAY-co) The Italian sparkling wine used, along with white peach puree, to make a *Bellini*.

Punt The indentation at the base of a wine or Champagne bottle, which reinforces the bottle's structure.

Q

Quinine (KWY-nine) It's a bitter tasting natural alkaloid having painkiller qualities. It comes from the bark of the cinchona tree of Central and South America. Quinine is used in tonic water and many bitters. On a soda gun the button for tonic water is sometimes Q. Also, clear spirits mixed with tonic water will glow a light blue under a black light. Some guests don't like the tonic that comes out of a soda gun and will ask if you have bottled tonic available.

R

Railroad A railroad is a list of cleaning duties divided up by each day and each shift. When you work your shift, you check the railroad to see what you are supposed to clean that day. This way the bar's icky parts get cleaned at least once a week.

Rain Vodka First introduced in 1996 and made from 100 percent organic American grains. Even the labels and shipping boxes are made from recycled paper, and the company gives a donation to the Wilderness Society with each bottle sold.

Ramos Fizz (RAY-mohss) Cocktail created in New Orleans by Henry Ramos in the late 1800s. It has gin, cream, lemon and lime juice, orange flower water, powered sugar, and club soda garnished with an orange slice. It's blended then topped with the soda water.

Real McCoy In the 1500s, rum runners were pirates who shipped illegal rum to colonies that were heavily taxed. During prohibition in the 1920s, the most famous *Rum Runner* was Captain William McCoy—he didn't add water to his spirits like the others. This is one story of how we got the phrase *the real McCoy.*

Red Bull Nonalcoholic high-energy drink used in *Jäger Bombs.*

Reinheitsgebot Law A 1516 law that was enacted in Bavaria, Germany, requiring that beer be made from malt, hops, yeast, and water only.

Richard Hennessy Was the founder of the best-known Cognac in the world in 1765. He was a son of an English lord, but grew up in Ireland and then later sailed with the Irish brigade as Captain Richard Hennessy. He was wounded in France and fell in love with the landscape, then decided to make Cognac for fun. With sailing skills and connections in England and Ireland, his product took off. He died in 1800, and his grandson, Maurice Hennessy, was the first to begin a labeling system for Cognacs in 1865. The system included VS, VSOP, and XO. Hennessy also produces very old and expensive brands: Private Reserve, Paradis Extra, Richard Hennessy, and Timeless.

Rickey A type of cocktail made with lime juice and soda from the 1800s.

Rimmer This holds your salt, sugar, and juice to help rim glasses. The most popular drinks it's used for are salt-rimmed *Margaritas* and sugar-rimmed *Lemondrops.* Most bartenders put lime cordial in the spongy part to get it wet. The proper way to rim is not on the rim itself but on the outside of the rim so that extra salt or sugar doesn't fall into the drink. Always clean it out after the closing shift.

Ring Your *ring* is what you sold while working your shift. The nickname came from the little ringing bell sound from the first cash registers.

Roll Method of mixing that involves filling a glass with ice and building a drink, pouring it into a shaker tin or glass, then pouring it back into the original glass.

Rose's Lime Cordial Popular brand name for lime juice cordial. It was first produced commercially in Edinburgh, Scotland, by Lauchlin Rose, who patented his method of preserving the juice without the addition of alcohol. That same year it was made mandatory for all ships in both the Royal Navy and British Merchant Navy to include lime juice in the sailors' daily rations, so Rose's Lime Cordial soon became known throughout the world.

Rotation When you are working in the food and beverage industry you will hear this term a lot. Rotation is simply rotating your product. For example, when you stock your beer bottles, you don't stock them in front of the ones already in the cooler. You must rotate your beer stock, bringing the older ones to the front and the newer ones to the back so nothing expires. This method is used for just about everything in a restaurant and bar.

Ruby Port Wood-aged Port.

Rum Spirit made from molasses or sugarcane. Columbus planted the Caribbean's first sugarcane in Haiti in 1493. It then spread to practically every location near the equator. The most popular rum is Bacardi, and Captain Morgan's Rum follows a close second.

Rumple Minze (ROOM-pull MINTS) German peppermint schnapps.

Rye Whiskey Aged two years with 51 percent or more rye in the mash. Popular brands are Old Overholt, Mount Vernon, and Wild Turkey Straight Rye.

S

Sambuca (sam-BOO-ka) Italian licorice/anise-flavored liqueur. Comes in a black version called *Opal Nera.* For good luck it should be served with three coffee beans dropped in. It can be served in a cordial glass or snifter.

Sangria A drink made with red or white wine with sugar and fruits added. It's a popular party drink. It's interesting to think that in 1694, the commander of the British Mediterranean fleet threw a huge officers' party using a garden fountain with over six hundred gallons of what one could say was sangria.

Sazerac (SAZ-uhr-ack) A cocktail first made in New Orleans and considered America's first cocktail. It's made with rye whiskey, Herbsaint Pernod, sugar water, and Peychaud's bitters with a lemon twist. It was first served at the Sazerac Coffee House.

Seagram's 7 Popular American blended whiskey made in Indiana.

Sec (seck) French word that means dry. When referring to wine it means *not sweet.* When referring to Champagne it means the opposite and something even sweeter for Champagnes is *demi-sec.* But it's most often seen as *triple sec,* which is an orange liqueur. Curacao is an orange liqueur as well, but sweeter, so the triple sec is a little dryer.

Service Bar Where servers order and pick up the drinks a bartender makes for them.

Shake Fill a glass with ice, build the ingredients, pour everything into a shaker tin, shake, then pour everything back into the original glass.

Shake and Strain Pour ingredients into a shaker tin filled half with ice, shake, and strain into the glass. This method is typical for Shooters and Martinis.

Shake and Strain Over Ice Pour ingredients into a shaker tin filled half with ice, shake, and strain into a glass of ice.

Shaker A shaker or shaker tin is used to shake a drink. You can find many novelty shakers in just about any shape or form. The two types are cobbler and Boston. Cobbler shakers consist of three pieces, and a real bartender would not be caught dead with one because it's a sure sign of an amateur home bar enthusiast. A Boston shaker consists of a mixing glass or tin and a shaker tin pieced together to shake a drink. You shake then break the seal by tapping where they meet.

Shandy Half beer, half Sprite/7-Up.

Shelf Mat Shelf mats are used to set glassware on. It keeps them slightly elevated so that air can get up and under to dry it out. They also protect the counter surface.

Sherry Fortified wine mostly made in Jerez, Spain. To fortify (flavor and preserve) it, brandy is added. There are two types of Sherry; fino (fee-NO, light and dry) and oloroso (O-lo-ROW-so, dark and full-bodied). A proper serving is 2 to 2 1/2 ounces. It's made with the solera system.

Shift Drink Some Ma and Pa-type local bars allow their bartenders to have one free drink after their shift called a *shift drink.*

Shoes For Crews Shoes For Crews is famous for making slip-resistant shoes for people working in the hospitality industry. They provide a payroll deduction program so that it's easy for employees to get some good shoes for work. Or you can buy them yourself online at www.shoesforcrews.com.

Shots Made are from 100 percent alcohol and served in a shot glass. You drink it quickly. Examples are a *B-52*, shot of Tequila, *Buttery Nipple*, etc.

Shooters Shooters are drunk quickly like shots, however they have a mix to them like a *Lemondrop*, *Woo Woo*, *Kamikaze*, etc.

Simple Syrup A mixture of sugar and boiling water. Some people make it without heat as well.

Single Barrel Bourbon Bottling of one single barrel of Bourbon.

Single Batch Bourbon Bottlings from a batch of barrels that have been mixed prior to the bottling.

Single Malt Refers to single malt Scotch whisky. It means that the whisky is 100 percent malted barley from only one distillery.

Skyy Vodka produced in San Francisco and invented by Maurice Kanbar. Comes in a cobalt blue bottle and claims to have almost no congeners, making hangovers unlikely.

Slammed Bartender term for *extremely busy.*

Sling A type of cocktail made with a sweet spirit, lemon, and carbonation from the 1800s.

Sloe Gin Sloe berry–flavored liqueur.

Smash A type of cocktail from the 1800s that is basically a short *Squatty Julep* with crushed ice.

Smirnoff The vodka responsible for introducing vodka to America. Ivan Smirnoff opened a Moscow distillery in 1815 then another in 1827. Wars came across Europe, and in 1873 Ivan's son Pierre rebuilt the original distillery. It's said that in 1886 Pierre dressed bartenders up in bear suits at a carnival booth in Moscow. In 1901 Pierre's sons, Vladimir and Nicolai, inherited the company. They grew up rich boys and were captured when communists came to Moscow. Nicolai was killed and after much torture Vlad was let go. He fled to France with only two things: the clothes on his back and the Smirnoff vodka recipe. Failing at trying to sell vodka to Frenchmen, he sold it to a Russian family friend named Rudolph Kunett who lived in America during 1933. Kunett set up a distillery in Connecticut but had the same problem selling it to Americans, so he sold it to an English gent named John G. Martin. Martin ran a Massachusetts company named G. E. Heublein that survived prohibition by developing and selling A-1 steak sauce. While in Hollywood in 1946, he was at a bar called the Cock 'n' Bull owned by a man named Jack Morgan. Jack had a bunch of ginger beer and John had a bunch of vodka. So they concocted a drink called the Moscow mule. Martin had an idea to combine the drink and a new piece of technology called the Polaroid camera. He would get bartenders interested in the camera then have them make the Moscow mule and take two pictures: one for the bar wall and one to keep. Soon, the drink spread and vodka was finally introduced to America. In 1962, James Bond exploded it by drinking Smirnoff vodka Martinis, shaken not stirred.

Sparkling Wine Any bubbly wine made outside of the Champagne region of France must be called and labeled sparkling wine.

Speed Rail Also called a *speed well* or a *speed rack.* It's a long stainless steel shelf about the height of your knees that holds the most commonly used well liquors. It's usually connected to the ice well. In time, you should never have to look down at the bottles but should just know where they are by feeling them. This would require them to be set up in the same order every time.

Spill Sheet A sheet kept behind the bar so when a mistake is made, the alcohol can be written on the spill sheet. It's needed so the manager can add it to the inventory.

Spritzer White wine & club soda over ice. A *cooler* is white wine and Sprite/7-Up over ice. Both are normally served with a lime wedge.

Steam Beer Beer that's half lager/half ale.

Straight up Chilled in a shaker tin and strained. The term *up* is the same as straight up.

Strainer A strainer allows you to shake a drink then strain it into a glass without the ice falling into the glass. A Hawthorne strainer has a metal coil on it and is used for a shaker tin. A julep strainer is used for the mixing glass.

Solera system. Wine is taken young and blended with older wine and vice versa. They say that the young wine refreshes the old wine, and old wine educates young ones.

Sommelier (sum-ul-YAY) is a trained and knowledgeable wine professional usually working at a fine restaurant. A *Master Sommelier* is certified, which is quite an honor.

Sour Mash When the yeast mixture is taken from a batch to start another batch—much like when you make sour dough bread. Scot James Crow of Old Crow Bourbon invented the method for making whiskey.

Southern Comfort Most people believe it has a whiskey base but it doesn't. There is zero whiskey in Southern Comfort. It's an apricot, peach, and honey liqueur invented by a bartender, M. W. Heron, in New Orleans in 1874; it won the gold medal at the 1904 World's Fair in St. Louis. He then moved to Memphis near Beale Street and opened a bar selling his liqueur with the phrase *None genuine but mine* on every bottle (plus he hand-signed every bottle). After prohibition and in tribute to the 1939 film *Gone with the Wind,* the company introduced the *Scarlett O'Hara* (Southern Comfort and cranberry juice with a lime wedge garnish). It's available in 100, 76, and 70 proof and is nicknamed *SoCo.* Note: The first name for

Southern Comfort was Cuffs and Buttons, which was in direct competition with another liqueur named White Tie and Tails.

Speakeasy An illegal club selling illegal booze during prohibition. Most times you had to know a secret word to enter and speak it easy. Some were camouflaged by soda shops, ice cream shops, barbershops, etc.

Stir Fill a glass with ice, build, then stir with a straw. In the case of stirring a classic *Martini* or *Manhattan,* you are stirring the mixture in a shaker glass of ice with a bar spoon then straining with a julep strainer.

Stone Sour Stone sour means the mix is half sour mix and half orange juice. A guest might order a *Whiskey Stone Sour.*

Stout Dark ale beer. It looks almost black.

Sweet-n-Sour Sweetened lemon or lime juice.

Sweet Vermouth A fortified wine with caramelized sugar added to make it sweet.

Swizzle A type of cocktail in the 1800s that was tall and tropical and stirred with a long swizzle stick until the outside of the glass turns frosty.

Swizzle Stick It's said that Jay Sindler invented the swizzle stick in 1934. Yes, they say that he actually got a real patent for this long thin stick used to stir cocktails.

T

Tall Drink A tall drink is simply a drink made in a tall glass. There's a misconception with the general public that if they ask a bartender for a tall drink then the bartender will pour more alcohol. This is not the case (unless they ask for a double). Tall drinks have the same portion of alcohol used in a short glass, just more mixer is added.

Teetotaler A term from the 1800s that means a person who doesn't drink alcohol. The teetotalers were the people who pushed for prohibition.

Tanqueray Gin made in Finsbury, England. The green emerald bottle is supposed to resemble an English fire hydrant or cobbler shaker.

Tawny Port Wood-aged Port.

Tequila A spirit made from at least 51 percent blue agave plant hearts in Mexico. Really good Tequila will be made from 100 percent blue agave hearts.

Tequila Rose A creamy strawberry Tequila liqueur that was introduced in 1997. There was no other liqueur of its type on the market and still isn't. It's pink and tastes like melted strawberry ice cream and is packaged in a black bottle.

The Woman's Christian Temperance Union Organization founded by American women who were concerned about the problems alcohol was causing their families and society in 1874.

Tia Maria A rum-based coffee liqueur produced in Jamaica.

Tiki Glass Glasses that look like totem pole carvings and come in 12- to 24-ounce sizes.

Toddy Today, most people think of a *Toddy* as being hot water, honey, lemon, and whiskey. Guests with sore throats will ask for it because they saw it in a classic film somewhere.

Tonic Water A carbonated water containing quinine and sugar. Many people are surprised that tonic water contains sugar because to the virgin tongue tonic water just tastes bitter and nasty. That's the quinine. You'll see that grocery stores sell diet tonic water next to the regular tonic water. Also, tonic water glows light blue under a black light.

Top Shelf Top shelf are the premium/best spirits your bar carries. They are usually kept up on the top shelf of the back bar.

Triple Sec Orange liqueur made with triple sec oranges.

Tuaca Italian citrus vanilla liqueur made from a five hundred-year-old recipe (they say).

Twist A twist is a long, thin piece of lemon rind that is twisted over a drink to release the lemon oils, then the oils are rubbed on the rim of the glass and the piece is dropped in. It's not to be confused with when a guest orders a soda water and asks for a twist. In this case they mean a wedge of lime.

U

Up-sell Up-sell is when you suggest a substitute spirit of higher value. If a guest asks for a vodka tonic you could say, "Would you like me to use your favorite vodka?" as you point to the shelf with the better quality vodkas. You're trying to up-sell to a more expensive vodka.

Upside Down Refers to when guests lays their head back on the bar and a drink is poured into their mouth, like an upside-down margarita.

V

Vermouth Fortified wine. Comes in dry/clear and sweet/dark red. The most popular cocktails it's used in are the classic *Martini* and the *Manhattan*.

Vesper In 1953, Ian Fleming wrote about a fictional British spy named James Bond in the novel *Casino Royale*. Bond orders a cocktail called a *Vesper* (the name of his love interest) containing of gin, vodka, and Kina Lillet aperitif, shaken, not stirred, with a lemon twist. By the second Bond novel the handsome and debonair spy was drinking vodka Martinis with a coined catch phrase; *shaken not stirred*. So the Vesper is the first Martini James Bond drank.

Vodka Clear spirit made from grain that is practically odorless and tasteless. Russia and Poland still fight over who invented it first.

VS Very Special; also known as *three star* and aged for a minimum of three years.

VSOP Very Superior Old Pale; also known as *five star* and aged for five years.

XO Extra Old; aged for six plus years.

W

Well Your well is where you make drinks. It's a bartender's workstation. It contains your ice, ice well, speed rail filled with the most common bottles you pick up, juices, soda gun, bar mats, and anything else you need to make drinks. Most of what you need should be no more than one step away from the well.

Well, Call, Premium, and Ultra Premium This refers to the quality and/or price level of spirits you offer at your bar. Everything in life has levels. Behind the bar the vodka that you keep in your speed rail is the *well* vodka. Next, Smirnoff will probably be the *call* vodka, then Absolut for a *premium* vodka, and Ketel One for *ultra premium* vodka. Just so you know, there wasn't an ultra premium category until Ketel One and Grey Goose hit the market.

Whiskey Spirit made by distilling fermented cereals then aging in oak barrels.

White Lightning Another word for moonshine.

Wild Turkey An American Kentucky Bourbon produced since 1855 in Lawrenceburg, Kentucky, by the Ripy family. However, it didn't get its name until 1940 when Thomas McCarthy brought a private supply of whiskey to share with friends on an annual wild turkey hunt. Today it comes in two proofs, 101 and 80.

Wormwood It's a plant that come in many forms, but when talking about spirits we are talking about the ingredient that was banned in absinthe called absinthe wormwood or green ginger. Its lab name is *artemisia absinthium* and it's supposed to have hallucinogenic properties.

Worcestershire (WOOS-tuhr-sheer) A sauce made with garlic, onions, molasses, lime, vinegar, soy sauce, tamarind, anchovies, and other seasonings. It's considered a condiment and can be used in a Bloody Mary. Its name comes from being first bottled in Worcester, England.

Wine Alcohol made from grapes or other fruits.

Y

Yard Long novelty beer glass that come with a wooden stand to hold it upright on the table. Originally, they hung on the wall.

Yukon Jack Canadian honey whisky liqueur.

Z

Zero Tolerance Refers to what happened in 1987 when the American government told the states that they would stop giving money for highway construction unless they raised their drinking age for alcohol to twenty-one. Of course, all complied.

Zester Also called a *channel knife*. This cuts curly, fancy twists from citrus fruit rinds for special drinks.

Know that like anything else, garnishes and decorations are limited only by your imagination, so try to present them a new way by spearing them differently, setting them on the glass differently, or anything else your pretty little head comes up with.

Indexes

Drink Names

197

General

About the Author

Cheryl Charming has been in the food and beverage industry since 1976. Twenty-five plus of those years has been tending bar from a cruise ship in the Caribbean to Walt Disney World. She is the author of many other bar- and cocktail-related books, and her teaching experience includes a mandatory bar trick and magic course to Walt Disney World servers and bartenders.

Cheryl also writes cocktail-related articles and frequents as a celebrity cocktail guest on various radio, television, and podcast shows. She is a member of The Bartenders Guild (www.usbg.org), FBA (Flair Bartenders Association, www.barflair.org), and The Museum of the American Cocktail (www.museumoftheamericancocktail.org).

She resides in downtown Orlando, Florida, and maintains the website www.misscharming.com.